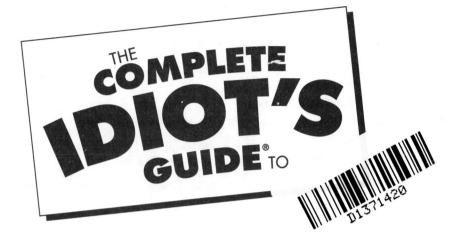

THE COMPLETE IDIOT'S GUIDE® TO

Frauds, Scams, and Cons

by Duane Swierczynski

ALPHA

A member of Penguin Group (USA) Inc.

This book is for Louis Wojciechowski, an upright man in a world full of grifters, punks, card-sharps, cheats, shortchangers, fakers, phonies, sharks, frauds, charlatans, swindlers, and con men. And Freddy Tenuto? You still owe this man five bucks.

International Standard Book Number: 0-02-864415-8
Library of Congress Catalog Card Number: 2002115303

06   05   04   8   7   6   5   4   3   2

Interpretation of the printing code: The rightmost number of the first series of numbers is the year of the book's printing; the rightmost number of the second series of numbers is the number of the book's printing. For example, a printing code of 02-1 shows that the first printing occurred in 2002.

Printed in the United States of America

Note: This publication contains the opinions and ideas of its author. It is intended to provide helpful and informative material on the subject matter covered. It is sold with the understanding that the author and publisher are not engaged in rendering professional services in the book. If the reader requires personal assistance or advice, a competent professional should be consulted.

The author and publisher specifically disclaim any responsibility for any liability, loss, or risk, personal or otherwise, which is incurred as a consequence, directly or indirectly, of the use and application of any of the contents of this book.

Publisher: *Marie Butler-Knight*
Product Manager: *Phil Kitchel*
Managing Editor: *Jennifer Chisholm*
Acquisitions Editor: *Gary Goldstein*
Development Editor: *Jennifer Moore*
Production Editor: *Billy Fields*
Copy Editor: *Ross Patty*
Illustrator: *Chris Eliopoulos*
Cover/Book Designer: *Trina Wurst*
Indexer: *Brad Herriman*
Layout/Proofreading: *Mary Hunt, Ayanna Lacey*

Contents at a Glance

Contents

Foreword

When I became a New York City police officer more than 20 years ago, my first six months were spent training at the Police Academy. Much of the classroom instruction was devoted to the law and, in particular, the crime of larceny, or stealing. Essentially, the Penal Law defines larceny as occurring when a person "… wrongfully takes, obtains, or withholds property from the owner …."

When your house has been burglarized, your wallet snatched, or your car ripped off, you *know* someone's committed larceny. But stealing can take much subtler forms—and that's where con artists enter the crime scene. Stealing may be accomplished by trick, false pretense, false promise, scheming to defraud, or issuing a bad check, all methods practiced with great skill by the ingenious con artist.

Over the past 100 years, various units within the New York City Police Department have waged battle against con artists—also known as confidence men. In earlier times it was the old Pickpocket and Confidence Squad. Today, it's the Special Frauds Squad, whose duties have been expanded to include investigating credit card fraud, cellular phone fraud, and other types of electronic fraud including ATM's and the Internet.

But the sad truth is that in a department of nearly 40,000 uniformed officers, little more than a handful of detectives are detailed on a full time basis to apprehending these fraudsters and cheats, and I imagine that's the same situation in most municipal police agencies. These dedicated investigators are not the first line of defense, they are the last line. As good of a job as they do, by the time they are contacted by an individual in need of assistance, chances are it's too late.

The trick, therefore, is to avoid becoming a victim in the first place. That's where this book can help and, in the process, save a potential victim—you—a lot more than its cover price.

Each one of the frauds, tricks, cons, scams, and schemes described in this book occur every single day in every single part of the country. I know because I've seen them firsthand and, on occasion, was lucky enough to catch the criminal in the act. But even though professional con artists can't be beat every single time, they can be neutralized on an individual basis by people who know—or even suspect—that a scam is being perpetrated. If a con artist can be convinced that you're not going to fall for his or her shenanigans, a small victory has been won. More importantly, early awareness that a scam is being committed may allow for time to get the police involved so they can apprehend the con artist in the act, which is the ultimate victory and the surest way to obtain a conviction.

Although this book's title indicates that it's for idiots, anyone who doesn't read it will find themselves feeling like one if they become victim of a scam that could easily have been avoided. I highly recommend it.

—Bernard J. Whalen

Lieutenant—NYPD, and author of *Justifiable Homicide*

Introduction

Con artists are everywhere. Oddly enough, they seemed to really pop out of the woodwork when I started to write this book.

On the very day my editor called to say, "Hey, congrats, you'll be writing the cons and frauds book," he stepped outside of his office to have a quick smoke. Within minutes, some shifty-looking guy approached him with a "travel opportunity you're not going to be able to resist." The guy wanted my editor to fork over some cash in exchange for a thick wad of airline and hotel discount "vouchers." My editor told him to buzz off, finished his cigarette, and went back inside to the relative safety of his office.

About a week later, my wife and I were out strolling in downtown Philadelphia with our newborn son. It was a week before his Christening, and we were passing our church, the oldest and largest in the city: the Cathedral of Saints. Peter and Paul. Right there—in the shadow of the church—a middle-aged man in slacks, collared shirt, and a sweater approached us. "Hi there," he said. "Cute baby. He looks like you, Dad. How old? Listen, I'm in a bit of a jam here. I'm down at the science museum with my fifth grade class, and I seemed to have lost my wallet. My Honda Civic is stuck in some parking garage, and I just need $5 to get my car back. I can send you the cash right back in the mail, once I get back to school."

Now maybe I was simply on high scam, alert—after all, I was a guy writing a book on the subject—but I politely said, "Sorry, we can't help you." What I wanted to say was: *Hey, buddy, let me find a cop for you. I'm sure he can give you a hand* but I didn't want to get into a confrontation, at least not with my wife and baby around.

As he shuffled away, the guilt started to creep in. What if the guy really needed my help? There I was, in the shadow of the church, turning away a man in need. I could almost imagine the Devil turning down the sheets on my soon-to-be bed in Hell.

Then we watched the same man, half a block ahead, take money from another pedestrian. And then a woman in a car, a block later. And then another woman. Now unless each person was giving him $1.78, I'd say it was a safe assumption that this "college professor" was working a pretty tidy little scam here. In less than 15 minutes, he probably made $15, if not more.

If you have been scammed in the past—who knows, maybe you're one of those poor saps I saw hand $5 to the "college professor"—the important thing is not to feel stupid. We can all be conned. It doesn't matter how smart or rich you are. Recently, I had the opportunity to personally meet with five real-life scam victims. They were gathered to speak on *Montel* about how they were scammed, and the stories ran from the amusingly frustrating (one couple learned that the justice of the peace who married them wasn't actually licensed to marry *anybody*) to the downright ghoulish (another woman learned that her mother was not actually cremated, but simply cast out like trash near that crooked crematorium in Georgia). The thing is: these were not stupid people. They didn't act foolishly, or out of greed. They were simply living their lives—paying bills, raising kids, smacking the side of the computer when the Internet is acting up again. How can they be expected to guard against swindles that seem to appear from every unexpected angle? The answer: they can't. But there is one basic thing all of us can do to protect ourselves.

Somewhere out there is the *Great Book of Cons*. Inside is every single con ever conceived by mankind. This book in your hands is not the *Great Book of Cons*. But it is an abridged version of that book. (Trust me—you wouldn't want to read all of the *Great Book of Cons*, anyway; it gets kind of slow in the middle.) Your first line of defense with any con, fraud, or scam is to *know* about the con, fraud, and scam. Sure, my editor and I were on high alert for scams; we had scams on the brain. But by picking up a copy of this book, you'll have scams on the brain, too. Even if a particular scam isn't covered here, you'll learn the framework of just about every scam on the planet. And that's your first step on the road to not ever being taken for a ride.

What You'll Find Inside

With *The Complete Idiot's Guide to Frauds, Scams, and Cons*, I wanted to give you the lay of the scamming land. First, I'll introduce you to the average con artist, and try to put you in his thieving, conniving little mind for a while. Then I'll describe the things that can make you a more attractive sucke… er, I mean, victim of a con game. You might be surprised to hear the types of people con artists routinely target. (Especially if you're a friendly, do-gooder senior citizen who happens to be African American.)

Next, I'll walk you through detailed descriptions of all kinds of individual scams—from the newest types of scams (identity theft, phone cons, and Internet fraud) to the age-old classics (street corner Three-Card Monte hustles and crooked carnival games). You'll also read about kinds of business and institutional rackets, including scams people try to pull on the least beloved-institutions in the United States, and learn why small business owners need to be especially vigilant.

In the fourth section, you'll finally get a chance to put faces to the scams in what I call the "Con Man Hall of Shame." Some names might be familiar (Charles Ponzi, Ivan Boesky, "Crazy Eddie" Antar), some not-so-familiar (Edward Zug, The Human Wreck, William "520 Percent" Miller). But all of them have pulled astounding swindles over the past 200 years, and some of their pioneering cons are still being used today. Finally, I'll tell you where to go if you have been the victim of a scam, from various local resources to federal agencies to a bunch of vigilant watchdog groups who are out there, watching your back.

My hope is that after reading this book, you'll have enough mental armor to ward off your average con artist as he tries to worm his way into your wallet or purse. At the very least, always remember that you have this book at home as a reference. If anybody approaches you with a line or an offer that sounds even the slightest bit shifty, tell them you have to go home and think it over first. Con artists thrive on the ticking clock; they want to pressure you to make a poor decision right then and there.

Don't let them.

A Few More Things About This Book

This book also features extra tidbits called sidebars. These asides are designed to supply you with extra information, tips, and cautions. Here's what you'll find:

Con-trary to Popular Belief

These will include surprising fraud facts, trivia, and real-life *scam*-ecdotes.

Grifter Speak

These sidebars include lingo and patter used by real con men, as well as other handy definitions.

Don't Be a Sucker

These give you detailed instructions on how to scam-proof your life.

It's a Scam

These will detail the various telltale signs of a con or scam.

Acknowledgments

Special thanks to Mike Connelley, my official consultant for this book, and April "Mad Dog" White, my official researcher; both put up with my annoying, last-minute, *gotta-know-right-now* requests. Also thanks to my partners in crime, Gary "Gibson" Goldstein and David "Hale" Smith, who have helped me perpetrate this long con I call a career. Jennifer "Bunco" Moore checked every single scam for flaws, and once again, saved me from getting pinched, as did Ross Patty. Honorary members of my own bunco squad include Rich "Dick" Rys, Sasha "Ice" Issenberg, Loren "Pretty Boy" Feldman, Larry Platt, Lynne Texter, "Kid Valentine" O'Connor, Greg Clark, Walt, Barb, Gregg, Kerry, Jamie, and Marcy. Most of all, special thanks to my son Parker Lennon—for not crying as much as he could have during the writing of this book—and to my wife Meredith—for taking care of Parker when he did.

Special Thanks to the Technical Reviewer

The Complete Idiot's Guide to Frauds, Scams, and Cons was reviewed by an expert who double-checked the accuracy of what you'll learn here, to help us ensure that this book gives you everything you need to know so you can spot the cons in the carnival game of life. Extra special thanks are extended to Mike Connelley for his insight, candor, and patience.

Trademarks

All terms mentioned in this book that are known to be or are suspected of being trademarks or service marks have been appropriately capitalized. Alpha Books and Penguin Group (USA) Inc. cannot attest to the accuracy of this information. Use of a term in this book should not be regarded as affecting the validity of any trademark or service mark.

Part 1

The Anatomy of a Con

You ever stub your toe really, *really* hard, but for a few wonderful seconds you don't feel any pain?

That's the essence of any successful confidence game: the delayed reaction. One minute, you're minding your own business and something out of the ordinary happens. You've been hit, but it feels good. Sooner or later, however, comes the sting, and it takes a while before you realize how much it actually hurts. Con games are crimes of stealth, and its operators are like magicians, using an array of tricks and speech to fool you into a false sense of security.

The first step in protecting yourself from con games? Take them apart to see what makes them tick.

The first step in protecting yourself from a stubbed toe? Wear some shoes, for goodness' sake.

Chapter 1

What Is a Con?

In This Chapter

- ◆ What makes a con different from other crimes
- ◆ How to tell a swindle from a con from a fraud
- ◆ Cons: big and short
- ◆ The essential elements of every con

If you've ever been the victim of a con game, you might have been so angry that you didn't quite know how to describe what happened to you. All you know is, goshdarn it, somebody *messed** with you! Here's the chapter where we define exactly what a con game is, and break it into its many parts. Once you know what con games are, you'll be able to spot many of them from a mile away.

Cons Are a Many Splendored Thing

Con is a shortened version of *confidence*, and that word says it all. While other criminals might use guns, knives, crowbars, incriminating evidence, or simply a deft hand to separate money from their victims, a con artist

*(*When you've been suckered, you might feel the need to substitute this word with a stronger word. Perhaps a word that rhymes with* hockey-pucked.)*

uses one simple tool: the victim's confidence in the con artist. When you trust the con artist, it's all over. He'll pretty much be able to take what he wants, when he wants, and as often as he wants.

Con games are crimes of persuasion and deception. Or to put it another way, the old bait-and-switch: you think you are getting one thing, but actually you are receiving something completely different. Other crimes involve brutal methods—threats of violence, or physical destruction—to achieve their goals. Not con games. Con artists are the magicians of the crime world, relying on sleight of hand techniques and clever patter to perpetrate their crimes. A carrot is promised, but instead you receive the stick. (If you're lucky.)

The con is probably the second oldest crime in human history—the first, of course, being murder. Then again, Cain probably pulled a scam on his poor brother Abel right before bludgeoning him with a hambone. (Cain: "Look, Abel, it's Elvis!" Abel: "Who?" *Th-wack*.) Cavemen probably scammed each other for better caves and wheels made of stone. There is much historical evidence that Ancient Romans were conning each other all of the time. (Brutus: "Look, Caesar, it's Elvis!" Caesar: "Who?" *Th-wack*.) As human beings, it's in our nature to want to get something for nothing. (Even if it involves a little larceny.) This is the operating principle that motivates con artists, and the same principle that guarantees that they'll never have to search far to find a willing victim.

What separates con artists from the rest of their criminal brethren is that they almost never use violence. They rely on their brains and mouths, not guns and bullets. If you were to force a pacifist to take up a life of crime, he would most likely choose the life of a con artist. (And then he could use the money he scammed from senior citizens to save humpbacked whales, or something.)

> ### It's a Scam
>
> The grift has a gentle touch. It takes its toll from the verdant sucker by means of the skilled hand or the sharp wit. In this, it differs from all other forms of crime, and especially from the heavy-rackets. It never employs violence to separate the mark from his money.
>
> —From "A Word About Confidence Man" in David W. Maurer's *The Big Con* (1940)

That's not to say that con artists are fey wimps who schlump home with only nickels and dimes while tough-guy muggers and pro heisters speed away with the big money. In fact, if anything, the opposite is true. Collectively, con artists are responsible for the theft of billions of dollars every year. Compare that with the total amount stolen by bank robbers in the year 2000—a paltry $78 million. Heck, most bank robbers couldn't afford to pick up a con artist's lunch check.

Let's take that crime—bank robbery—to further illustrate the difference between con artists and other criminals. A traditional bank robber will go about his trade in three basic ways: scribbling a demand note and handing it to a frightened teller (*"Gimme all of your money, or I'll pump you so full of lead you'll be able to sharpen your head and do* The New York Times *Crossword"*), recruiting a bunch of tough guys with shotguns to take over the bank, or by sneaking into the bank after hours and drilling through the vault. All three techniques can work, but they are full of risk. A teller might laugh at your demand note, or may give you baited cash that will spray you with purple dye the moment you leave the bank. A takeover heist is even worse. A silent alarm might be pulled, and before you can say "Gimme the money," the place might be hopping with Virginia farm boys carrying heavy artillery and FBI badges. A takeover-style bank robber might leave the bank lobby with thousands of dollars in a vinyl bag … or with dozens of bullets firmly planted in his chest. A bank burglar faces less risk of physical violence, but also faces an array of obstacles, including heat sensors, extra-thick vault walls, and hidden surveillance cameras.

Now, let's see how a con artist could go about the same crime. For starters, he wouldn't use the direct approach—no notes, no guns, no drills. Most likely, he'd simply apply for a job at the bank. There is almost always a demand for bank tellers, since they're not exactly glamorous, highly-paid positions (wages vary, but few tellers earn more than $25,000 a year). Once he's worked a week or two, the con artist will have everything he needs to steal money

from the bank. He'll know what times the manager goes to lunch and how money is tracked and logged into the system. Sooner or later, the con artist will find a way to embezzle thousands of dollars from the bank—or maybe, just a couple of hundred bucks at a time. By the time the bank realizes what has happened, the con artist has already moved on. No shots fired, no broken drill bits left on the vault floor.

A con artist doesn't even have to do that much work to steal money from a bank. One con game, called the bank examiner's scheme, involves the con artist simply standing outside of the bank and convincing customers leaving the bank that he's a bank examiner (or a U.S. Marshal, or a U.S. Treasury officer) on the trail of embezzlers. He usually waits for an older victim, someone who doesn't look very sophisticated. The con artist gives her the story, usually flashing some sort of badge identification at her. The examiner asks the victim if she's withdrawn any money. Of course she has; he watched her do it. Then he asks to see the money, so he can check the serial numbers. The victim, wanting nothing more than to do her civic duty, shows the examiner the bills. It's $300. He scrutinizes the cash, brow furrowed, eyes narrowed. "I'm afraid these are the bills we're looking for," the examiner says. "The teller who gave you these is stealing from personal accounts. I'm going to have to seize this money as evidence." The victim looks shocked, mostly at the thought that her bank teller might have been stealing from her.

"Here's what you do, ma'am," the examiner says, pulling out a pad with forms on it. "Take this receipt back into the bank, walk up to the manager's office, and tell them you'd like this amount withdrawn from the bank's security fund." The examiner thanks the victim for her time and effort in stopping crime, then sends her back into the bank. But inside, the bank manager doesn't know what she's talking about. Bank examiner? Embezzlers? When the pair walk back outside, the "bank examiner"—and the victim's $300—are long gone.

Think back to the root of the word "con": confidence. The victim put her confidence in that phony bank examiner. Maybe it was the badge. Maybe it was his no-nonsense, just-the-facts speech that reminded her so much of that nice Sam Waterston on *Law & Order*. Maybe it was his good looks. Either way, trust was given, and the con artist walked away with her money. He didn't need a gun or a threatening demand note, either.

Don't Be a Sucker

If someone approaches you outside of your bank branch—or calls you, claiming to be an officer of your bank—and asks for your help in catching a crook, hang up. Law enforcement almost never involves civilians when investigating bank fraud. (If it makes you feel better, call your bank directly and ask to speak with a manager and tell him what the "bank examiner" told you.)

Have I Been Conned? Scammed? Bamboozled?

It's amazing that the English language has dozens of words for the act of being scammed, conned, defrauded, bamboozled, tricked, schnookered, taken, duped, suckered, fooled, cheated, gypped, clipped, hornswaggled, gulled, snowed, bait-and-switched, shortchanged, shaved, rooked, flimflammed, screwed, stung, burned, gouged, chiseled, played, diddled, dipsy-doodled, hustled, roped, and hoodwinked*.

Geez—even baloney only has a first name.

The working title for this book was actually The Complete Idiot's Guide to Flimflams, Hornswaggles, and Dipsy-Doodles, *but my editor didn't think it was commercial enough. What does he know?*

The language itself acts like a con artist: It obscures the truth and clouds good judgment. Sometimes, people don't even know they've been conned, because it seems like there isn't even a name for what happened to them. Murder is easier to understand. Somebody kills you, you've been murdered.

To clear things up—and for the purposes of this book—let me simplify things a bit. Out of all the synonyms for the word *"con,"* only *fraud* has any real legal definition. Put simply, it's intentional deception to cause a person to give up property or some lawful right. When con artists are arrested, they're usually charged with some variation of fraud, be it *actual fraud*—which is a scheme intentionally designed to cheat somebody—or *constructive fraud*, which is basically cheating somebody with misleading words or actions. When a con artist tries to sell you the Brooklyn Bridge, that's actual fraud. When a con artist tries to sell you the Brooklyn Bridge, and actually owns the Brooklyn Bridge, but doesn't tell you that some sections of the roadway are missing, that's constructive fraud. (Important tip: never agree to buy the Brooklyn Bridge. You see, it's actually owned by the City of New York, and it's not for sale.)

Con-trary to Popular Belief

Of all the landmarks in the world, the Brooklyn Bridge is one that will forever be linked with a con game. Somewhere, at some undetermined point in time, some con artist convinced some poor sucker that he could buy the Brooklyn Bridge—cheap. The scam turned into a punchline that has spanned the decades. "Nobody really knows where it comes from," said David McCullough, author of *The Great Bridge*, in an interview with *The New York Times*. "But it's suspected that it comes from the confusion over who owned it, whether it was Brooklyn or New York who owned the bridge. And since the bridge is the most conspicuous symbol of New York and all its grandeur and accomplishment, the easiest way for tricking the rube would be selling the Brooklyn Bridge."

Boiled down to its basics, fraud is: *I promise you this, but instead I give you that.* "That" being an inferior product, an envelope full of shredded paper, a bogus receipt, or nothing at all. Every other word—be it con, scam, or swindle—is essentially the same thing. Word use depends on the situation; for instance, nobody calls a street corner game of three-card monte a "fraud," which implies some grander scheme. It's not. It's a scam, or a swindle.

Another word you might hear is *bunco*. The word is probably a distortion of the Spanish card game *banco*, but it's not limited to gambling. Like con, fraud, and scam, it is used to describe "swindling an unsuspecting person." You'll hear it mostly used in terms of law enforcement; chances are, your local police department has a bunco squad. (I guess it's easier to pronounce than "swindle squad." Go ahead, try saying *that* three times fast.) There is also, apparently, a popular suburban game called "bunco" that involves three dice and a whole lot of free time. You'll find sites dedicated to it on the Internet. This is not the same kind of bunco I'll be discussing in this book, however.

In short: Don't let the words bamboozle you. A con is a fraud is a scam is a bunco is a flimflam. Throughout the rest of this book, if there's an important distinction to be made, don't you worry. I'll make it.

Con-fused: Making Sense of the Modern Con

More confusing than the words, however, is making sense of the endless variations of cons, frauds, and scams out there. I have to admit, when my editor first approached me to write a book about cons, frauds, and scams, a shiver ran up my spine. How on earth was I going to organize every single type of con game into a structure that made sense? There are street cons and corporate cons and sweetheart cons and gambling cons and real estate cons and tax cons and Internet cons and raindrops on roses and whiskers on kittens and bright copper kettles and warm winter mittens. And those are just a few of my favorite cons!

But then I took a deep breath, and realized that con games can be broken down into two general categories: scams that target individual people, and scams that target institutions and businesses. There is some overlap; for instance, gambling cons can target both the individual (when rigged casinos scam tourists) and the institution (when cardsharking con artists scam reputable casinos). But I still think it's a useful distinction, so that's how I organized this book. In Part Two, you'll read about the wide variety of modern con games targeted at ordinary schmoes like you and me. In Part Three, I turn my attention to the con games that scammers launch on businesses and institutions.

Grifter Speak

The word **con** has two different meanings; one is shorthand for *confidence game*, while the other is shorthand for *convict*. And while a con can perpetrate a con, not all cons are perpetrated by cons. You dig?

No matter who the target, however, we all should care about con artists and their games. Even if we don't work for the IRS, all of us are hurt when some grifter pulls a tax scam. Even if we don't exactly love our car insurance company, we're collectively penalized when somebody pulls a fast one on them.

The cynics may see modern business practices as one big con—who hasn't felt the sting of opening up a product that was nothing like the product advertised on TV? I hear you, brother. We've all been there. But for the purposes of this book, we're going to stick with the con games recognized by the law, and leave the corporate ranting to Michael Moore.

The Essential Elements of Classic Cons

The simple con game only requires two people: the con artist himself, and the victim—typically referred to as "the mark." The word "mark" comes from the freaky world of carnivals. When a crooked game operator found someone who fell for his tricks, he would palm a small chunk of chalk and clap that person on the back. The chalk would leave a mark, which would tell other crooked game operators that this person was Grade-A, USDA-approved sucker. (For more about crooked carnival operators and their shifty games, see Chapter 10.)

The two basic types of con games are the *short con* and the big con.

The Short Con

Basically, this is the "hit and run" version of a con game. Short cons require a small number of meetings—perhaps only one—between the con artist and his mark. Many of the con games described in this book—and most likely, all of the con games you are familiar with—are short cons. San Francisco private detective Fay Faron, who writes a newspaper column on con games called "Ask Rat Dog," breaks a short con game into six components: the motivation, the come-on, the shill, the swap, the stress, and the block. Here's how it works:

1. **The motivation:** The carrot at the end of the stick; the pot of gold at the end of the rainbow. The con artist promises to give some kind of reward to the mark. This doesn't have to be money (although greed is a huge motivator for many marks). It could be the happy, self-satisfied feeling you get when you help out a fellow human being in need. Or it can be the smug, do-gooder feeling you get when you help the police bag a criminal. Whatever it may be, the motivation is what stops the mark in his tracks, and makes him at least listen to …

2. **The come-on:** This is where the con artist pitches his tale to the mark. In the previous example of the bank examiner scheme, this refers to the badge-flashing and the story about catching that evil bank embezzler. The badge held the mark's attention, and the

Grifter Speak

The **short con** is also sometimes known as a "one-liner."

story kept her planted there, eating up every detail. If the "bank examiner" really wanted to cement the deal, he may have employed ...

3. **The shill:** A co-conspirator who does nothing more than reinforce the scam. After all, there's safety in numbers. In the bank examiner case, a shill might pose as a fellow bank employee—or even better, as another bank customer, who willingly forks over hundreds of dollars to the "examiner." If the con artist really wanted to milk his mark, he'd use a shill to convince her to go back inside and withdraw even *more* money, so he'd have a better chance of catching that evil embezzler in her tracks. Once the mark agrees, then comes ...

4. **The swap:** Quite literally the physical trade of the genuine with the phony. The mark gives the con artist her $300; the con artist in return gives the mark a bogus receipt that isn't worth the paper it's printed on.

5. **The stress:** This is the time-is-running-out portion of the scam, meant to ensure that the mark won't have any time to think about what's happening to him. Our bank examiner con artist didn't need to apply much stress; the mark seemed willing to help. But the stress is highly effective when used with a doubting mark, who will be led to believe that if he walks away, he'd be missing out on the opportunity of a lifetime.

6. **The block:** The sting at the end of the con that is meant to dissuade marks from going to the police. This is easier when the con game plays on the mark's greed. If the deal is shady, and he willingly participates, he'll be very hesitant to report it to the authorities. The block is why short cons can be so successful—they're rarely reported, since the mark feels either guilty or foolish. Faron calls this "insuring the happy ending."

Some short cons skip some steps; some involve more complex steps. But all of them involve at least two critical components: the motivation and the swap. In other words, you have to put yourself out there first before you're scammed. If you don't put yourself out there, you can't be conned. Of course, there are many ways to define "putting yourself out there." It might mean listening to some bunco man's street patter, or it might mean slapping down $10 on a three-card monte table. But as you'll see in Chapter 4, it might simply mean owning a credit card. The technological explosion of global financial systems and the Internet have been a boon to con artists everywhere. In the twenty-first century, it's extremely different to not be "out there." You, your identity, your vital numbers, can be found in any number of places. And con artists are waiting to take advantage of it.

The Big Con (a.k.a. Long Con)

The opposite of the short con is the big con. These are con games that can take days, weeks, even months to set up, but for all of that work, the payoff is usually very high. A hundred years ago, big cons started to appear in the form of big stores. These were illegal gambling dens, hidden behind what appeared to be an authentic dry goods store, or a shop that sold various items for only $1. Marks would flock to these minia-ture casinos, hoping to make a quick buck, but they had no idea how much the deck was stacked against them. Not only were the games more crooked then a crippled flamingo's leg, but the employees of the big store were gifted actors who knew when to scare the mark into running away—usually leaving his betting money on the table. I'll describe more of these operations—also called dollar stores and smack games—in Part 4.

Today, you won't find too many people pulling big cons in the traditional sense of the word, although managed earnings scams like Enron and WorldCom might be seen as a modern update of the big con. (For more on these, see Chapter 17.)

The Least You Need to Know

- Con games are crimes of persuasion and deception.

- A con artist rarely uses violence to perpetrate his crimes.

- There are dozens of words that mean "con," but all of them boil down to the same thing: an act that deceives people into voluntarily surrendering property.

- Most modern con games are "short cons"—hit and run-type crimes.

The Confidence Man and His Mark

In This Chapter

- ◆ Common traits of the garden variety con artist
- ◆ The five types of con man
- ◆ The most wanted marks
- ◆ How to avoid being a sucker

Do you want to know what the average con artist looks like? Take a look in the mirror. Want to know what the average mark looks like? Take another look in the mirror. The thing is, you can't tell a con artist (or his victim, for that matter) by his looks. Most con artists want to look like Joe Average—a friendly, easy-going, honest kind of guy. But certain psychological factors set con men apart, and in this chapter, I'll walk you through some of them. These factors won't necessarily help you spot a grifter operating in your neighborhood, but they will help you understand who we're all up against.

More importantly, I'll also discuss the psychological makeup of your average mark—in other words, the victim. (That's you, chump.) If any of the characteristics of the mark sound familiar, you'd better take this book to the cash register at the front of the store right away. Your life could depend on it. Yes, you! Go now! Purchase this book, or suffer the life-altering consequences!*

The Common Traits of the Con Artist

Like snowflakes, no two con artists are exactly alike. (Unlike snowflakes, most con artists won't melt when exposed to a temperature greater than 32° Fahrenheit.) Classifying them isn't as easy as, say, classifying a serial killer. There's no hard-and-fast sociology rule that says, "If you were raised in a middle-class suburb of a large American city, you stand a 40 percent chance of growing up a swindler." It doesn't work that way. Con artists come from all kinds of socioeconomic backgrounds and ethnic groups and parts of the world. Not all come from a hard life on the streets, or drug and alcohol problems, or an abusive home—all factors that can influence other types of criminal behavior.

Grifter Speak

Dennis M. Marlock, a member of Professionals Against Confidence Crime (PACC) once interviewed a man who was married to a fake fortune teller. How, Marlock asked, can you justify taking advantage of people's misery and ignorance? "You must be kidding," the guy replied. "I buy a new car every year, my wife brings in over $500,000 a year without any real effort, and I don't pay any taxes. I never had to work a day in my life. Suddenly you come along and suggest that I give it up. For what? I should work like those other suckers, give half my income to the government, and be happy with a lot less. You've got to be kidding."

But experts and investigators *have* uncovered some common personality traits of the typical swindler. Not every con man you meet will possess all of these qualities, but at least some of them will ring true.

He Thinks Hard Work Is for Suckers

As Chaz Palminteri said in *A Bronx Tale*: "The working man is a chump." Only a fool would clock in 40, 50, 60 hours in a cheap fabric-lined cubicle, squandering the best years of his life for a company that neither cares for his well-being nor is concerned with his future. Even a man who works for himself or runs his own business is at the mercy of a fickle public or cutthroat competitors—in the world of business, no man is

(* See how easy it was to convince you to buy something you didn't necessarily want?)

an island. Except, perhaps, in the fraud business, where the lone wolf can be wildly successful, and the profit margins are only as large as the con man's imagination. At least, that's what probably goes through a con artist's mind. He's not a criminal; he's simply being smart. He's playing the game. "Con artists commit crimes because it pays and because swindling is easier and more exciting than working for a living," writes FBI agent Scott O'Neal in *The FBI Law Enforcement Bulletin*.

He Thinks Fraud Is Fun

A con artist isn't necessarily only in it for the money. "Con artists also tend to act irrationally," writes O'Neal. "Their criminal behavior is more the result of flawed character than of adverse social conditions or greed alone." In other words: he gets off on it. The thrill of outsmarting others is a high, and he might pursue that high even when presented with the opportunity to make a lot of money the legit way. He's always on the lookout for a new mark, for a new victim to feed a line about the pot of gold at the end of the rainbow. It's a thrill to see them fall for it. And it doesn't matter who he hurts, because …

He Has a Conscience the Size of a Cashew

Con men believe they operate on a different plane of morality than the rest of us suckers. They may believe that beating or killing someone for money is morally wrong, but it's totally fine to steal money if you use your wits. And what about the poor slob who gets suckered? Who cares? They should have been smarter. The weak and stupid deserve everything they get. "Con artists will generally be individuals who lack any remorse for what they do," says retired FBI agent Mike Connelley, who served as my official consultant on this book. "They tend to rationalize it, and say that someone else made them do it. They lack any real compassion for people, which allows them to screw somebody and still sleep at night."

Con artists are geniuses at rationalizing their behavior and explaining away their crimes. Chuck Whitlock, professional scam-buster and author of *Scam School*, has interviewed hundreds of con men. "They all seemed to be very sincere, very candid—until I started to ask some hard questions," he writes. "At that point they all became hostile and angry—and in a couple of instances, near violent. Male or female, they pleaded their innocence to me, claiming that their convictions were all misunderstandings. So while there are no obvious identifying features common to con artists, there is one thing they share: they are always able to rationalize away accusations against them and to justify their actions, at least in their own minds."

Grifter Speak

"Count" Victor Lustig, a notorious charlatan, had 10 Commandments for being a con man:

1. Be a patient listener.
2. Never look bored.
3. Wait for the other person to reveal political opinions, then agree with them.
4. Let the other person reveal religious views, then have the same ones.
5. Hint at sex talk, but don't follow it up unless the other fellow shows interest.
6. Never discuss illness, unless some special concern is shown.
7. Never pry into a person's personal circumstances (they'll tell you eventually).
8. Never boast—let your importance be quietly obvious.
9. Never be untidy.
10. Never get drunk.

He Believes He Is a Criminal Mastermind

Fraud is the thinking man's crime. Any thug can pick up a .38 Saturday Night Special in the neighborhood pawn shop and start sticking up mom and pop shops. Any idiot can resort to brute violence to make money. But it takes real skill to get what you want using only your brains. And con artists are proud of this fact. Even Frank W. Abagnale, a former con man who now consults law enforcement agencies and private businesses on how to prevent fraud, can't resist bragging about himself in his autobiography, *Catch Me If You Can*. "I've been described by authorities and news reporters as one of this century's cleverest bum-check passers, flimflam artists and crooks, a con man of Academy Award caliber," he writes. "I was a swindler and poseur of astonishing ability. I sometimes astonished myself with some of my impersonations and shenanigans." (Abagnale sometimes astonishes me with his humility.)

Con artists also like to think they're smarter than all of law enforcement, which creates particular problems for investigators who question them. "The con artist often sizes up an interviewer to determine their expertise in the particular financial/business dealings involved in the fraud and then attempts to explain the 'misunderstanding' using jargon the con artist perceives the interviewer will not understand," writes

O'Neal in the *Bulletin*. The scammer assumes he'll be able to talk rings around his inquisitors—especially if they're low-level bunco squad members from a lowly city precinct—and as a result isn't too afraid of being questioned.

This kind of pride, however, can get them in trouble. A clever investigator will use it against them by allowing them to talk themselves into a corner, and then carefully pick apart the discrepancies one by one. But it's not easy, and it's extremely rare to break down a con artist to the point where he'll want to sign a confession. That's because …

He Knows He'll Probably Get Away with It

The sad truth is: He's probably right. A successful con man will arrange his games so that the victim will be either too embarrassed or too confused to report what happened. If it does get reported, it's very tough to catch a con man—descriptions are often vague, and names and addresses given (if any are given at all) never lead anywhere. Even if you do slap the metal cuffs on a con man, it's much tougher to prosecute him than any other kind of criminal. Some district attorneys won't touch a fraud case unless it hits a certain dollar figure—say, $5,000—otherwise, it's not worth the money or manpower. Con artists who *are* prosecuted know that the odds are heavily stacked in their favor. In 1998, the Department of Justice reported 1474 cases of check forgers. Of those, only 122 were convicted of a crime. (And of those, only 26 received jail time.) In general, only 9.4 percent of fraud cases result in a felony conviction.

Let's say all of the planets are in alignment, and you manage to arrest and successfully prosecute a con man. The penalties? Fairly light. Judges are more concerned with putting drug dealers and murderers in jail, not small-time bunco artists. Even though fraudsters and scammers take a huge financial bite out of everyone, we as a society are just not as concerned about locking them up as we are other criminals.

The Five Types of Con Man

Psychological traits are fine and dandy, but they don't do much to help you visualize who we're all up against. I've found that con artists can be broken down into five general types: the Grifter, the Impostor, the Business Opportunist, the Insider, and the Guy Next Door. What follows are brief character sketches of each, to help you visualize them in case one of them ever tries to feed you a line, or a pitch, or a plea. Of course, some con artists can be two or more of these types at the same time: the Grifter who is the Guy Next Door, or the Insider who's also an Impostor. But for now, let's take them one at a time.

The Grifter

In *The Big Con*, David W. Maurer defines a grifter as "one who lives by his wits as contrasted to the heavy-men who use violence." But the definition of "grifter" has narrowed since then. A grifter is the guy working the street corner scams—asking for $20 because his car ran out of gas, or shortchanging a bartender when ordering a beer. He's not into the big institutional scams, or any kind of scam that lasts for more than a couple of hours. He might pass some bad checks, but he won't try to embark on some grand counterfeiting scheme. He's in it for the short con. He's like that John Cusack character in the Stephen Frears film, *The Grifters* (1990), a small-time operator just looking to make a buck any way he can except by working. I'll describe some classic grifts in the next chapter.

Con-trary to Popular Belief _____

Back in the late 1800s, the word "confidence man" wasn't in use. The preferred term: diddler. Edgar Allan Poe wrote an essay on "diddling" which said that "a crow thieves; a fox cheats; a weasel outwits; a man diddles. To diddle is his destiny." Today, the word "diddle" may have a slightly different connotation, although the end result may be the same: screwed.

The Impostor

To some degree or another, all con artists are impostors—they pretend to be someone (a stranger in need of help, a financial whiz, a lover) they're not. But the impostors I'm talking about here are people who assume the actual identity of someone else, or a profession or job they don't have, to achieve some goal—be it money or power. I'll be outlining the various types of impostors in Chapter 10, and boy are there some humdingers. (Including the guy who pretended to be Robert DeNiro. You don't just go messing with Bobby D., you know?) But more typical is the impostor who steals a uniform or credentials to pose as an official of some sort. The thrill here is perhaps slightly different than with other con games; in a way, this is childhood fantasy fulfillment. There may be financial gain, but that's almost secondary to living a completely different life. Frank W. Abagnale is perhaps the most gifted impostor in recent history, and appears to have loved every single minute of it. At a young age, he managed to pose as a pilot and receive free air travel all over the country (don't worry, he never took the controls—by himself, anyway), as a doctor, a lawyer (although he did pass the bar for real), and a college professor. You'll read more about him in the "Hall of Shame" portion of this book.

The Business Opportunist

If fraud is a profession, here are the entrepreneurs. These con artists set up operations to defraud people and institutions with a staggeringly wide array of cons. They can be as simple as a phony business opportunity with a 1-900 number attached (you call the number, hear a lame recorded message, and then later receive a phone bill that reaches into hundreds of dollars), as complex as a scheme to defraud an entire city out of millions in pension funds, or as shocking as the recent financial cons perpetrated by well-respected execs at large American companies (cough, cough, Enron, WorldCom, cough, cough). If any one type of con artist dominates newspaper headlines (and this book), it's these guys.

The Insider

Related to the Business Opportunist is the Insider, the term I use for anyone who agrees to work for a company with the intention to rob it blind. Here are your embezzlers and corporate con men, the ones who find ways to subvert their company's financial systems so that a small stream of revenue is diverted directly into their personal savings accounts. Embezzlement is the number one financial crime, so much so that one out of every three businesses you see going belly-up is thanks to someone (or a group) inside the company siphoning the profits right out of it. We'll get to these guys in Chapter 11, appropriately enough.

> **Grifter Speak**
>
> But you're a con artist! And you blew it like a pimp!
> —Luther Coleman (Robert Earl Jones) in *The Sting* (1973)

The Guy Next Door

These are the scariest kinds of con artists. They don't stop you on the street requesting money or help. They don't cold call you with a business opportunity. No, the Guy Next Door appears in a completely innocent way—maybe it's a chance encounter on the street—and then proceeds to insert himself into your life, so deeply that before you know it, your life savings are gone and your credit is shattered. You'll read more about these vampires in Chapter 8, specifically the "Let Me Scam You, Sweetheart" section. Some victims are so completely bamboozled by these people, they don't even fully realize they've fallen prey to a professional con artist—they just think it was another bad relationship.

Cont-rary to Popular Belief

Most con artists are nonviolent criminals. But once in a while you get somebody like J.E. Robinson, a sadistic con man/killer from Kansas City who was profiled by David McClintick in *Vanity Fair*. Allegedly, Robinson found women on the Internet, lured them into his life, exploited them financially—in some cases, draining their life savings and retirement accounts—before beating some of them to death with a hammer. "I've dealt with a wide variety of characters," said one probation officer in the *Vanity Fair* story. "But never anyone like Robinson. He's just chilling. There are so many sides to him. There is the con man after the money. There is the murderer. There is the sexual deviant. There is the cover-up artist—the lies, endless lies."

Are You a Mark?

Now that you've seen the face of the enemy, it's time to take a look at yourself. Not just to admire your pretty eyes, but to see yourself how con men see you. Are you a tough target? Or a prime, Grade-A, USDA-certified sucker?

Contrary to what you may think, not all scam victims are stupid, naïve, or gullible. (Though it helps). The problem is, all of us—yes, you, me, Einstein, Alan Greenspan—can be stupid, naïve, or gullible at times. "All of us fall for scams," writes private detective Fay Faron, who writes "Ask the Rat Dog," a syndicated column about scams. "As long as there is a lottery, we the people of the United States must believe in getting something for nothing. It's the law." It's tough to keep your guard up 24/7. And even if you do manage to be at the top of your game all of the time, there's still a chance you'll be suckered. "Some sophisticated schemes can fool even the most intelligent and experienced business person," says ex-FBI agent Mike Connelley. Some con artists spend years perfecting their techniques; you've been busy working and eating and sleeping and playing with your kids and brushing your teeth and, basically, living your life.

Don't Be a Sucker

The surest way to be deceived is to consider oneself cleverer than others.

—Francois Duc de La Rochefoucauld

That said, there are certain mindsets that can make you particularly attractive to con artists. Their particular favorite: the "good deal syndrome"—in other words, the bargain hunter who's always looking out to save a buck. "Many marks are people who believe they are getting something for nothing," says retired FBI agent Mike Connelley. "When I was 19—and this is back in 1961—my family went to Las Vegas for vacation. My dad and I were walking back to our hotel, The Sands, when this guy came up. He showed us this 'expensive watch with diamonds.' He explained that he was a business man who had lost his money, but was willing to sell his watch cheap so he could get back to Los Angeles. My dad shook his head no, but I thought this was too good a deal to pass up. I offered $25, and said I wanted a receipt. Smart move on my part, correct? The guy said, 'Kid, you drive a hard bargain,' and gave me the watch. I'm proud. I'm now the owner of an expensive watch that cost me only $25. Well, you know the rest of the story. I got back home, took it to a jeweler friend, and he broke the news to me." As it turned out, the watch was worth no more than $5, meaning that Connelley was suckered out of $20. "The guy probably had a trunk full of those watches," Connelly adds. "The point is, I thought I was getting a good deal, which clouded my judgment. That, and the fact that I was a stupid 19-year-old kid."

> **Grifter Speak**
>
> **Good Deal Syndrome**
> The desire in some people to get something for far less than its perceived worth. Con artists love marks afflicted with "good deal syndrome"—it makes their job that much easier.

That's not the only mindset that con artists find attractive. Are you a wild dreamer? A guy who always plays by the rules? A gambler? Slightly greedy? Slightly desperate? Easy-going? Swindlers know how to spot all of the above personality traits and the proper swindle to deploy for each of them.

For instance, a wild dreamer might jump at an investment scam that sounds like the sure opportunity she's been waiting for all of her life (see Chapter 13). A guy who walks the straight and narrow might cross paths with a guy who just needs $30 to get his car out of the garage, because, you see, he's lost his wallet and he needs to get home to the suburbs (Chapter 3). A man who likes to gamble might be transfixed by a three card monte set up on a Manhattan street corner, and decide he knows how to beat it (Chapter 9). If you're greedy, forget about it. Con artists love greedy people the way Larry King loves getting married. Desperate people are prone to be schnookered by phony healers, psychics, and even Guy Next Door-type scammers. And the easy-going, Walter Mitty-types are a con artist's dream. You know the kind—the kind who would sooner buy an expensive sump pump system for their backyard than to insult a complete stranger?

Most Wanted Marks

U.S. Post Offices hang posters of wanted fugitives on their bulletin boards. Con Artists hang posters of these typical victims on *their* bulletin boards.

Senior citizens. Far and away, the elderly—or as my grandfather likes to call them, "AARPies"—are the most-scammed segment of our population. According to some reports, 60 percent of all fraud victims are 65 or older. In certain small town newspapers, you can count on reading a senior fraud story every couple of days. What makes them so attractive? Older adults tend to be easily confused, too trusting—with values dating back to a different generation—and just not as sharp as they used to be. It's sad, but sometimes senior citizens are so lonely, they'll listen to anybody who'll talk to them, even a swindler. They're generally retired, so most times either alone at home or out at the bank or the grocery store, right where a con man can easily find them. Plus, they're more likely to have a nest egg tucked away somewhere that is worth looting. And even more insidiously, con artists count on more senior citizens to keep their mouths shut. If a victim admits that he was suckered by some smooth-talking scammer, he might wonder, "What will my kids think? Maybe they'll think I'm not able to take care of myself, and they'll put me in that group home, after all." For many seniors, this fear outweighs any financial loss, so they're very loath to report the crime.

Con-trary to Popular Belief

Florida has a program called "Seniors Versus Crime," which deploys about 800 elderly people to go undercover as "Senior Sleuths" to trap con artists. The group recently nailed three companies involved in a water filtration scam in which they tried to convince senior citizens that their water was bad, and they needed an expensive system to fix the problem. One of the Sleuths who cracked the case—an 83-year-old from St. Petersburg known as "Granny Super-Sleuth"—told the *Las Vegas Sun* that swindlers should be looking over their shoulders. "These days, you may not know it," she said, "but the older lady listening to your spiel so intently with big eyes could be a senior sleuth. We could be anywhere." And you thought *Matlock* was hardboiled.

College students. Or young people in general. They don't have the life experience of adults, and they tend to be rather impulsive when faced with a decision. You've already read about Mike Connelley's encounter with a grifter in Las Vegas. And Connelley would grow up to be an extremely shrewd fraud investigator. The sad thing is, many youngsters just aren't cynical yet. They still believe that their worries and concerns are at the center of the known universe, and that the world was created for their benefit. The fools. (Note: the preceding lines were written by a very cynical 30-year-old.)

Sick people. When you are sick, your immune system is generally working overtime. That goes for your brain, too—nobody makes good decisions when they're feeling like dog poop. The con artists who go after these marks—as well as marks who feel too fat, too ugly, or too weak—are more than happy to supply the "cure." For more so-called "vanity scams," check out Chapter 7.

Small business owners. Huge corporations have fraud departments and fully-manned security desks. Small business owners? They're lucky if they remember to set the store alarm code over the weekend and maybe give the books a good once-over every couple of weeks. Con artists will hit them with bogus machine repair scams, shortchanging, bogus invoices, and more. For more skinny on the most common forms of business bunco, hit Chapter 11.

Minorities. Some con artists will take particular advantage of people of various ethnic backgrounds. Whether they're new to this country and don't fully understand the local customs and laws, or are native-born but generally mistrustful of government and law enforcement, minorities tend to have feelings of being "outsiders" that con artists can use to their advantage. The most recent example is the Slave Reparation Scam, in which bogus "tax experts" claim to be able to secure huge checks from the I.R.S. thanks to a little-known—and completely fake—statute in the tax laws that says African American descendants of slaves are entitled to fat tax breaks. (For more on this, see Chapter 8, specifically "40 Acres and a Fraud.")

Grifter Speak

Synonyms for "mark": sucker, patsy, pigeon, chicken, fall guy, doormat, mug, fish, jay, easy mark, sitting duck, juggin, pushover, cinch, vic, easy pickings, greeny, greener, chump, boob, schlemiel, sap, saphead, prize sap, easy touch, soft touch.
—*Roget's International Thesaurus*

How to Avoid Being a Mark

Well, you've already taken your first step: you've purchased this book. (Or at least checked it out of the library. Or scammed it away from your best friend.) Congrats. Inside these pages, you'll find dozens of specific tips on how to scam-proof your life.

But maybe you're looking for general wisdom. In that case, I've found healthy skepticism to be the best defense against fraud. Now, I'm not suggesting you live your life completely paranoid. Let's face it: the only way to completely protect yourself from all kinds of fraud is to stay indoors, never answer the phone, live alone, avoid all other people, stop receiving mail, stay off the Internet, and not have a Social Security number, credit cards, insurance policies, or a driver's license. That's no way to live, unless you're the Unabomber.

I'm talking about "healthy" skepticism, the kind that causes you to question any kind of plea, request, proposal, or opportunity, especially those involving your money. Remember: a con artist can't succeed unless you willingly give him money or surrender some kind of right. You always reserve the right to think about any kind of proposal; any legit businessman will give you all the time you need, not pressure you into a decision. Sure, some kinds of fraud are beyond your control—I'm thinking of identity theft, where you're not even aware you've been scammed until you start receiving bills in the mail (see Chapter 4). But for most scams, the scam artist needs your willing approval. Your confidence. So what I'm saying is, don't give your confidence lightly. To anyone. If that makes me sound paranoid, tell Oliver Stone to give me a call. We'll do lunch.

I'm not the only one who thinks this way. Most fraud experts recommend healthy skepticism as a first line of defense against the con man. "Always remember—if it sounds too good to be true, then it probably is," says Mike Connelley.

Don't Be a Sucker

The moment you suspect something is a scam, immediately sever contact with the con artist—walk away, hang up the phone, close the door, file for divorce, whatever. The longer you hang on, trying to find a polite way out, the more the con artist will think you're vulnerable to his patter. Forget polite. This joker is trying to steal your money!

The Least You Need to Know

- You can't tell a con artist or mark just by looking at them.

- Most con artists are gifted with big brains, but tiny consciences.

- Senior citizens are very popular targets of con artists.

- Remember: If something sounds too good to be true, it probably is.

Classic American Cons

In This Chapter

◆ Taking a con for a test drive

◆ Learn how to avoid being the pigeon

◆ Shortchanging scams

◆ How bartenders set you up

Now that you know what a con is, who perpetrates 'em, and who usually falls for 'em, you're ready to start learning about every con game under the sun—from small-time swindles to huge corporate cons. Con artists are cooking up new schemes all the time, but that doesn't mean they don't go back to the classics time and time again. In fact, some con artists prefer going with the tried-n-true; if it's suckered people for decades, there's no reason why it won't work now. (That is, unless those people have read the book you're holding in your hands. Aren't you lucky?)

But before I toss you head-first and screaming into the big ol' cauldron of cons, let's start with a few simple ones. These are short cons that you can find in ordinary places—the street outside your house, the neighborhood store, the ballpark, the corner bar. The first con game, one I like to call "The Trapped Car," is the perfect one for you to test drive.

The Trapped Car

You're walking down the street on your way to the video store, wondering if it's possible to find a comedy that doesn't star Freddie Prinze, Jr. when all of a sudden a guy approaches you. He's clearly not a bum; he's wearing a forest green sweater over a collared shirt and tie, corduroy pants, and Hush Puppies. He looks to be somewhere in his mid-40s, with turtle shell glasses and a vaguely academic look to him. "Sorry to bother you," he says, looking pained and embarrassed. "But I've run into some trouble."

The man will point to the nearby science museum and explain that he's in town with his archeology students—he's a professor at the nearby university—but then lost his wallet somewhere inside. The students left, the museum closed, and now he's left without a way to spring his 1989 Ford Taurus from the local park-n-lock. Could you possibly loan him $8, which he will promptly mail back to you when he returns to campus?

Unless he produces a syllabus and a T-Rex leg bone, my inclination would be to direct him to the nearest police officer. You see, Mr. Trapped Car most likely belongs to the fraternity of con artists known as *panhandlers*. Sure, he wasn't leaning on a crutch or shaking a Starbucks cup full of change at you, but his intent was the same: to use a sob story to convince you to give him money. Panhandling is a classic *short con*. There's little risk to the con artist (the worst you can do is say no), and the earnings potential is nice (in this case, our professor could have pocketed $8 in under three minutes). If he repeats this con just six times, he's walking away with close to $50—probably far more than adjunct faculty at some universities make for an hour's teaching. Begging can be so lucrative, one former con even opened his own Manhattan school in 1979 to teach the art of panhandling, according to Carl Sifakis in his book *Frauds, Deceptions and Swindles*. "Lesson One," Sifakis writes, "On the subway, pick out one target, stand before him and whine loudly, 'Please!' If that doesn't work, get on one knee and continue to plead until he does give."

Be wary of anyone who wants to discuss finances with you on the street—even if the finances in question are only 25 cents. Pro panhandling con men won't make it easy for you to say no. They'll plead, beg, yell, or even insult you. *The Onion*, the satiric weekly newspaper based in New York City, once ran a news brief entitled: "Panhandler Demands Explanation for Failure to Provide Quarter." The item ends with the line: "After explaining that he had no change on him and that he was sorry, DiCostanzo walked two blocks before realizing he'd just apologized for not handing free money to a complete stranger." If you've ever been harassed by a guy begging for change, you know the feeling.

Panhandling cons are effective because they play on our tendencies to be decent, caring human beings. (Those bastards!) On top of that, there's also that nagging thought that some people who beg for money are genuinely hungry and in need of help. If that's what keeps you handing out quarters to complete strangers, I commend your humanitarian spirit. But if you want to really help the ones who need it, you might consider alternate forms of charity.

One way? Give them what they want. One man in Indianapolis reports that he was approached in April 2002 by a stranger who said he desperately needed money to get a ride to a job interview elsewhere in the city. The 43-year-old offered the stranger a ride to his interview. "Man, I tell you, he couldn't have been more shocked," he told a columnist at the *Indianapolis Star*. "He said, 'Um, that's all right. I don't need a ride anymore,' then walked away."

Grifter Speak

You can make a good living panhandling. For somebody who's addicted, why would they want to do anything else?

—a 32-year-old Philadelphia panhandler, speaking to a reporter from the *Philadelphia Daily News*. The same man claimed to make $250 to 300 per week. (By the way, minimum wage for a 40-hour week is $206.)

Don't Be a Sucker

You don't have to be walking down the street to fall victim to a panhandling con man—you can be just sitting at home. Some towns are reporting incidents of strangers knocking on doors and asking for a few bucks because their car ran out of gasoline. Not only do you stand to lose a few dollars (more often than not, the con artist doesn't even have a car nearby), but he might also be casing your house for valuables, and either break into your home later, or sell the information to pro burglars operating in the area.

Some cities, like Indianapolis, have outreach programs. If you're approached by a panhandler, simply call a number, and within 20 minutes, an outreach worker will be on the scene to assess the panhandler's needs. If the person genuinely needs help, it will be given. If con's just looking to fatten his (or her) bankroll, he's out of luck. Some people do a little digging and find the addresses and numbers of local community outreach shelters. They simply type up a list, run off a few copies, then keep them in their briefcase or purse. When a panhandler comes looking for a hand-out, they give the list to them. The genuinely needy can only benefit from such information; the con artists will likely crumple it up and throw it away.

Con-trary to Popular Belief

At www.pbs.org/needcom, you'll find a site dedicated to fine-tuning panhandling techniques, approaching the topic from a market-research point of view. (No, I'm not making this up. Log on for yourself.) One forum asks, "Who's the best panhandler you've ever met?" Some of the more amusing nominations:

- A Texas beggar whose sign is designed to look like an oversized credit card. On one side it reads: AMERICAN DISTRESS CARD. And on the back: DON'T BE HOMELESS WITHOUT IT.
- An L.A.-area panhandler who holds a sign that reads, PLEASE GIVE TO THE HOMELESS. If you chose not to give, the man will show you the other side of the sign: DIE, YUPPIE SCUM.
- A San Francisco-based man who pleads with the sign: HELP, I NEED A BEER!

The Pigeon Drop

Okay, you've walked through (and survived) a simple street con. Now let's discuss a slightly more complex con game, one that involves a team of at least two other people. It's called the "Pigeon Drop," and it's probably the most widely-cited example of a street con. The Pigeon Drop has thousands of variations, but I'm going to boil the drama down to its basic form, then give you a few real-life examples.

You're walking down Main Street, and your attention is drawn to a stranger. He's stooping over in front of something. "Oh my God," he says, lifting the object up. It turns out to be a briefcase with its lid ajar. He locks eyes with you. "You're never going to believe what's in here." The stranger looks back down at the briefcase, then back at you. "There's got to be thousands of dollars in here."

Out of nowhere, a second stranger approaches. "Hey, I see what you guys have got there. I saw it first. I want my share!"

"You want what?" says the first stranger. "No way, man. This is none of your business." Then he turns to you. "Right?"

Before you have a chance to answer, the second stranger gets more insistent. "No way. You're not squeezing me out. Fair is fair."

Begrudgingly, the first stranger allows the second stranger into the fold. (The first stranger even rolls his eyes, gesturing to the second stranger.) Soon, talk turns to what to do with the money. You look inside the case, and the first stranger is right—there's got to be thousands of dollars inside. "Should we turn it in for a reward?" the first stranger asks. "No way," asserts the second. "Look at it. That's drug money. Nobody's going to offer a reward. Cops will probably keep it for themselves."

The first stranger looks insulted. "Screw you, pal. My brother's a cop."

"Look," the second stranger says, "I'm just being honest. There ain't nobody offering a reward for this loot. Trust me."

"Tell you what," says the first stranger. "Let me give my brother a call. He's at the 15th Precinct. If the loot is stolen or part of a drug deal, he'll give it to me straight."

The second stranger agrees. So do you—better to know what you're getting yourself into. That's when the first stranger says, "Look, if you don't want to be bothered with this, we can handle it from here."

You know what's going on. This is a bum's rush. "No way," you say. "I'm in this, too. Call your brother."

The first stranger pulls out a cell phone, then wanders a few steps away. He has a short conversation, then walks back over. "It's like you thought," he says, gesturing at the second stranger. "My brother says it's probably drug money or stolen. We'd be fools to report it. So we split it."

"Hold on now," says the second stranger. "I don't know either of you from Adam. I think we need some kind of good faith gesture, just to make sure we can all we trusted."

"What you mean?" asks the first stranger.

The second stranger says each of the three should show a substantial sum of money, and then and only then will the split be made. "Otherwise, how can we know we can trust each other not to rat?"

You're getting a queasy feeling. "Why do you need to see money? Isn't my word good enough?"

"No, he's right," says the first stranger. "We got to make a good faith gesture. If you don't want to bother, no worries on my part. We can split this two ways, can't we?"

"Yeah, we can," says the second stranger.

You're no fool. You quickly agree to the conditions. But who's going to hold the money in the meantime? Of course—the brother who's a cop. Another cell phone call is made, and within 15 minutes, the brother—a plainclothes detective—is on the scene. Soon, all three of you disperse to withdraw the agreed-upon sum—$3,000 out of the bank—and return to the detective to collect your share. You hand over your money to the cop, and his beeper goes off. "Shit," he says. "Gotta return this call. Excuse me."

That's the last time you see the cop, or his brother, or the second stranger, for that matter. And you're $3,000 poorer.

The term *Pigeon Drop* most likely refers to the underworld courier (i.e., the "Pigeon") who dropped the ill-gotten gains while making a delivery, and it depends on convincing the mark that he has to produce "good faith" money, otherwise he'll miss out on a fat pile of free money. Of course, reading about this con might make you roll your eyes and ask, Who would ever fall for *that?* But right there, you're underestimating the skill of the con artist, and the power of greed. It's very tough to walk away from free cash. The fact that a cop is involved, and has given his blessing to the scheme, is often all the convincing a potential mark needs. *Let's make the deal.* As crazy it may sound, the Pigeon Drop is successfully perpetrated dozens of times across the country every year.

Grifter Speak

Pigeon Drop a "found money" scam in which an unsuspecting passerby is encouraged to offer up "good faith" money, only to have it swindled away from him.

Grifter Speak

Michigan Roll the fake roll of money flashed to marks in Pigeon Drop schemes. Often, it's real money on top, but shredded newspaper or bogus bills stacked beneath. Also known as boodle, flash roll, or nut.

An 81-year-old man in Fort Worth, Texas fell for a rather simple variation of the Pigeon Drop in early August 2002. At 10 A.M., in front of a Target department store, the victim was approached by a guy in a suit and carrying a black briefcase. "Sorry to bother you, sir, but I'll give you $50 if you could give me a lift to McDonald's." The victim declined the cash and gave him the ride anyway. "This other fellow came out of the McDonald's and I thought he was the manager," the victim told the *Fort Worth Star-Telegram*. "That fellow started talking with the guy I had driven to the restaurant. Pretty soon, they started arguing about money."

The argument? That the second man couldn't come up with $15,000. Soon, this argument involved the 81-year-old victim, and a bet was made: The first man said he'd give $15,000 to the older gentleman if he proved he could come up with his own $15,000. Dutifully, the victim drove to his bank—accompanied by the second man, just to make sure things were on the up and up—and withdrew $15 Gs. When the victim handed the money over to the first man, the two fled. "He was a real friendly man," said the victim. "He didn't look like any criminal to me." Of course, that was the idea.

Other varieties of the Pigeon Drop rely not on the victim's greed, but their do-gooder instincts. One such variation is called the "Jamaican Switch." In it, a foreigner approaches a kindly-looking mark (many times a priest) and shows him a bag full of cash—over $20,000, he claims. The mark looks into the bag and sees a ton of green. The foreigner explains that he's been here in the United States raising money for needy children, and that he needs to find a certain church to offer his donation. The only problem: He has a plane to catch, and he doesn't trust American banks. And if he took the money home, it would be confiscated, and he would be executed. Would the mark mind dropping it off at the church? The mark agrees, but then the foreigner asks for a sign of trust—maybe $5,000. When the mark withdraws the money from the bank, the foreigner takes it, and hands over the bag full of cash. Happily, the mark walks away with it, either to promptly deliver it to the church, or perhaps to make a private donation to himself. (Maybe that foreigner was right to mistrust the mark.) The mark opens the bag, but sees nothing but shredded paper. No money. And the $5,000 is presumably on a plane out of the country.

In 1997, this exact scheme happened to a retired minister in Dayton, Ohio. "I was so excited," the minister told the *Dayton Daily News*. "I got home and pulled the table up in front of me, and I put the blue handkerchief on the table and opened it up. Oh man. I felt so bad. There was nothing there but rolled-up scraps of paper. I had really been conned. I called the police."

It's a Scam

Another popular street con is something that fraud expert Frank Abagnale calls the "mustard squirter." You're walking down the street, and a concerned passerby stops you. "Do you know you have mustard all over your back?" she'll ask. Oh no, you say, and twist your neck around to inspect the damage. "Here, here … let me help you," she'll say, removing a wet-nap from her purse. *She must be somebody's mom to carry around wet-naps* like that, you think to yourself, turning your back to her. "Now this will stain if you don't take it to a dry cleaner's in the next 24 hours," she says. "But it'll do for now." You thank her profusely, your faith in humanity restored. Restored, that is, until an hour later, when you're in front of an ATM, but can't seem to find your wallet. *Why, it was in my back pocket this afternoon …* Some con artists use ketchup, some use sweet and sour sauce, some use mustard—but all of them leave a rotten taste in their victim's mouth.

Your best defense? Remember that the Pigeon Drop can only work with one key ingredient: your money. If you follow the rule of never giving a stranger money on the street—no matter how good the reason sounds—you'll stop a con artist from getting the drop on *you*.

One Buck at a Time: Shortchangers

As David Bowie sang, "Don't want to be a richer man … ch-ch-ch-ch-changes." Well, some con artists *do* get rich playing around with *ch-ch-ch-ch-change*—namely, your change from a purchase. They're commonly referred to as "shortchange artists," and they make their living $1, $10, or sometimes even $99 at a time. It's really tough to find accurate statistics on how much cash shortchangers steal every year—some place the figure at over $500 million, because not many people even realize they've been shortchanged until it's too late, and even then they loathe to report it because they're embarrassed.

Shortchanging is an especially appealing game to a con artist because the risk is relatively low. If the game is played right, a shortchanger can always play innocent ("What? You gave me an extra $20? Golly, I'm sorry—I didn't even notice!"), and the truth is, most police bunco squads are chasing after bigger fish. That leaves the policing up to you—the careful consumer. You work too hard for your money to have some slippery, smooth-talking *hype*—that's slang for shortchange artist—pocketing some of it. In this next section, I'll tell you how to catch them in the act.

Grifter Speak

Hype Slang term for a shortchange artist.

—Source: William Denton's *Twists, Slugs and Roscoes: A Glossary of Hardboiled Slang.*

How Sales Clerks Shortchange You

Every time you hand someone money expecting change in return, you're potentially setting yourself up for a shortchange con. Think about *that* the next time you give your little nephew $6 for an oversized Snickers bar for a school fundraiser. (Don't let the oh-so innocent smile fool you; the boy is milking this candy gig for all it's worth.) But the most frequent offenders are sales clerks—cashiers, ticket sellers, street vendors, check cashers, register-jockeys, and bartenders.

We're going to save bartenders for the next section, since they have their own devious tricks. Let's start with the most innocuous salesman we can think of. How about the guy who sells beer at baseball games? Beloved by fathers and uncles everywhere, beer men have the ability to make any tedious ball game bearable. Somehow, that $4 plastic cup of watered-down Coors Light tastes like the nectar of the gods, especially when paired with a greasy $3 hot dog. But the stadium owner might not be the only ones getting rich. Pay attention to the change the beer man hands you. He may tick it off from the fat wad of cash in his hand, dollar by dollar, but count it anyway—one common vendor trick is to fold a dollar bill in half, then count it twice when ticking off the change. Sure, it's only a buck to you, but think about how many times he can pull this trick in an hour. If the beer man keeps it up for even just an inning or two, he'll be able to buy a whole truckload of that overpriced beer.

For that matter, think back to the lady who sold you the ticket at the front gate. Let's say the tickets came to a grand total of $16.25. Notice how she slid you the bills first, then the change behind it? She might have been hoping you would grab the green and completely forget about the silver. This is an old carnival trick. Even if only one out of ten customers falls for it, it's a nice hourly wage. (Carnivals at the turn of the century, by the way, used to intentionally hire shortchange artists to work the change booths. The shortchangers were expected to scam so much money from the paying customers, they were often asked to pay *the carnival* a fee just to work there.)

Other times, you won't even be given the opportunity to take the correct change. Some register-jockeys will count off coins from their right hand to the left—quarter, dime, dime, nickel—but then use the old magician's sleight-of-hand trick to "palm" the quarter and merely slide you the two dimes and a nickel. (Palming can be as simple as trapping the quarter between two fingers, out of the customer's line of vision.) Since you've already seen him count the change, you simply take it and shove it in your pocket and think nothing of it.

> **Don't Be a Sucker**
>
> Always count your change, even if the vendor has already counted it in front of you. Sometimes, shortchangers will fold a bill in half and count it twice.

Most shortchange artists take advantage one of the realities of modern life: you're too damn busy to worry about something as inconsequential as counting your change. But others purposefully want to slow you down and distract you with conversation. Some might use a number trick. Say you're with your wife and you go to buy tickets to an amusement park ride. "What a lovely couple you are," the ticket-taker might say. "The total comes to $1.50." You hand her a $20. "Thanks. That's two, three, four … how long you guys been married anyway?" You beam, clutching your wife closer to you, and say, "Eleven blissful years." "Wow, eleven, that's terrific … twelve, thirteen, fourteen, and five makes twenty. Enjoy the ride!" You're so happy to be reminded how happy you are, you don't even realize that the ticket-taker has already taken you for a ride—to the tune of ten bucks.

Con-trary to Popular Belief _____

Former con man and fraud expert Frank W. Abagnale once shortchanged the country's most beloved talk show host. "Johnny Carson once invited me onto the 'Tonight Show' and dared me to fool him while he was fully expecting to be scammed," writes Abagnale in *The Art of the Steal* (2001). "I had no problem shortchanging Johnny out twenty dollars twice in five minutes. The audience loved it."

When Con Men Shortchange Sales Clerks

Now let's turn the tables. Some serious con artists don't want to bother with you—a buck here, a buck there. That means getting a job as a clerk, and that's just too much work. Why bother, when you can make just as much—if not more—shortchanging businesses?

Shortchangers who target businesses rely on their lightning-quick tongues and the hopes that the person running the register can be easily distracted. Personally, I feel bad for register-jockeys who go up against an experienced shortchanger. Even the most basic shortchanging con can leave the average person's head spinning, even if that average person has a graduate degree in advanced mathematics.

The most basic form of shortchanging scams is something I'll call "Nine Will Get You Twenty." It's simple and brilliantly complex, and unless a sales clerk is paying attention, he'll fall for it every time. Here's how it works (and stop me if this gets too confusing, because it can be): a con man walks into a corner store. He picks up a pack of gum for 98 cents—one of those new, ultra-powerful, bad-breath-killing brands—and pays for it with a $20.

The cashier hands back the change: two pennies, four ones, a five and a ten.

Now the scam begins.

The con man asks for a favor: would the cashier mind giving him a $10 for five and five ones? No problem, says the cashier, who hands him a ten, while the con man hands over the five and four ones, saying, "There's five and five ones. But you'd better count it." The cashier does, and realizes she's a buck short. "There is only nine dollars here."

Now the con man acts irritated. "I'm running late. Look, I've changed my mind about the gum. Here it is. You say you have nine dollars there? Good. Here's a ten and a one. Can I have my $20 back?"

At this point, the flustered cashier hands back the $20. She's forgotten that she's already handed over a ten dollar bill. The con man leaves $10 richer. Then he goes in search of another store to pull a similar stunt. Hmmm, maybe he'll use a $50 this time.

If you own a store, the best investment you can make is to train your cashiers to be on the lookout for shortchangers using tricks like the one I just described. There are dozens of variations, but they all depend on the same essential factors: a confused cashier. Tell your employees to take payment from only one customer at a time, and never to be in a hurry—the world's not going to end if they don't get their 98-cent can of Burma Shave in the next 30 seconds. Shortchange artists love to have rapid-fire conversations that confuse or rattle your workers; make sure your employees know to follow the money.

Also, tell them to keep it over the counter: When they take a bill from a customer, lay it on top of the drawer while making change and handing the change to the customer—this prevents some mook from saying he's been short-changed.

It's a Scam
A shortchanger almost always buys something for less than a buck, pays with a large bill ($20 or $50), tries to ask for his change in a specific order, and then makes a fuss about a mistake he claims the cashier has made.

Set 'Em Up, Joe: When Bartenders Cheat Drinkers

As you've seen in the Pigeon Drop, con artists often work in teams. Well, shady bartenders often work in teams, too. They team up with the three martinis you've downed this evening—alcohol consumption and con men go together like gin and vermouth. Think about it: most con artists want to impair your better judgement. When you've had a few drinks, your judgement has already been impaired!

I've certainly been there—and scammed. In my younger and wilder days, I was known to frequent a bar now and again. As an underpaid magazine employee, sometimes I had only $40 to last a weekend, so I was very fond of dive bars where pints of Yuengling Lager were only 90 cents, and on Wednesdays, hot dogs could be had for a quarter. (If scientists were to analyze my DNA in my early 20s, I'm sure they'd find it was comprised of adenine, cytosine, guanine, lager, and hot dog.) Anyway, once in a while I'd wander in, drink for a few hours with some friends, then wake up the next morning and realize I had $7 to my name. Now, I know that I couldn't have consumed $33 worth of 90-cent beers. If I had, my liver would be the size of Rob Reiner.

What happened? Most likely one of the waitresses or bartenders took me for a ride. Maybe I handed over a five, and got only three ones and a dime back. Or bought a round for two friends, handed over a $20, but only received change for a $10. Or maybe the bartender decided to charge us $1.40 for those pints instead of 90 cents. I wouldn't know. After all, it was a bar. I was probably in the middle of a very important beer-fueled conversation. The Ramones were on the jukebox, wailing about wanting to be sedated. Everyone in the world was my friend. Why should I count my change? Because I don't want to wake up the next morning with only $7 to my name. (Thank God you could sell CDs for cash.)

It's a Scam

The Orange County Weekly has a unique feature called "Hey, You!" in which readers can anonymously praise or accuse their fellow citizens. Here's one rant from 1998, when a reader watched a bartender pull scam after scam:

> After a particularly stressful day at work recently, I sat at the bar of a popular beach-city watering hole. You were the bartender there. It was easy to see that most of your customers think you're a likable, easygoing guy. What they don't know is that you are also a thief. During the time it took me to drink two beers, I watched you brazenly shortchange or overcharge several bar patrons. The scam might have gone unnoticed if it hadn't been for the one alert guy who caught you giving him change for a $10 after he had given you a $20. Your innocent act—which I later realized was designed to make the customer feel petty for calling attention to the "error"— seemed genuine to me at the time ... The two women you overcharged $4 on two glasses of wine don't know what a scumbag you are, either.

Sometimes, bar scams are perpetrated by the bar owners themselves. Such places are known as "gyp-joints," and there, all bartending staff are encouraged to save the boss money by employing the following booze bunco tricks:

- **Dice ice** A professional cocktail tastes better when shaved, crushed, or diced ice is used (as opposed to those clunky Fisher-Price blocks of ice you have in your home freezer.) But some bars take this idea too far. They'll make buckets of "dice ice"—ice cubes that are roughly the size of playing dice, or sugar cubes—and pack them into highball glasses so very little liquor can fit in between them. The average mixed drink uses anywhere from 1 to 3 ounces of spirits; but with dice ice, the bar might get away with using a measly quarter or half ounce of booze.

- **Slyball glasses** Ordinary highball glasses hold 8 to 12 ounces. But certain sleazy joints will buy "slyball" glasses, with thick sides or bases, that hold only

6 ounces. The drink will taste the same, but you'll seem to blow through them a lot quicker.

◆ **Short shots**   You belly up the bar and ask for a shot of Jack Daniels. The bartender slams down the thick shot glass, which echoes on the wooden bar top, then tips the end of the J.D. bottle skyward. You see that he fills it a bit past the "fill line" at the top of the glass. You appreciate that. You do the shot, and instantly feel ready for your 10 A.M. production meeting. (Just kidding, folks. Remember: Drinking and office work do not mix.) But you might have just been shorted half your shot. Some bars use short shot glasses—much like the slyball glasses—which have thick bases, and use an inner conical shape that starts wide up top, but funnels down to a rounded point. Sure, your drink appeared to go above the fill line, but if you were to pour it into a measuring cup, you'd see you're only getting an ounce of booze, instead of the usual 2 ounces in the average shot. That's not enough to start your work day, damnit! (Kidding again, folks. And remember: Don't photocopy and collate while drunk.)

◆ **The poorer pourer**   Sometimes, a bartender will mix a weak drink right before your thirsty eyes. Remember the 1988 stinker *Cocktail*, where Tom Cruise made a big deal of juggling bottles and pouring booze into martini glasses from absurd heights? That was all for show. Shady bartenders will put on a similar show by pouring vodka—to, say, the count of four—into your martini glass. So where's the scam? It's in the speed pourer, that silver spout that regulates the flow of booze. When you use a standard pourer and tip the bottle to the count of four, you'll get the proper amount for a cocktail. But if you use a pourer with a narrow tip, you can pour to the count of four, but the result will be a weaker drink.

Con-trary to Popular Belief

A few years ago, investigative magazine reporters found that many bars don't use any vodka in their Bloody Maries. We're not sure which is more shocking: the stinginess of the bars, or the fact that investigative reporters are so intently focused on Bloody Maries.

If you receive any drinks with the above tell-tale scam signs, send it back. You deserve better for your $5. (In my book, a con artist who tries to swindle a drinker belongs in the same corner of Hell as people who try to swindle schoolchildren and little old Catholic nuns.) And if you suspect that a bartender is serving you the same drink twice, you can catch him with the clear button trick. Simply drop one into your drink, and see if it comes back to you—it'll be very hard for the bartender to see, if he's even looking at your drink. If it does, you should take your liver elsewhere.

And you thought the neighborhood bar was a safe haven. Guess you'd better find a bar you can trust, or just stick to six-packs at home.

The Least You Need to Know

- ◆ Don't fall for panhandler's pleas—it's one of the oldest scams in the book. If you really want to help, direct them to the nearest police officer or homeless shelter.

- ◆ The Pigeon Drop is a very popular scam that involves a large sum of "found money" on the street.

- ◆ Store clerks try to shortchange you with a little slight-of-hand when returning your change. Always count it again, even if the clerk has ticked it down for you, buck by buck.

- ◆ Be careful where you get tipsy—some bartenders love to swindler their customers with a variety of penny-ante scams.

Part  Pigeons, Pills, and Predators: Scams Against Individuals

Some con artists refuse to pull scams on individuals. It violates their code of ethics—after all, most folks are working chumps, just like them, trying to make a go of it in a world where the odds are stacked against the working chump. What fun or challenge is there in bilking the average Joe?

Other con artists, however, have no such moral qualms. They'll target you at birth (adoption scams), at your wedding (sweetheart scams), and even after your death (a variety of inheritance and fake billing scams). In this chapter, I'll describe what happens when con men turn their attention to you, and what you can do to protect yourself.

Chapter 4

Identity Theft and Credit Fraud

In This Chapter

- ◆ The sneaky ways crooks steal your identity
- ◆ How to steal back your life
- ◆ Credit gangs who sell your numbers
- ◆ Avoiding phony credit offers

In the 1974 horror movie *The Exorcist*, a supernatural demon takes over the body of an innocent 14-year-old girl, forcing her to do all kinds of unpleasant things—mouth off to her mother, stay up way past her bedtime, vomit pea soup on priests. In the 1990s, some con artists fashioned their own version of possession—identity theft—the fastest-growing con on the planet. Thieves snap up your date of birth and Social Security number to create a shadow identity—another virtual you, who suddenly applies for new bank accounts and credit cards and likes to do a lot of shopping.

Here's how con artists pull off the trick of financial possession, and how you can perform an identity theft exorcism. Read on. The power of MasterCard compels you!

An Identity Crisis

Throughout history, successful con artists have found ways to crawl inside their victim's heads. They learn their strengths, their weaknesses, and how they'll react to certain situations. But twenty-first century con artists have upped the ante. Not only can they crawl inside their victim's head, but they've found a way to hang out for a while. And order a lot of junk using their victims' good names (and credit reports).

Identity thieves—the latest and most frightening breed of con artist—operate by stealing your personal numbers: a bank account, a credit card number, your Social Security number. Using that single string of digits, an identity thief can weave himself a shadow You.

In spring 2002, Attorney General Richard Ashcroft called *identity theft* "one of the fastest growing crimes in the United States," and added that U.S. attorneys brought 25 new cases against these identity-jackers in the "last 24 hours alone." The Justice Department estimates that 500,000 to 700,000 people are victimized each year. Even the September 11 hijackers were believed to have been identity thieves, using stolen passports and Social Security numbers to obscure their trail.

Grifter Speak

Identity theft is when a con artist uses your personal data—name, address, Social Security number, credit card accounts, birth date—to create a shadow identity, which then buys merchandise, takes out loans, and makes other financial transactions. The con man keeps the loot; you get stuck with the bad credit.

Identity theft makes headlines more and more every day. One recent case involved a Memphis, Tennessee man who cooked up a clever identity theft scheme: theft by *Who's Who*. James Rinaldo Jackson, 41, purchased a copy of *Who's Who in America* and made a list of prominent people—including the chief operating officer of Coca-Cola Enterprises, the chief executive of Hilton Hotels, and the president of Wendy's International. Then, Jackson paid illegal Internet brokers between $50 and $100 each for the Social Security numbers to go with those names. Once he had matching sets, Jackson used the information to impersonate his victims on the phone to order $730,000 worth of diamonds and Rolex watches.

After he was caught and pleaded guilty, Jackson told the court how easy it had been. "I got credit card numbers and I started ordering diamonds," he said. And once Jackson had his victims' SSN and credit card numbers, it was easy to swipe more personal data, including the expiration date on those credit cards and even spending limits. "If American Express gave them an opportunity to spend $22,000 with their company last month," Jackson told the court, "I know that I could spend $22,000 plus for the next month because the credit is going to be heightened somewhat."

The judge responded: "Amazing, Mr. Jackson. Absolutely amazing." Then he sentenced Jackson to eight years in prison and ordered him to pay back $376,704 in restitution, which was the amount police were unable to recover.

Con-trary to Popular Belief

Identity theft is considered a nonviolent crime, but that isn't always the case. One thief from Chicago was charged with suffocating a homeless man to death. The thief was already facing trial on a host of charges—counterfeiting birth certificates, Social Security cards, and driver's licenses—and thought he would pull the ultimate identity switch: cremate the homeless guy under the thief's real identity, thereby making it impossible for the Feds to prosecute him. (It didn't work. The thief—under his real name—faced a murder rap in addition to his counterfeiting charges.)

Nice Life–We'll Take It!

Of course, to steal your identity, a thief needs your most vital numbers. You probably think they're safely locked away in your wallet, a filing cabinet at home, or behind impenetrable bank vault doors. Please. More people have your most vital digits—your Social Security, bank account and credit card numbers—than you can possibly imagine. Ever use a calling card at a pay phone? Pay for lunch with a credit card? Order something online? Get divorced? Stay over in a hospital? Receive mail? Then your numbers are out there. You might as well use a magic marker to scrawl them on a bathroom wall. *For A Good Identity Theft, Call Jenny 867-5309.*

So how do identity thieves get their grubby little digits on your personal digits? Let us count only some of the ways:

1. *Shoulder Surfing*   You punch in your credit card or calling card number into a pay phone in a hotel lobby. Little do you know that, mere feet behind you, an identity thief is watching your hand movements, and can discern your number from them.

2. **Trash Picking**   You toss away old bills, tax records, credit card statements, even those "Congrats! You've Been Pre-Approved for a Ridiculous New Credit Card" offers. The identity thief loves it when you do that. He simply takes your trash, and fishes around until he finds that

Grifter Speak

Shoulder Surfing   the method a con artist uses to watch a victim's hand movements to learn their secret PIN and credit card numbers.

unopened, intact pre-approval and takes the liberty of mailing it in for you. Of course you never see the card, until it's too late.

3. **Courthouse Digging**   Ever been involved in a civil suit or divorce? A ton of your personal numbers are sitting in a big fat court file, which are public records. Anybody can stop by City Hall and have a look.

4. **Personnel File Filching**   Identity thieves—or their assistants—may be lurking in the human resources department of your own company, or institutions you depend on. One hospital employee was accused of stealing the identities of 393 hospital patients, which he used to obtain one heck of a lot of credit cards. It's enough to make you sick.

5. **Old-Fashioned Filching**   Some identity thieves simply steal your purse or wallet, and use your I.D. and credit cards they find inside. Or they might even take letters of your mailbox to glom some personal info.

6. **Who's Who Scanning**   You're proud. After years of dues-paying and personal struggle, you're prominently listed in *Who's Who in America*. But so is your birthday, hometown, mother's maiden name, and home address. Identity thieves—like James Rinaldo Jackson, mentioned previously—use this informa- tion to request your birth certificate, which in turn can be used to forge a shadow identity. Congrats!

7. **Mail Moving**   You've lived at your present address for 12 years. All of a sud- den, you stop receiving mail—not even so much as a piece of junk mail. When you call the post office to find out what happened, it turns out that you filled out a change of address form a couple of weeks ago. But of course, you didn't. Your identity thief did.

8. **Online Purchasing**   Some crooks make a business out of selling your personal numbers. One brazen thief even offered Social Security numbers on eBay. His listing read: "100 (one hundred) social Security # Numbers Obtain False Credit Cards Identity Theft I Don't Care Bid Starts At a Dollar a Piece USPS Money Orders only all Different [sic]."

9. **Credit Report Ripping**   All an identity thief has to do is call one of the big three credit reporting companies—Equifax, Experian, or TransUnion—and pre- tend to be a prospective landlord. With the right info, one of the companies will simply fax over your detailed credit history.

Once he gets your number, an identity thief gets busy. He may call your credit card issuer, pretend to be you, and ask to change the mailing address on your account.

Then the thief goes off and hits your plastic hard, taking out cash advances and buying expensive items (which in turn might be pawned or sold). But since your bills will start going to a new address, it'll be a while before you realize what's happening. Or, he may simply apply for a stack of brand new credit cards—all he needs is your name, birthday, and Social Security number. When the bills come in, the identity thief uses them as beer coasters. After a while, the delinquent account lands on your credit report.

But that's not all. An identity thief can also open wireless phone service in your name, buy cars with auto loans (also taken out in your name), order checks and debit cards to drain your bank account, open a new bank account in your name and write rubber checks on that account, and in general make you look like a total weenie.

> **It's a Scam**
>
> Beware if your phone number suddenly becomes unlisted—and you never requested it. Sometimes an identity thief will go ahead and make your number unlisted, so curious creditors won't know where to reach you.

The scamming possibilities are endless. One trio of identity thieves in Detroit used their purloined info to execute $1.7 in stock options that were owned by a retired Kmart executive.

Keeping Your Identity to Yourself

The last thing you want is somebody stealing vital info and giving you a bad name. (Most of us manage that just fine on our own, thank you very much.) So how can you protect yourself?

1. **Pay close attention to those little envelopes with the plastic windows.** In other words, your bills. Missing a credit card statement? It might have been lifted from your mailbox by an identity thief. Call your creditor to follow up, and see if any odd purchases have been made in past week or two. Use the chance to get to know your creditor, and compliment him on the lovely tie he's wearing today.

2. **Guard your mailbox.** Don't be one of those chumps who lets his mailbox fill up until it cries "Uncle!" Empty it as soon as you can. Going on vacation? Ask a trusted friend to pick up your mail for you. Don't have any friends? Call the U.S. Postal service at 1-800-275-8777 and ask for a "vacation hold." Your friendly neighborhood post office will hold your mail until you return.

3. **Only give out personal info on a need-to-know basis.** And truth is, legitimate companies don't "need to know"—they should already have your vital info on file and not have to ask you for it. So be wary of callers who claim to be representatives of your bank or credit card companies, and ask you for your mother's maiden name or your Social Security card.

4. **Secure your Social Security card.** The last place you want to keep it is in your wallet or purse—when a crook finds one, he considers it hitting the lottery. Also, many agencies and banks use your SSN as an identification number. If possible, ask them to use something else. The fewer places your SSN is flashed around town, the fewer opportunities an identity thief will have to swipe it.

5. **Run a credit check on yourself.** The Federal Trade Commission recommends checking up on yourself once a year. Order a copy of your credit report from each of the three credit reporting agencies—by law, this can't cost you more than $9 each—and give it a good look. Each report shows where you work and live, the accounts that are open under your name, and how often you pay (or don't pay) your bills. Someday, when the bomb drops, this may be all that you leave behind. Don't you want to take a look first? To order yours, contact:

   Equifax: www.equifax.com, 1-800-685-1111, P.O. Box 740241, Atlanta, GA 30374-0241.

   Experian: www.experian.com, 1-888-EXPERIAN (397-3742), P.O. Box 2104, Allen, TX 75013.

   TransUnion: www.transunion.com, 1-800-916-8800, P.O. Box 1000, Chester, PA 19022.

6. **Close the (pre) screen.** Remember that trick where identity thieves fish a pre-approved credit card offer out of the trash? You can stop receiving them in the first place by calling 1-888-5-OPTOUT (567-8688). The three major credit bureaus all use this same number, which give you to option of not receiving these offers in the future. And while you're at it, give Experian a call at 1-800-407-1088 and tell them to remove your name from lists that are used for marketing and promotional purposes. (The other two, Equifax and TransUnion, won't let you do this.)

[handwritten margin note: free reports from all three at www. annual credit report. com]

How to Reclaim Your Identity

Your identity has been stolen. You have two new cars and three mortgages you didn't know about. Someone has been snapping up Barbara Streisand Collectible Plates in your name on eBay, then stiffing the seller. And you really, *really* hate Barbara Streisand.

ut it? First off, don't feel bad—virtually anybody can become an
t any time. Even our smart-as-a-tack technical consultant (and
ike Connelley fell victim to this kind of scam. "A year and a half
y AmEx number and used it to purchase about $9,000 worth of
tomobile engines from a dealer in Utah," says Connelley. "I
a pain in the neck to get straightened out." Here's how to do it,
eral Trade Commission:

aud department of all three major credit bureaus. You'll find
and numbers in the previous section. You can tell them to issue a
vhich will make it tougher for the identity thief to wreak more
sk for copies of your report—by law, they're required to send
them to you for free in cases of fraud—and scan them carefully. Especially keep
an eye out for the section that lists "inquiries"—these mean that somebody has
been inquiring about opening a new account using your info. Tell the credit
bureaus to delete these from your report, then check back again in a few months
to make sure they're gone.

◆ **Call your creditors, and tell them what happened.** Especially be sure to
notify accounts that have been used by the identity thief. Make sure you do it in
writing—that's how the law says you're supposed to resolve credit discrepancies—and make sure you ask to speak with each company's fraud or security
department. (Believe me, these days, every company or creditor, including
phone and utility companies, has a fraud department.) Also, open new accounts,
with new passwords and PIN numbers.

◆ **File a report with the cops in your area.** While Sgt. Friday down at the 12th
Precinct isn't likely to catch your identity thief, having a police report on hand is
an invaluable tool, especially when try-
ing to clear your good name with your
creditors. It establishes that a crime has
been committed, and can be easily faxed
to the creditors who demand proof of the
crime before wiping your accounts clean.

Beginning in 2002, the FTC began publishing
ID Theft checklists and affidavits, available for
free by calling 1-877-IDTHEFT or download-
ing them from www.consumer.gov/idtheft. The
charts are extremely handy—they walk you
through every step of the process of clearing

Don't Be a Sucker

Think someone jacked
your identity? Called the Federal
Trade Commission's Identity Theft
Hotline at 1-877-IDTHEFT (438-
4338). The FTC also has a
handy "ID Theft Affidavit," which
you can copy and send to companies where an account has
been opened in your name. You
can download a copy at
www.consumer.gov/idtheft..

your name, and include boxes to record the date and time you contacted the fraud representative at each company. If some jerk steals your identity, you'll be confused enough. These lists give you some semblance of order in a life that's suddenly gone haywire.

Frustratingly, identity thieves typically receive light sentences—maybe a year at most. Compare that with the years that most identity theft victims will spend putting their lives—and credit reports—back together again. But in 2002, Attorney General John Ashcroft asked Congress for legislation that would lead to tougher sentences. When the original legislation was passed back in 1998, there were fewer than 600 cases; in the first eight months of 2002, there were approximately 1,400 cases. Apparently, a year in the pokey is a risk identity thieves are willing to make.

Give Them Some Credit

Some con artists don't want to bother stealing your identity. All they want is your name, credit card number, and expiration date. And they don't need your wallet or identity to get it.

These thieves hang out in what *The New York Times* called "cyberbazaars"—online trading places where stolen credit card numbers are offered to the highest bidder. Actually, I shouldn't say "highest" bidder, since the cost of a single credit card number can fluctuate between 40 cents and five bucks. There are even bulk discounts; $100 might get you 250 cards, and $1,000 can net a crook an astounding 5,000 cards. The card numbers come to the thieves with an exclusive "It's valid, or your money back guarantee" from the sellers.

Where do these thousands of stolen card numbers come from? Well, somebody certainly isn't mugging 5,000 people just to make $1,000 online. No, hackers are doing the heavy work—cracking into online merchants and rifling through the credit card files of the customers. In one astounding case in spring 2002, hackers posed as employees of Ford Motor Credit Company, then filched 13,000 credit reports, which gave thieves access to each customer's address, Social Security number, bank and credit accounts. (Ford immediately sent out certified letters to every single victim, warning them that their reports had been snatched.) "In the old days, people robbed stagecoaches and knocked off armored trucks," said Richard Power, editorial director of the Computer Security Institute. "Now, they're knocking off servers."

> **It's a Scam**
>
> A big fat technology order with a foreign shipping address is usually a red flag that a credit gang might be at play. However, some overseas credit gangs have started to recruit U.S. assistants, just so that merchandise can be shipped to a U.S. address first.

Of course, the online merchants and credit card companies largely take the hit from credit gangs—who operate overseas, mostly in the former Soviet Union. Some estimate that online credit card theft costs the industry over $1 billion a year. However, you'll feel the pinch, too, especially if credit card companies decide to raise their interest rates to cover the losses, or if your card number has been sold to somebody for 40 cents, and they decide to buy a laptop computer with it.

Credit, Declined

Credit gangs sound like the worst thing since Hell's Angels made the scene. But there is hope. Not from the overburdened FBI or Secret Service but from private antifraud groups like CardCops.com. Consider them the Charles Bronsons of the credit world: vigilantes who use the punks' own weapons against them. Funded by credit card companies and online sellers, new groups like the Malibu, California-based CardCops. com and the Atlanta-based Internet Security Systems actually lay traps for credit gangs.

Take this CardCops.com sting that went down in June 2002. First, a phony website called Laptops4Now.com, was established. (Among credit gangs, laptops are like hubcabs, since they can easily be purchased online and resold for cash.) Then, CardCops.com operatives made it into credit gang chat rooms and let it drop that Laptops4Now.com's credit-verifying system was fairly lame. "Our guys floated this information to the chat rooms at 5 P.M., and within 12 hours we got 16 orders for about $27,000 worth of product," said Dan Clements, CardCops.com chief operative, to *The New York Times*. Many of the buyers were in foreign countries like Indonesia and Bulgaria—usually, a big credit gang tip-off.

But when the credit gang members ripped open their USPS boxes a week later, they must have been surprised. Instead of shiny new laptops, CardCops.com loaded the boxes with junk, including old John Grisham paperbacks. Unless the credit gang members were *Pelican Brief* fans, it must have been a big disappointment.

The real score, however, was the 29 leads that the sting generated, which CardCops. com turned over to various law enforcement agencies, including the FBI, the Secret Service, the U.S. Postal Inspector's office, and various local-level district attorneys. Instead of becoming irked at the competition, the pros seemed to welcome the help.

Con-trary to Popular Belief

Online merchant CDUniverse.com told *The New York Times* that they estimate anywhere from 5 to 8 percent of their orders come from credit gangs.

(Especially at a time when terrorist hunting is the FBI's number one priority.) There's also an added legal bonus: If a government stings you, your lawyer can plead entrapment. But if private citizens do it, the government can use the evidence in court.

Now, if only some private vigilan ... er, I mean, *security* companies could figure out a way to turn the tables on identity thieves. How cool would it be to steal an identity thief's own real identity, and hold it hostage? And in the meantime, charge something really embarrassing to his accounts, like a membership in the Skeet Ulrich Fan Club?

The Least You Need to Know

- Identity theft is the fastest-growing crime in the country.

- Thieves use a variety of clever tricks to steal your most vital numbers.

- You can't completely protect yourself from identity thieves, but you can lessen the odds your identity will be swiped.

- Credit card gangs steal your digits, but private companies have started hunting them.

Chapter 5

Dot.Con: Internet and E-Mail Scams

In This Chapter

- ◆ The number one e-fraud: bogus auctions
- ◆ The infamous 419 con
- ◆ Get-rich-quick and work-at-home schemes
- ◆ The verification trick

Back in the days of cowboys and Indians and saddle-sores, the Old West—newly opened up to settlers—was seen as lawless turf, operating grounds for every kind of thief in the book. Today, we have another Old West. It's called the Internet. And just like in the old Old West, traditional law enforcement agencies are overwhelmed by the sheer size and scope of the landscape. No agency can police every square inch of cyberspace. It's up to you, pilgrim, to learn how to make your way safely across the data prairie. (Can I possibly fit another Old West allusion into this paragraph? No, I don't think so, buckaroo.)

The computer is great … for separating a mark from his cash. There is no need for a clean getaway; the con artist could be separated from his mark by thousands of miles. "This borderless phenomenon is a unique characteristic of Internet crime and is not found with many other types of traditional crime," says Thomas Richardson, Deputy Assistant Director of the FBI's Criminal Investigative Division. As a result, many agencies have to pull together to untangle the jurisdictional problems when pursuing an Internet scammer. The problem is only growing, too. There were 16,775 Internet fraud complaints made in 2001, the highest number ever.

Fortunately, the FBI and the National White Collar Crime Center have teamed up to create the Internet Fraud Complaint Center (IFCC), a clearinghouse of Internet fraud. Thanks to "Operation Cyber Loss," launched in May 2001, over 90 online scammers were brought to justice. That may not sound like many, but consider this: Those 90 scammers were responsible for bilking over 56,000 victims who suffered more than $117 million in losses. (Feel free to whistle now.)

If you want to reach the IFCC to file a complaint, log on to www.ifccfbi.gov. Hopefully, though, you won't have to do that. You have a copy of this book in your hands, and in this chapter, I'm going to tell you how to protect yourself while cruising the Wild, Wild Internet.

Con-trary to Popular Belief

Here are the Top Ten forms of internet swindles according to the Internet Fraud Complaint Center (IFCC), based on percentages of complaints:

1. Auction fraud	42.8%
2. Non-delivery	20.3%
3. Nigerian letter fraud	15.5%
4. Credit/debit card fraud*	9.4%
5. Confidence fraud	3.1%
6. Investment fraud*	1.7%
7. Business fraud	1.4%
8. Identity theft*	1.3%
9. Check fraud	0.7%
10. Communications fraud	0.6%

* For more on credit fraud and identity theft, flip back to Chapter 4. For investment and business frauds, skip head to Chapters 11 and 13. Check fraud? Try Chapter 12. We'll be hitting the rest in this chapter.

Going Once, Going Forever ...

Online auctions are great for digging up stuff long buried in the pop culture past. Where else can you find an unopened box of Fruit Brute—the forgotten cereal in the classic General Mills monster cereal line—for just $39.95? Or a signed Leonard Nimoy album for just $79.95? Or an Aurora plastic model kit of Frankenstein for a mere $219.95? (My wife still hasn't forgiven me for that one.)

Sometimes, however, an object posted on an Internet auction site is too good to be true. That's because it exists only in the mind of a con artist, who conceived it to steal your money. According to the U.S. Department of Justice, about 43 percent of all reported Internet fraud involves an online auction. But damn the statistics—they've even hit me twice. Once was when I found an incredibly oddball item on eBay: an ashtray with a machine-gun toting bank robber painted along the bottom. I had just finished writing a book about bank robbery, so I figured it'd be a funny gift for my editor. I paid my money, but the ashtray never showed. Not even after repeated e-mails and complaints. It wasn't as if I lost my life savings on the ashtray, but it still made me mad. Where the heck else am I going to find so tasteless a gift for my editor?

Con-trary to Popular Belief

Internet crime occurs in cyberspace, but its practitioners have to make their beds somewhere. According to the IFCC, most Internet scammers live in these "top ten" states.

1.	Nevada	11.9*
2.	Florida	9.4
3.	New York	6.8
4.	California	6.0
5.	District of Columbia	5.7
6.	Nebraska	5.2
7.	Virginia	4.3
8.	Arizona	3.8
9.	Georgia	3.8
10.	Utah	3.8

Perpetrators per 100,000 population.

Another time, I ordered a DVD copy of an obscure Steve McQueen movie, *The St. Louis Bank Robbery*. (You might be sensing a theme here.) This time, I actually received the product. But it turned out to be a cheap knockoff, with a horrible picture that was grainier than a pair of swimming trunks after a trip to the beach. When I went back to eBay to check on the seller, it turned out that he was selling dozens of these crappy copies—no returns, the fine print read. I was $12 lighter, and stuck with an unwatchable Steve McQueen flick. And there's almost no such thing as an unwatchable Steve McQueen flick, my friend.

My small-time fraud experiences illustrate the two ways con artists defraud unsuspecting online bidders: non-delivery, and the ol' bait and switch. *Nondelivery* is easy enough—the seller takes your cash, but never delivers the promised item. *Bait and switch* is when you are promised one item, but given another. This kind of fraud isn't limited to auctions, either. You might purchase an item—a printer, a bottle of perfume, a printer that spritzes perfume at you while you print—at a deep discount online, only to receive some other piece of crap instead. Here's how to avoid risky bid-ness:

- **Check the fine print.** Make sure you understand how the particular auction site works, and how they deal with problems. For instance, eBay has a detailed fraud reporting process in which you might be eligible for a $200 reimbursement if you can prove you've been swindled.

- **Stay out of the box.** If the seller asks you to send payment to a P.O. box only, be cautious—you'll have no way of tracing him in case he rips you off. Ask for a physical address and a phone number. To be sure, try the phone number to make sure it actually works and doesn't connect you to, say, Dial-A-Prayer in Wilkes-Barre, Pennsylvania.

- **Be wary of free-mail.** If the seller uses a free e-mail service—such Hotmail or Juno—that doesn't require a credit card, you may want to think twice. Anybody can sign up for these services. You. Your cousin Ray. Your cousin Ray's dog. And your cousin Ray's dog can easily cancel the service to disappear in case he's accused of scamming someone. (We always knew Ray's dog was trouble.)

- **Read the feedback.** Auction sites like eBay usually have a "feedback" section, in which other people who have purchased goods from the same seller leave their two cents. Ignore the praise, and look for any negative responses and the reasons given. Be especially wary of sellers who have racked up more than one or two negative responses—or worse yet, don't seem to have any feedback at all, which means they're brand-spanking new. (That, or they've been booted off the auction site before, and now have re-registered under a different name.)

- **Introduce a third party.** Using an auction payment service like PayPal will protect you in two ways: it'll keep your credit card info out of a stranger's hands, and it'll give you the option of stopping payment if you never receive the promised goods.

♦ **Hang on to your digits.** There's no reason to ever give a seller your Social Security number or your driver's license number. Anyone who asks for it is trying to pull a fast one. Also, be cautious if someone asks your shoe size … unless you're buying shoes.

♦ **Ask about returns.** The seller should tell you what kind of return policy he has, and if the goods he's shipping are covered under any kind of warranty. A "Full Money-Back Guarantee" policy? Good. A "Sucks To Be You, Chump" policy? Not so good.

> **CAUTION**
>
> **Don't Be a Sucker**
>
> Are you considering making an online purchase from someone who uses only a P.O. box or e-mails you from a free service (such as Hotmail or Juno)? Don't. If you're scammed, you'll have no way of tracing the culprit, since P.O. boxes and free-mail services can be cancelled in an instant.

Out of Africa

One of the most infamous e-mail frauds is the so-called "Nigerian" or "419 fraud." Here's how it works: You or your company receive an e-mail (or a mailed letter or fax, in some cases) from someone in West Africa who is trying to move a large sum of money to American banks, and if you'll do him the simple favor of allowing him to deposit this money into your bank account, you'll be able to keep a sizeable chunk of it. The letters are humble, charming ("Compliments of the season. Grace and peace and love from this part of the Atlantic to you …") and hint that this deal is not exactly the most legal thing in the world, which is why you have the potential to make a lot of dough. Take this opening salutation from an authentic 419 fraud letter:

> Dear Sir:
>
> REQUEST FOR URGENT TRANSER OF $22,500,000.00 INTO YOUR ACCOUNT
>
> My name is Chief Collins Ozobia. I am the deputy director of finance in the Federal Ministry of Petroleum (F.M.P.) I have been assigned to seek for the assistance of reliable foreign company through which we can transfer the sum of US$22,500,00.00 …

Where did this windfall come from? Why, it's an insurance payout after a horrible plane crash. Or (another version goes) it's money right from the Nigerian government, in return for completing a contract. Or it's a big fat family inheritance. Or it's a juicy real estate deal. Or it's from the sale of crude oil at below market prices. Whatever the tale, it's a ton of money—anywhere from 10 to 30 percent of the total haul, which usually reaches into the tens of millions—that needs to be moved out of the country for safe keeping as soon as possible. How can you refuse? How can your checking account refuse?

Con-trary to Popular Belief

Salon.com writer Douglas Cruickshank wrote a highly amusing essay about the 419 scam in which he praised the pitch letters' literary merits: "I've fallen for them—not the scam part, but for the writing, the plots (fragmented as they are), the characters, the earnest, alluring evocations of dark deeds and urgent needs, Lebanese mistresses, governments spun out of control, people abruptly "sacked" for "official misdemeanors" and all manner of other imaginative details all delivered in a prose style that is as awkward and archaic as it is enchanting. It's some of the most entertaining short fiction around these days."

Once you're hooked, your new Nigerian business partner hits you with the catch: first, you must wire some money to cover expenses—banking fees, transfer tax, administrative costs. In some cases, it's a couple of thousand dollars; other suckers have wired over hundreds of thousands. Often, you're encouraged to travel Nigeria to help close the deal—and here's where it can get really creepy. Once you arrive, you are treated like a king ... until some official discovers there is something wrong with your passport and/or legal papers, and you are detained in a Nigerian jail until your relatives can bail you out for thousands of additional dollars. Sometimes—although very rarely—these scams can turn fatal, and 17 people have been reported murdered due to a *419* scam gone wrong.

These schemes may sound a bit ridiculous, but hundreds of Americans are suckered by the 419 every year. According to the U.S. Secret Service, who's in charge of polic-ing this particular scam, various 419 scam artists have suckered victims out of $5 bil-lion since 1989. And they're always looking for more victims; every month, over 9,000 scamming e-mails are forwarded to the Secret Service. Chances are, you've received one of these e-mails in the past year, especially if you own your own business. The Nigerian government has been coop-erating with the Secret Service in attempting to crack down on these types of scams, but like all Internet crime, it's not so easy to raid something that exists largely in cyberspace. (The Secret Service does

Grifter Speak

419 refers to the section of the Nigerian criminal code that deals with fraud.

have agents on hand in Lagos, Nigeria, and has assisted in the rescue of U.S. Citizens who have been abducted by 419 scam gangs.)

Avoiding this scam is as easy as reading this chapter—once you know about it, you won't be hooked. While it's true that some legitimate Nigerian companies do seek out American investors, they won't be promising millions in return. (As with any business opportunity, take the offer to a lawyer first.) Of course, you're doubly-protected if you adopt a policy of never giving out your savings, checking, credit or other financial account numbers to other people.

If you have been schnookered by the 419, contact the U.S. Secret Service at 202-406-5850, or www.secretservice.gov.

Get Scammed ... Without Leaving Your Home!

You receive a strange e-mail. Lazily, you open it. WORK AT HOME, it says. *Earn Up to $6,000 A Month! No special skills or experience required. This is not a get-rich-quick scheme!*

There you are, sitting in your bathrobe, munching on a granola bar and sipping the dark lake of swill you call coffee. Work at home? Well, that certainly sounds good. I'd have more time to spend with the kids, you reason. No pain-in-the-butt commute on the Long Island Railroad. And best of all, working at home means there is no compelling reason to wear pants. Six bones a month? No special skills required? Sign me up, you say. Sure thing. Just sign right here, on the dotted line above the word SUCKER.

Home business opportunities are not new, but the Internet has certainly given them new life. "For some reason," said FTC spokeswoman Brenda Mack, "people think everything they see on the Internet has got to be real." As you are about to see, nothing could be further from the truth.

Con-trary to Popular Belief

In 2002, the FTC launched an ambitious dragnet called "Project Biz-illion$" which aimed to shut down phony business scammers. In its first major takedown, Biz-illion$ made 35 cases against these scammers in California, Arizona, Florida, and 26 other states. One scammer settled for $81,000; another refused to settle and was hit with a $4.9 million default judgment. The FTC also convinced many newspapers to help screen out fraudulent ads. The Internet, however, is not so easily policed.

E-mailed work-at-home scams have certain trademarks—come-ons that tap into every office drone's secret fantasies. They'll promise high pay ($30,000) in an absurdly short amount of time (just two months). They'll also say you will be your own boss—set your own hours, work where and when you'd like. They might mention the opportunity to travel, or avoid pesky taxes.

Take this e-mail pitch I received at work just a few days ago. It's the perfect example of a work-at-home scam. (I've left the punctuation intact. Shakespeare, these scammers are not.)

Does your boss allow you to:

* Work from home in your pj's?

* Receive 100% of your pay WITHOUT deductions?

* Earn six-figures tax-free every 90–120 days?

* Travel to Tropical Locations every 3–4 months?

If not, FIRE YOUR BOSS!

We can show you how!

Welcome to Prosperity

"The Informed People in Society Will Be Among the Wealthiest In The Coming Era." We Have the Information Needed To Be One of Those People … Do You?

1-800-645-7765

2-Minute Recorded Overview

Let us count the ways in which this one e-mail screams "scam." First of all, it promises an absurd amount of money in a very short period of time—hell, most lawyers don't make six figures in 120 days. Note the details about "WITHOUT deductions" and "tax-free" money. Last time we checked, not paying your local, state, and federal taxes is illegal. (Did they change this rule recently? If so, please drop me an e-mail.) Travel to "tropical locations" every 3 to 4 months? You mean, when you're not earning those six figures every 3 or 4 months? Finally, the e-mail completely mangles the plural form of "pajamas." This is not necessarily a scam, but it is a crime against grammar.

What really sets off alarm bells is the "2-minute recorded overview." As of this point, you have no idea what kind of work you might be doing. Could be stuffing envelopes … could be assassinating the president of some South American country . You simply don't know. You probably won't know until after you call that 1-800 number either, because it seems like an excuse to hook you with a lame message while you rack up toll charges. I'd call to confirm this, but I'm afraid the answer will cost me $49.95, and I'd end up on a "sucker list." (See Chapter 6.) Even if the number doesn't sting you, the "work-at-home" opportunity will, because inevitably, you'll be asked to lay out some cash beforehand. These scams all follow the same pattern: You send Company X an initial investment, and X promises set you up with everything you need to start earning big bucks immediately. The only thing you'll be set-up with, however, is a sure-to-fail business. These bogus opportunities can take many forms. The most common:

- ◆ **Work-At-Home**   *The pitch:* Make thousands stuffing envelopes, processing paperwork, or do some other menial task in the comfort of the family den! *The reality:* The "work" you're doing at home turns out to be incomprehensible—the directions are as convoluted as an Oliver Stone movie. Or, you find out that the "work" you're doing involves selling this same scam to other people. Even if you're successful in passing the buck to make a few bucks, those people will now be competing with you, all of you desperately trying to hook the next sucker. (Shame on you.)

- ◆ **Vending Machines, Display Racks, Pay Phones**   *The pitch:* Own and distribute your own army of candy bar machines/magazine spinners/public phones to earn a comfortable living. *The reality:* The machines you distribute are low-quality or even defective, and they're placed in out-of-way locations like small town gas stations or dying strip malls, where they don't have a prayer of attracting customers.

- ◆ **Employers List**   *The pitch:* Send us $65 for a list of companies that are looking for top-shelf employees like you! *The reality:* You receive a simple, directory-style listing of local businesses. That's it. Nothing else. In other words, information that can most likely be found in your free copy of the Yellow Pages, or at free Internet job listing sites like www.monster.com.

- ◆ **The Uncle Sam Scam**   *The pitch:* For only $50, you'll receive an exclusive form that practically guarantees a cushy government job. *The reality:* Send in that half-a-century note, and you'll get a bunch of photocopied pages on how to take a civil service test. You can skip the middle man and look for government jobs for free at www.usajobs.opm.gov.

Once you discover that you've been had, the scamming company usually has a funny way of disappearing. Your phone calls go unreturned. Mail inquiries are stamped "return to sender." Emails are bounced back like a rubber nickel off Rob Reiner's stomach. These scammers jump from state to state, leaving scores of unpaid bills and angry victims in their wake.

It's a Scam

The next time you see an ad that says you'll earn a particular income (Earn $20,000 In Your First Month!), look for a few more numbers. Legitimate businesses will list the number and percentage of other people who achieved those same amounts. If those numbers are not listed, they're probably breaking the law.

Still, some legitimate businesses do choose to advertise opportunities via the Internet. If you're unsure about a particular business enterprise, make sure you run them through this checklist:

- **Will they give you the details in writing?** Scammers will duck this one; legit companies know they are required by law to do so and will happily provide you with any information you request, especially verification of earnings claims. (Earnings claims = proof that 19-year-old Jenny Sue Johnson made over $17,000 in just two days cooped up in her double-wide trailer.)

- **Will they give you a franchise disclosure document?** This document will list vital info about the company—specifically, if anybody's tried to sue them. You should look for a section listing previous purchasers. If the company tap-dances around this and tries to offer a list of references instead, be wary. According to the FTC (which made the franchise disclosure document law in the first place), it's all too easy to list a bunch of phony references.

- **Will they give you a list of 10 other people who participated in this same venture?** Legit companies know that the FTC requires businesses to provide the names, addresses, and telephone numbers of at least 10 former "purchasers" into said venture. Scammers will also duck this one, or pass you off to one or two "shills," accomplices hired to sing the venture's praises. Don't believe a voice on the phone—ask for the specific contact info.

- **Are they selling a nationally-known product?** If so, it's simple to check 'em out. Simply call the legal department of that nationally-known product, and make sure that the company in question is legally affiliated with them. Also, ask if the nationally-known product has ever threatened to sue over trademark violations. Trust me—if this is the case, the lawyers will be thrilled to tell you all about it.

◆ **Are they rushing you?** Fraudsters will pull out all stops to make sure you send your check as quickly as humanly possible. Legit companies will allow you to take your time and mull over the fine print. This isn't Olympic speed skating; this is a potential business investment.

CAUTION

Don't Be a Sucker _____

If an Internet business opportunity sounds appealing, don't send a dime until you have the details in writing. Companies that ask for more than a $500 investment are required by the FTC Franchise Rule to give you a written document backing up the earnings claims—in other words, proof that their other investors are raking in as many greenbacks as they say. Companies that ask for investments under $500 aren't required to supply such proof, but don't let that stop you from asking for earnings info in writing. If they put you off, put them off.

Just Verifying a Few Things ...

Another variety of Internet scams relies on a pre-Internet trick: tricking people into giving the scammers information they don't have by claiming to be "verifying" that information. In general, be leery of anyone who calls or e-mails to "verify" something. Especially your mother, when she calls to "verify" who you're dating these days.

The IRS Scam

Most adult Americans are afraid of only two things: Freddie Prinze, Jr. movies and the Internal Revenue Service. Scammers take advantage of the latter fear by sending you a e-mail with the subject line: "IRS E-AUDIT." The message inside tells you that you're under audit (and this is pretty much where you clutch at your chest). You must fill out an extensive questionnaire within 48 hours, otherwise you'll face penalties, interest, and a public whipping in the nearest town square. Among the pieces of information the "IRS" requests: your Social Security number, bank accounts, and other confidential information.

Let me put your mind at ease: while the IRS does have a lot in common with Tourquemada and his gang of Spanish Inquisitors, they aren't cruel enough to notify you about an impending audit via e-mail. (They do it by registered mail.) And there is no such thing as an "e-audit." You can file your taxes online, but the IRS isn't going to accuse you of cheating on them online. Never give your personal information via e-mail, unless you're very sure you know who's receiving it. If you receive one of these "e-audit" scams, contact your local IRS office. This will probably be one of the few times you'll be happy to call them.

The Domain Game

It's been about a year since you've set up your website, www.ElvisUFOfans.com, and you're pretty happy with it. But then suddenly you receive an e-mail saying that it's time to renew your domain name (that's the name between the www. and the .com) and that if you don't, you could lose it. Be careful: this notice could be from a scam artist, and not your legitimate web hosting service. If you click the link they supply, you could be visiting a fake domain registration site, and giving a scam artist your account numbers, credit card number, and password.

Hey, Pal—This Is PayPal

Online auctions are great, but then there's the matter of paying for that velvet painting of dogs playing poker. In early days of eBay, buyers would be instructed to send a check to the seller, and he would have to wait until the check cleared before the velvet painting could be mailed. A money order would only speed things up so much. And buyers were leery of giving an unknown seller a credit card number.

Then came the online money transfer programs like PayPal, which act as the middle man between buyer and seller. It's very simple: The buyer gives PayPal his sensitive info—a credit card number or a bank account—and then PayPal pays the seller, without the seller seeing so much as an expiration date. Today, you can win an auction, immediately zap out a payment to the seller, and expect to be hanging that painting in your den within a few days. About 16 million people use services like PayPal to pay for auctions, or even credit card and utility bills.

Leave it to con artists to screw up this happy arrangement. Some scammers have been sending out phony e-mails to PayPal clients, claiming to need to verify some account information because of a "server upgrade." The e-mail includes a link which takes an unsuspecting PayPal user to a non-PayPal site (but cleverly designed to look like one). Type in your password and account information and it drops right

> ### It's a Scam
>
> E-mail and web pages are the most common mechanisms scammers use to hook their victims, according to the Internet Fraud Complaint Center's (IFCC) 2001 report. Nearly 70 percent of the victims reported that they had been in contact with the perpetrator via e-mail.

into a hacker's eagerly awaiting hands. Now the hacker will be able to buy all of the velvet paintings he wants—using your accounts.

There's a simple way to prevent this scam: never, under pain of death, give anyone your password or bank account info online. The only time you should give out this information is when you originally establish the account. If you receive an e-mail asking you to update info, no matter how legitimate it may seem, go to the original site—type in the URL yourself—and e-mail customer service about this supposed "update." Chances are, it's a scammer at work.

 **Don't Be a Sucker**

Whenever you receive an e-mail asking for your password, bank account info, or other personal data, be extremely skeptical. Legit companies almost never ask for this kind of information via e-mail.

The Least You Need to Know

◆ Almost half of all Internet fraud involves an online auction.

◆ The Nigerian 419 scam is a surprisingly effective con that involves your bank account and phony "millions" in overseas funds.

◆ Most Internet "work-at-home" offers are scams that pocket your initial investment and never produce the business opportunity.

◆ Some scammers try to trick you into "verifying" sensitive info by pretending they're the IRS, online money services, or your Internet service provider.

Never believe anybody who tells you they can get you a loan—or a credit card, or extension of credit—by paying an upfront fee. No legit company in the world does business that way. Sure, you may eventually have to pay an application or credit report fee, but nothing upfront and urgent. Many variations of this scam exist, and some even appear in your local newspapers or advertise on local radio stations. A tell-tale sign that loan and credit offers are bogus? A 1-900 contact number, which means toll charges will appear on your phone bill. (No legit companies will pull a fast one like this.) Also, legit lenders never absolutely guarantee you a loan. Be wary of ads that claim "Bad Credit? No Credit? No Problem!"

Bogus Prizes

The phone rings. You answer it. The voice on the other end tells you that you've won hundreds of thousands of dollars in valuable prizes. You say "That's nice" and hang up. What, are you crazy? Nope. That's a perfectly sane reaction to any caller who says you've won a prize. Because unless it's Ed MacMahon calling you from his beachfront home in Florida—and you can verify it, because Dick Clark is sitting right there to vouch for him—you can bet that the caller is trying to perpetrate a scam.

> **It's a Scam**
>
> If a telemarketer calls you before 8 A.M. or after 9 P.M., hang up. This is a sure sign that the caller is a con artist.

One increasingly popular prize cons use the international lottery scam. In this one, the telescammer offers you a chance to place a bet in a foreign lottery, where the odds of winning are 1 in 6—and the prize money is tax free, to boot. All you have to do is purchase tickets right over the phone, using your credit card. But according to the FTC, the large majority of these international lotteries are scams—the operators pocket your money instead of using it to buy tickets. Besides, betting in foreign lotteries is just like burning an American flag or squashing a praying mantis: expressly *against the law*. Also, if you buy even a single foreign lottery ticket—even if it is on the level, albeit illegally—you're opening yourself up to a world of telescamming. You might not have simply purchased a lottery ticket; you may have bought your way onto a con artist's "sucker list."

One sure sign that a prize/lottery caller is pulling a scam is if they ask for some kind of "fee" or "taxes" to arrange for delivery of a prize. No legit contest works this way. Free is supposed to be free, period, end of story, have a good night.

Unfortunately, this is what one telescammer was trying to pull in Arkansas in November 2001. The man claiming to be a representative of Publisher's Clearing

House called Little Rock residents and told them that they'd won big money. All they had to do, the caller continued, was pay a small bit of taxes on their new winnings before it could be mailed to them. "The scary part is that he was using Publisher's Clearing House, a nationally-known company," said a local police spokesperson. In one case, the caller told an 80-year-old woman that she'd won $36,000, and it was being mailed to her in two separate checks. However, due to an anthrax mail scare, he said, the envelopes had been opened, and couldn't be claimed until the taxes were paid up. The caller then insisted that the transaction be paid in person, and that the woman read her bank account number to him over the phone. Wisely, the woman hung up and notified the police.

Sucker Lists: How Telescammers Get Your Number

What did you ever do to deserve all of these fraudulent phone calls? Chances are, you were a victim of a phone phraud in the past, and now your name appears on a *sucker list*. Some con artists sell these lists to other con artists in the hopes that if you've fallen for a scam once, you'll probably do it again. Even if you haven't been suckered in the past, you're still listed in telephone directories and legit mailing lists, which sometimes fall into crooked hands.

Your first line of defense: ask the caller to remove you from their list. If the same scammer calls again later, they're breaking the law. Feel free to slam down the receiver. Or if you really want a little payback, you can ask for their name and number and promptly report them to your state attorney general, or the FTC's toll-free complaint line: 1-877- FTC-HELP (1-877-382-4357).

> **Grifter Speak**
>
> **Sucker List** a telescammer's Bible. This phone/mailing list includes the name, address, phone numbers, and other personal details about anyone who may have fallen for a telemarketing scam in the past. Con artists sell these lists to other con artists, theorizing that once a sucker, always a sucker.

How to Tell a Telescammer from a Telemarketer

In my opinion, anybody who uses a phone to call unsuspecting citizens and try to sell something over the phone deserves to be thrown into a burlap sack and beaten with sticks. This punishment should include me. I admit it: One summer in my teenage years, in a fit of sheer financial desperation, I worked at a job as telemarketer. At the time, I justified my actions by telling myself I was doing a public service—the job entailed selling copies of a local newspaper to raise funds for a children's hospital.

Nevertheless, I still feel pangs of guilt whenever I think about all of those plates of meat loaf growing cold on suburban Philadelphia tables, all because I wanted to meet my hourly quota.

You may feel sorry for telemarketers, and may even welcome calls from the legit ones. So how can you tell the difference between someone trying to (sniff, sniff) make good in this tough cruel world, and someone trying to fleece the living daylights out of you? Pay attention to these tell-tale scam signs:

- **Hidden Agendas.** A scammer will barrel right into a conversation, trying to befriend you before making their pitch. A legit telemarketer tells you, right up front, that this is sales call, and names their company.

- **Pressure Tactics.** A scammer will do everything in his power to close whatever deal he's trying to make, just short of kidnapping your pet goldfish and threatening to dump out the water. A legit telemarketer will respect your right to say no, and not apply high-pressure tactics to make a sale. (They may tap dance around a few times, but they should peaceably accept your firm "no.")

- **Money Upfront.** A scammer will often ask you to pay a "fee" for a prize, or ask for cash, a check, or a credit card number to enroll you right then and there, over the phone. They'll tell you how easy it is to read the numbers from the bottom of your check, so they can easily transfer the funds right from your account. Never agree to make any payments immediately. If an offer is legit, payment details can always be arranged later, after you've had a chance to think about the pitch.

- **Early and Late Calls.** Some scammers don't care what time of the day they call. Legitimate companies know and follow the FTC rules: No telemarketing calls before 8 A.M. or after 9 P.M.

- **No Writing.** Scammers will be awfully hesitant about sending you written info on their deal; legit companies will be more than happy to send you literature.

CAUTION   Don't Be a Sucker _____

Remove yourself from "sucker lists" by telling the next telemarketer who calls that you would like to be removed from their calling lists. By law, they have to do so, and if they call again, they're breaking the law. Hang up on their felonious butts.

Phonejacked

Some con artists have developed ways of turning your own phone against you, often using quirks in long distance telephone service. One popular long-distance trick is the 809 Scam. Here's how it works: You press play on your answering machine, and hear a frantic voice message, urging you to call a phone number with an 809 area code. That code doesn't ring a bell, but these days—with the proliferation of cell phones—new area codes seem to be popping up all of the time. (Hell, your teenaged daughter probably has her own area code by now.) So you dial the number, completely unaware that your phone is now connecting you to the Caribbean, where a weird recorded message keeps you on the line for a couple of minutes. What you don't know is that you've just made a toll call—similar to a 1-900 call—and you're being charged $25 per minute. Two minutes, a scam artist somewhere is $50 richer.

Area codes change all of the time; right now, people are reporting phone scams using 500 and 700 area codes. The best way to avoid these cons is to be aware of the area codes you're dialing. If one of them seems odd to you, consult your most recent telephone directory, which includes pages that break down the latest area codes around the globe. Don't know anybody in Zimbabwe? Don't bother returning the call.

Another variation is the phone service credit scam. You receive a call from someone claiming to work for your local phone carrier. "Do you know you overpaid your local phone bill?" he'll ask. Then he'll offer to immediately credit your account if you will simply confirm some personal information. What could be easier? The only problem is the caller doesn't work for your phone company; he's in business for himself. And he'll use your personal info to order a long distance calling card in your name, then use it to call his con artist buddies seven states away. He knows he'll be able to use the card for at least a month, because that's how long it'll take you to receive your first bill and realize you've been scammed. Also, watch out for scammers who cram and slam. (Say *that* three times fast.) Cramming is when a salesperson tries to pack in extra services into an existing order. For instance, you order basic cable, but the sales guy tacks on HBO, Cinemax, Showtime, and the Spice Channel into your TV. Sadly, this scam is perpetrated by over-zealous sales people at legit companies just to boost their commissions. Watch out for this on your phone bill, where you might see that you're being billed for Caller ID and paging services without ever having ordered them. This even happened to me once, when I bought a new cell phone. I clearly remember the salesman describing the joys of wireless internet access via cell phone, and I clearly remember telling him that I wasn't interested. Lo and behold, on my first bill was a $29.95 charge for wireless internet access—a charge that might have gone unnoticed, since my membership fee was also absorbed into that same bill. One phone call straightened it out, but if it had gone for a few months, things would have gotten ugly. And I would have been out $90.

Slamming is the art of a long distance carrier switching your service without your permission. They may trick you into it by having you sign a coupon or a "sweep-stakes" form, or just go ahead and make you switch teams, no matter what you do. Of course, this is highly illegal, and unfortunately, highly difficult to detect, unless you know how. Here's how: call 1-700-555-4141 ten days after you receive a sales call. This toll-free call will tell you which long distance carrier you're currently signed up with. If you've been slammed, you should make four calls:

1. Your local service carrier. Explain what happened, and ask to be switched back to your original carrier with no "change charges." (These are fees that might occur if you were to have voluntarily switched.)

2. Your original long distance carrier. Explain what happened, and insist you be placed back in whatever special plans you had before.

3. The slamming carrier. Demand that your charges be rebilled to what they would have been with your original carrier. Inform them that you'll be reporting them to the National Consumers League. (It also helps if, under your breath, you cough the words "Lousy jerks.")

4. Then follow through and call the National Consumer's League toll free at 1-800-876-7060.

There's an easy way to prevent slamming, however—and that's by calling your local telephone carrier and asking that they never change your long distance unless you give them written permission. This is a free service, required by law, and will keep the slam-hounds at bay. The lousy jerks.

Giving Until It Hurts

You should also be wary of people who call, claiming that they're collecting donations for a charity or some other do-gooding organizations. Because often, the only people they're helping are themselves.

One charity fraud based in Queens, New York called itself the "Police Survivors' Fund" and solicited donations over the phone for the

It's a Scam
If someone calls you claiming to be from your phone company, and then proceeds to ask for personal information, hang up—this is a tell-tale sign of a con artist workin' the phone. Legit phone companies will never ask for this kind of information unless you contact them directly.

surviving families of slain police officers. Investigators discovered that from October 1999 until March 2002, the Fund collected $441,000 from generous donors—but paid out a measly $14,500 to six families. Their telephone techniques were shameless. First, the telemarketers were instructed to ask people to "go all out for the widows and children"—"all out" meaning a lifetime membership that cost $1,000 or a year membership that cost $395. If the victim demurred, the telemarketer asked for $99. "Surely you can do that for the widows and children." (Note the repetition of the phrase "widows and children.") The hard sell became even more shameless after the terrorist attacks of September 11, in which dozens of police officers were killed. The telemarketers first assured potential donors that "we are currently coordinating our fund drive with the World Trade Center tragedy." Then, they asked for a contribution of $911—after all, many other donors were giving this very special amount. If that didn't work, the victim was asked to give $50, just to "save face in the community."

Another con artist worked the September 11 tragedy by posing as a representative of Publishers Clearing House (clearly, a scammer favorite) and claiming that the purchase of magazines would help the national recovery and rescue efforts. Of course, no donations were ever sent—and no magazines arrived, either.

If you're moved by a call from a charity, do the needy folks out there a favor and ask for written literature from the organization. If material arrives, check out the organization with your local or state consumer protection office—they'll have records of all legit charities out there.

The Least You Need to Know

- More than half of all consumer fraud involves the phone.
- Telemarketers have to play by certain rules, otherwise they're breaking the law.
- Be wary of strange area codes or offers to change your phone service.

Chapter 7

If Looks Could Kill: Vanity Scams

In This Chapter

◆ The skinny on weight-loss scams

◆ The lure of other vanity cons

◆ Fake glamour products

Jim Carrey is known for a variety of over-the-top characters—Ace Ventura, Andy Kaufman, Jim Carrey. But none hold a candle to Jimmy Tango. In a May 1996 episode of *Saturday Night Live*, Carrey portrayed Tango, a freaky weight loss guru who had come up with a novel concept: heat beads and … well, crystal meth. "Yes, you heard me right!" Tango screamed. "I lost 155 pounds in less than three weeks! How did I lose all that gross fat? By combining the miracle of technology with ordinary street junkies! Fatties, here's my promise: Wear my vibrating heat beads while blasting down handfuls of crystal meth, and you'll drop weight so fast you'll lose your mind!"

If only more scam artists were like Jimmy Tango—patently ridiculous and downright scary—maybe fewer people would be suckered by fat-busting scams. But miracle cure scams are designed to sound reasonable, backed up by "medical studies" and live testimonials from allegedly happy customers. In this chapter, I'll walk you through some of the most common and surprising quack cures and products that promise to make you slimmer, sexier, smarter, and richer, but only succeed in making your poorer.

Weighting Is the Hardest Part

Almost everybody could stand to lose a few pounds—recent statistics show that more than half of us Americans are overweight. Con artists know this, and they're counting on another statistic: Most overweight Americans are too lazy to want to lose weight the traditional way, in other words, a proper balanced diet and a modest routine of daily exercise. They know that you'd rather just pop a pill, or rub some cream over your Buddha belly, or maybe even wear something goofy to nuke the blubber. After all, modern science has found a way to split the atom, eradicate static cling, and make Michael Jackson white. Is it too much to ask for a miracle fat buster?

Yes, it is.

It's impossible to keep track of all of the weight-loss scams and phony cures out there. Even the Federal Trade Commission seems to want to throw up its hands and cry uncle "We're in the Wild West of advertising right now," said an FTC spokesperson to *The New York Times*. "We're seeing claims being made on a whim without a scintilla of evidence, and there's such a huge proliferation of products it's very hard for the regulatory world to get hold of it."

Looks like it's up to you, the wary consumer. Actually, it's not hard to tell the weight-loss scams from legitimate programs. If the program involves dietary changes in combination with an exercise regimen, it might actually be real, because that's the only safe, tried 'n' true way to nuke the fat. But if the program sounds like one of the following, hang on to your money.

> **Grifter Speak**
>
> **Snake Oil** The common term for bogus health cures or products. This term originated with Old West traveling salesman who would sell all kinds of exotic oils and extracts, claiming they'd cure any ailment, from heart disease to hangnails.

> **Con-trary to Popular Belief**
>
> Over the past five years, sales of traditional weight-loss products and services—diet soft drinks, low-calorie snacks, commercial weight loss centers—have plummeted, while sales of quick-fix pills and supplements have quadrupled. These days, nobody wants to wait to lose the weight.

Take a Pill

We're a nation preconditioned to swallow pills whenever our minds or bodies feel out of sort. There's pretty much zero effort in swallowing a pill—the toughest thing is remembering when to take them. But unless you happen to be a chemist at a pharmaceutical company, there's no way to tell what's in those pills you're popping. Con artists capitalize on this.

One Minneapolis scammer marketed a "Teen Diet Pill" by direct mail to unsuspecting teenaged girls—a demographic already afflicted with body image problems and eating disorders. "I lost 27 POUNDS quickly, easily, safely," read one ad, which also included a testimonial from an allegedly happy consumer: "TDP didn't just change my body … it changed my life." Of course, the creator of the TDP didn't offer one shred of medical evidence that the pills even worked. The attorney general's office in Minnesota filed suit, charging him with false advertising and deceptive trade practices.

Who knows what's really in the Teen Diet Pill? The jury is also out on SeQuester, a plant fiber that is supposed to block fat from being absorbed into your body. Ditto with "Fat Burners," a supplement that is supposed to be used in conjunction with diet and exercise. Strangely, in the fine print, the following statement appears: "The dietary supplement in this system does not contribute to the loss of body fat." At least there's some truth in advertising.

Some weight-loss pills may contain ingredients that actually will help your body burn fat, but at an awful price. Beware of pills touting a substance called ephedra, ephedrine, or Ma Huang—variations of the same dangerous substance. The Food and Drug Administration has been inundated with complaints about them, yet dozens of manufacturers use it as a key ingredient in their weight suppressors. "This is the substance that has reportedly caused over 80 deaths and over 1,400 complaints of adverse effects," said Samantha Heller, senior clinical nutritionist at NYU Medical Center, to CBS' *48 Hours*. "Everything from heart palpitations, muscle spasms, hypertension, cardiac arrhythmias … it's a stimulant." Stimulants can suppress your appetite, but they can also end your life prematurely. (Remember Jimmy Tango and his crystal meth/heat bead plan?)

Don't assume that just because the FDA hasn't swooped down out of the sky and squashed a new weight-loss drug means it's probably safe. There are simply too many products out there—too many Jimmy Tangos cranking this stuff out on a daily basis for the beleaguered agency to keep up with. If you're unsure about a new weight loss drug, always check with your doctor first.

Don't Be a Sucker _____

According to the Federal Trade Commission, a weight-loss product is probably a scam if their ads show one of these red flags:

- ◆ Lose 30 Pounds in Just 30 Days!
- ◆ Lose Weight And Keep it Off for Good!
- ◆ David Smith Lost 40 Pounds in Two Weeks—So Can You!
- ◆ Scientific Breakthrough! New Miracle Cure!
- ◆ Lose Weight While You Watch TV!

Ah, There's the Rub

Too lazy to swallow a pill with a glass of water? No problem. Scam artists have just the product for you.

The same Minneapolis guy who gave the world the Teen Diet Pill also cooked up a Miracle Thigh Crème, which would give you "the smooth beautiful thighs you want." Simply spread it over those ham hocks you call your legs and watch them wither away. Another company came up with Defat Seaweed Soap, and promised that you could watch "the fat go down the drain!" Yet another, a company based in Guangxi, China, cooked up Aoqili soap. Aside from breaking the long-standing rule that the "q" is always supposed to be paired with the letter "u," Aoqili is also supposed to break the rules of nature: penetrating your pores in the shower to jump-start your metabolism and help you lose 25 pounds in two months.

Let's be clear on this: Nothing you can apply to the outside of your body can burn fat on the inside of your body. If such a miracle substance existed, we would have intervened and tossed Dom DeLuise into a vat of it years ago.

Don't Be a Sucker _____

Found the perfect weight-loss drug or cream? Tell your doctor about it to ask his opinion.(If you're to embarrassed to tell your doc, it's probably a scam, and you know it, deep down inside.) Scamming manufacturers love to tell people not to trust their doctors, that they're simply too old-fashioned to understand the benefits of "alternative medicine." But would you trust someone who has studied the human body for close to a decade, or some guy named "Dr. Cody" who operates out of a shack near Olympia, Washington.

Press a Button, Lose the Pounds

If pills and creams sound too taxing, no sweat! Con artists have come up with all kinds of machines to do the fat-burning for you.

Take the "Fat-Be-Gone Ring." According to its maker, all you had to do to lose weight in a particular part of your body was place the coiled ring on the appropriate finger. Got chipmunk cheeks? Slide the Fat-Be-Gone Ring on your index finger. Your hips too wide? Slide the ring on your thumb. The manufacturers, American Design, claimed that the ring uses the principles of acupuncture and acupressure to help you slough off the pounds without doing a damn thing. "No drugs, no starving, no sweating," the ad read. "Get the same benefits as jogging up to six miles a day!" The Fat-Be-Gone ring sounded so powerful, one could imagine the effects of wearing more than one at a single time—the discovery of your withered corpse, wearing baggy clothes and ten coiled rings, on your living room sofa.

Don't laugh too hard at people suckered into the fellowship of the Ring. Legitimate companies and otherwise sane individuals believed the hype, too. Walgreen's used to carry the product—until it disappeared after a reporter from *The New York Times* started asking questions. Lynne McAfee, director of the Council on Size and Weight Discrimination, even admitted to the *Times* that she had purchased a Fat-Be-Gone Ring. "In the back of my mind, I say, Well, maybe it will work," she said.

The finger is just one place to stick these fraudulent fat-burners. Another is your ear. Chuck Whitlock, author of *Scam School*, once set up his own phony weight loss product booth for a *Hard Copy* television segment. The product "Dr. Charles Whitlock" hawked was called Acu-Stop 2000, and it was pretty much a little piece of plastic that you would stick in your ear. Whitlock rented a booth at a convention, slapped on a lab coat and stethoscope, and started telling people that Acu-Stop—only $39.99—actually blocks the hunger impulse between your stomach and brain. "People ate up my sales pitch—no pun intended," writes Whitlock. "If I had been a real con artist, I could have sold scores of the devices in just one day at the mall." Acu-Stop may sound ridiculous, but Whitlock didn't make it up. It was a real product that was shut down by the FDA years before Whitlock's test.

Other freaky fat gizmos include: "Slimming Insole," which you slapped into the bottom of your shoe. Walk a little, and the insoles would trigger fat-busting nerves in your feet. (On the upside, at least Slimming Insoles promoted walking. Sort of.) There's also Le Patch, which costs $39.95 and is supposed to speed your metabolism while bitch-slapping fatty tissue. The active ingredient? A seaweed mold called "fucus," which some doctors have said doesn't even exist. The only conceivable way Le Patch could make you lose Le Weight is if you slapped the patch over your pie-hole.

My all-time favorite weight-loss device, however, is the Incredible Fat-Burning Cookie. That's right—it's a high-fiber snack that's allegedly the "only fat-burning cookie in the world." It's also the most expensive cookie in the world: 14 cookies for $24.95. As the furry blue monster on *Sesame Street* once said, "C is for Con Artist, and that's good enough for me."

Con-trary to Popular Belief

Even if you happen to find the one miracle cure that does blast away fat like there's no tomorrow, don't start snarfing Big Macs like there is no tomorrow. Studies show that 95 percent of people who lose weight too quickly gain it right back, and then some. Slow, gradual weight loss—and the lifestyle change required to achieve that weight loss—is the only way you'll keep the blubber off permanently.

Vanity Fare

As we've seen, scammers love to prey on human flaws, promising quick and easy fixes for every personal problem. But the scamming doesn't stop with fat-busting. Con artists target other people's … er, *short*-comings. Take the next scam for example.

One company, C. P. Direct in Scottsdale, Arizona, sold a pill called Longitude over the Internet. The pills cost $59.99 (plus shipping and handling) for a one-month supply, and $39.99 every month after that. What kind of bang did you get for that kind of buck? Well, C. P. Direct claimed that their pills would promote penile enlargement—guaranteed, within a few months. The only thing enlarging, however, was C. P. Direct's bank account—to the tune of $2 million, plus $3 million in cash. The owners purchased fancy cars, including a Lamborghini, Rolls Royce, Ferrari, and Bentley, along with pounds of jewelry. The pills? Fakes, which cost $2.50 per bottle to make. And their customers? Short-changed, in more ways than one.

Women aren't free from this kind of con, either. Breast-enhancement pills are—pardon the term—the biggest scam going. If you're bored some night, type in "breast enhancement pill" into your favorite search engine, and watch the countless sites pop up, all promising the va-va-voom of Jayne Mansfield for only $79.95 per month. Many of these chest-boosting pills claim to work because they contain natural estrogens, either in the form of plants like palmetto or in grains like barley and hops. (Which sounds more like a decent beer than a miracle cure.) You simply buy a few months' supply, and wait for your chest to swell up like you've got helium balloons beneath your blouse.

The only problem is that natural estrogen does not enhance breast size whatsoever. The thousands of women who take prescribed doses of estrogen to help combat the symptoms of menopause aren't growing a couple cup sizes thanks to the pills. In fact, if the estrogen has any effect, it will make your breasts more dense, not visibly larger. If you have a history of breast cancer in your family, you definitely shouldn't take any extra estrogen—that will only increase your risk of cancer.

The Big Knockoff

Sometimes, looking better isn't a matter of losing weight or gaining a cup size—it's what you carry under your arm.

In one episode of *Sex and the City*, Carrie (Sarah Jessica Parker) and Samantha (Kim Catrall) find a hidden treasure while combing the streets of Hollywood: some swarthy guy selling fake Fendi bags out of the back of his car. ("A Fendi bag," one fashionable friend tells me, "is the one accessory that's worth taking out that second mortgage for.") Samantha eagerly snaps up a purse for a fraction of the cost of a real Fendi bag, while Carrie decides against it. Smart move on Carrie's part. Samantha pays the full price later when her Fendi is revealed as a fake—in front of Hugh Hefner and a bevy of super-models, no less, all of whom (except Hef) have real Fendis.

It may seem like an innocent crime, but counterfeit merchandise is a huge international industry—the International Chamber of Commerce says that anywhere from 5 to 7 percent of global trade involves the sale of knockoff items. The cost to you and me? Well, one study pegged the cost of unpaid taxes at $350 million, which means we all share the hidden costs of knockoffs. (Now don't you feel guilty about buying that $8 Rolex on the street corner?) Also, con artists take advantage of counterfeit goods by passing them off as the Real McCoy, which means that some might pay thousands of bucks for that $8 Rolex that will stop ticking after a few weeks.

Con-trary to Popular Belief

Knockoff artists don't stop at fake designer products like Kate Spade bags and Rolex watches. Other products routinely counterfeited include: prescription drugs, food, cigarettes, booze, baby formula, auto parts, audio CDs, computer software, and perfume.

It's a Scam

Want to know how to tell a fake Rolex from the real thing? Watch the second hand. If it ticks along, second by second, it's a fake. The second hands on genuine Rolexes move in a nonstop sweeping motion.

New York City is the unofficial capital of knockoff merchandise. Squads of private investigators routinely sweep particular knockoff districts—like the stores along Canal Street in lower Manhattan—looking to catch a merchant passing phony Oakley sunglasses or Armani scarves or Microsoft software. Some people aren't bothered by purchasing counterfeit goods, because they know they're getting what they pay for. "That's the fun of being a tourist in New York City," says one shopaholic friend of mine. "You go out, eat great food, and buy a $16 purse that would normally cost you a car payment."

Even my wife—who I love and respect and think the world of—isn't immune to the temptation. We lived in New York City for two years, and one sunny afternoon in the East Village she was enraptured by a table full of Donna Karan bags. Against her better judgment, she decided to buy one for $15. But Karma (if not Karan) works in mysterious ways, my brothers and sisters. Just a few months later, my wife was mugged right down the street from our Brooklyn apartment, in broad daylight. The punk tried to swipe the fake DKNY bag out of her hands, but my wife held firm and screamed so loudly that her attacker got freaked and ran away empty-handed. Later, my wife discovered that her prized knockoff bag had been ripped badly in the struggle. New York City has a funny sense of justice, doesn't it?

Now let's assume for a minute that you want nothing to do with street corner knockoffs—you want the genuine article. Still, knockoff merchandise can find its way into your hands, even if you're shopping in a reputable store. How can you spot the fakes?

- **Check the spelling.** You know you've got a fake when the label says "Rolexx" or "Shah-Nell." One consumer who bought a $16 Prada bag was amused to see the word "Drada" on a label inside.

- **Look at the zipper.** Knockoff artists aren't as concerned with the little details, like stamping the brand name on the zipper.

- **Examine the leather strap.** Is it a single piece of material? Chances are it's real. A couple of pieces stitched together? Probably a fake.

- **Examine the bindings.** Knockoff artists save money when stitching the purse together, so it won't be as finished or smooth as the real thing. If the seams are rough, seems like you've been taken.

- **Don't fall for a sticker on your specs.** If you're looking at a pair of "Oakley" sunglasses and see a UV sticker on the lens, it's a fake.

- **Check for certification.** Some designer goods come with a certificate of authenticity, complete with serial number. Many knockoff artists don't bother to fake these.

◆ **Listen for the ticking.** If you're presented with a Rolex, hold it up to your ear. If you hear ticking, it's a fake. The second hands of genuine Rolexes move in a quiet, sweeping motion.

Con-trary to Popular Belief

The foot soldier in the war against counterfeit merchandise is your friendly neighborhood private eye. Law firms (acting on behalf of large corporations who have been stung by knockoff artists) will hire teams of private dicks to go undercover and buy enough fake purses to warrant a court order to seize the whole fake lot. According to a *New York Times* article, the booty from one recent counterfeit seizure—in which the private security firm Holmes Hi-Tech raided five lower Manhattan shops—included $100 million worth of fake sunglasses, DVDs, handbags, and watches.

Of course, some con artists don't even have to go through the trouble of manufacturing a fake item. Take the rocks-in-a-box scam. Here's how it works: You're approached by a guy with a truck who says he works for a large electronics chain and needs to unload some stuff quick. He opens the door, and there are piles of boxes of DVD players, still sealed in plastic. You've been wanting a DVD player for some time now; there's a director's commentary track on *Goodfellas* you've been dying to hear.

Normally, the guy will tell you, these beauties go for $400 bucks—they're top of the line. But since he needs to get rid of a few quick, he'll let you have it for $100. Then he'll slice open one box, rip open the plastic, and show you the sleek black DVD player inside, complete with warranty and instructions. The offer sounds awesome—hey, stuff like this happens all the time, right? Sure, the player may be a little on the hot side, but what's that to you? You happily hand the guy $100, and he hands you an unopened, plastic-sealed box.

You get home, and eagerly slice open the top of the box. You even have the TV pulled away from the wall, ready to install your new DVD player. But inside the box is nothing but a carefully-packed set of rocks. Unless your name happens to be Fred Flintstone, those rocks aren't going to do you a bit of good in terms of home entertainment.

The rocks-in-a-box scams has two essential parts: The contact, where the con artist makes the pitch and shows you the merchandise, and the sting, in which you give him money in exchange for a sealed box full of rocks. A variation of this scam is called the block hustle, in which the con artist makes it clear that he's selling stolen merchandise, making it extremely unlikely that you'll contact the authorities after getting stung.

The Least You Need to Know

◆ The only way to effectively burn fat is through diet and exercise, not miracle drugs.

◆ Check with your doctor before taking any drugs or supplements.

◆ You might find fake designer products in legitimate stores.

◆ Beware of "hot off the truck" sales; they're often scams.

Chapter 8

Take It and Leave It: Family and Inheritance Swindles

In This Chapter

- ◆ A con artist in the family
- ◆ Inheritance fraud
- ◆ Adoption scams
- ◆ Sweetheart cons
- ◆ Slave reparation swindles

The goal of every con artist is to gain access to your circle of trust—people you believe are looking out for your best interests, no matter what. But sometimes, a con artist just so happens to be *born* into your circle of trust. Maybe he's your brother. Your daughter. Your grandmother. Maybe you share a bed with him. And sooner or later, he might try to pull a scam.

Now I'm not talking about the innocent everyday scams we all perpetrate on our family members. Yes, even you. Like you really had the flu during your second cousin's wedding in Scranton, Pennsylvania? (Next time, try a more believable medical condition, like a cerebral hemorrhage. Works wonders for me.) I'm talking about criminal fraud, perpetrated by trusted family members who use that trust against us. Or by someone who's hoping to become a member of your family, like a boyfriend or girlfriend, and uses the mists of love to hide their misdeeds. Or maybe even someone who is pretending to be part of your family.

In this chapter, I'm going to detail some of the ways in which family—or other people close to you—can swindle you out of money or property. Also, I'll hit other family-related con games, the most recent being the Slave Reparation Scam, in which an African American family is told they're owed thousands of dollars in "slave reparation" settlement money. The money isn't real, but the legal and "transaction" fees are, unfortunately.

Family Affairs

As I just mentioned, we've all conned members of our own family. Remember the time you convinced your mom that you needed a buck for school supplies, but instead spent it on *Amazing Spider-Man* #187? Or the time you convinced your little brother to share his ice cream cone with you, giving you the first 100 licks? Or even the time you set up your Aunt Diane to take the fall for that $11 billion Russian diamond caper?

Family cons can take all forms. The simplest? Lying to your relatives. One 22-year-old man in Missouri told his 88-year-old great aunt that he had colon cancer, and desperately needed money for medication and radiation treatments. Of course, this great nephew—who had once used his grandmother's bank account to write a bad check—and his colon were quite fine. The scam was uncovered when relatives noticed the 88-year-old woman taking huge amounts of cash out of the bank, but by that time, the not-so-great nephew had already pocketed $129,000. "I still love him," the great aunt said. "He just got in with the wrong crowd. They talked him into this stuff." The nephew and an accomplice were both charged with unlawful financial exploitation of an elderly person and theft of more than $100,000, offenses that could result in a 4- to 15-year prison term.

Actually, damn near every con game in this book could potentially be perpetrated by a family member. Being a relative doesn't create the con game, but it does allow the con artist a short cut. Does this mean you should never trust any relatives with money? Well, uh … yeah. There's no hard-and-fast advice here to help you through matters of finances and family … heck, a great deal of Western Literature, when you boil it down, is all about whether or not you should have lent your cousin Ray that $500. My advice is this: when you're unsure about some kind of financial arrangement or business opportunity with a family member, take the family out of the equation. In other words, if Joe Blow came to you with this same deal, what would you do?

Con-trary to Popular Belief

Best-selling spy novelist John LeCarre admitted in 2002 that his father was a "five-star con man," and that as a child, the young LeCarre (real name: David Cornwell) would be recruited to help his father swindle people. When the elder Cornwell's victims would complain, little David and his brother Tony would be sent to reassure them that the money was on its way. The swindling didn't stop, even as LeCarre grew into adulthood. The writer recalls that, after the publication of *The Spy Who Came in From the Cold*, his father smooth-talked his way into VIP treatment at a film studio by claiming he was his son's "business advisor."

Luke, I Am Not Your Father

The flip side of family swindles, of course, are cons perpetrated by folks claiming to be family. Celebrities are frequent targets of fraudulent paternity claims—Bill Cosby is a recent example. But paternity claims can work both ways: either by a child who wants to glom on to a desirable family, or by an adult parent who wants another adult to take financial responsibility for their child.

Usually, these scams are unraveled with the ever-popular DNA paternity test, in which samples from the child are matched with samples from the alleged parent. (Sometimes, I like to use DNA tests to mess with people's minds. When passersby stop me, my wife, and my infant son and comment on how much he looks like me, I feign indignation and say: "Yeah, well tell it to the blood test!" This behavior does not please my wife.) Don't bother trying to figure out a way to fake this test, unless you've found a way for your consciousness to leave your body and inhabit another body. The tests are 99.99 percent accurate, and all the courts need is 99.00 percent proof positive.

But that doesn't mean that every DNA paternity test goes smoothly. In 1998 in Missouri, a 23-year-old man was accused of fathering the child of a 17-year-old girl. The state required the guy to come in and submit DNA samples to be used in a paternity test. A Polaroid photo was taken, a thumbprint inked, and a blood sample drawn. The result: The guy wasn't the father!

However, the 17-year-old mother refused to believe the results, and demanded to see the evidence. Strangely, she didn't recognize the guy in the photo. It was later revealed the 23-year-old had paid a friend to take his place. (*Dude, you totally hooked me up on that p-test. Yeeaaah!*) The state charged the 23-year-old with two counts of felony forgery and two misdemeanors of tampering with physical evidence, and then forced him to take the paternity test all over again. The shocking result: The guy really wasn't the father! "But even if you are not the dad, you can't try to avoid responsibility by fraud," said the prosecuting attorney involved in the case.

It's a Scam
Pets are part of the family, too, so imagine the heartbreak when forlorn pet owners discovered that the man they hired to find their pets turned out to be a con man. A 39-year-old scammer in California glommed at least $10,000 from 16 pet owners who'd wired him money, but never saw their beloved furry friends in return. Ace Ventura, Pet Detective, would be ashamed.

Triumph of the Will

Trillions of dollars are currently being passed down from the so-called "Greatest Generation"—the World War II generation—to Baby Boomers and their families. (Did you catch that, Grandpa? I just referred to your generation as "Great." And you, in particular, are a damned fine example of that shining, exemplary generation of Americans. I get woozy just thinking about your many accomplishments … oh, sorry. Back to the chapter.) That's one fat river of cash that attracts greedy con artists, looking to dip their own cup into the flowing waters.

There are two basic types of people who commit will fraud. One is an actual family member who tries to carve himself a bigger piece of the inheritance pie, or somehow grab a slice he was never intended to have. (And you thought Grandpa Jennings was kidding when he said that if you slouched at the Thanksgiving table, you were out of the will.) The other type involves nonfamily members who hunt for a good prospect, then attempt to forge documents naming them as inheritors. Some of the latter fraudsters are successful to a spectacular degree.

San Antonio native Mel Spillman loved Ferraris. Some would say Spillman loved them a little too much. The walls in his garage were painted red and yellow (like a Ferrari), and the floor was checkered in black and white. He kept framed photos of Ferraris over his bed and toilet. He also owned five of the damned things. Funny thing is, he only made $33,000 a year probating wills at the Bexar County courthouse. Where did the moola come from? Oh, inherited from relatives, Spillman would say. There was just one wrinkle. According to *The New York Times*, Spillman never specified *whose* relatives.

As it turned out, Spillman had pulled a fast one: stealing over $5 million from 122 dead people by using his office to produce phony wills and forged documents. One signature, and suddenly Spillman was the "temporary administrator" of an estate, which enabled him to sell property and transfer funds to his own accounts. Sometimes, he'd seize a property, then rent it out to make money. Precious objects, like vases and paintings, were taken and placed in Spillman's private home. (It's amazing there was any room next to the Ferrari memorabilia.) Spillman's money-siphoning scam lasted 15 years, until a probate judge noticed Spillman's name on a particular case and launched an investigation. A sting operation caught Spillman walking away from a bank with $900 in ill-gotten gains. He plead guilty to fraud, and was forced to watch as the court sold off each and every one of his precious little Ferraris.

> **It's a Scam**
>
> Another popular inheritance-type swindle is the so-called Nigerian Letter Scam, which I cover in Chapter 5 on Internet fraud.

Other con artists have smaller, sneakier ways of preying on the dead. Many grifters scan the newspaper obits every day, searching for a ripe target. When they find one, they visit the home of the bereaved family and attempt to deliver a C.O.D. package—the delivery charges, of course, highly exceeding the value of the object inside the box—or attempt to collect on an old debt.

Don't Lie to Me, Baby

Con artists prey on your needs. Maybe it's your need for money. Good looks. Love. Some con artists, however, cruelly prey on your need to start a family. Adoption fraud usually involves two parties: A married couple desperate for a child, and a birth mother—who may or may not actually be pregnant—who tries to milk every dollar she can out of the couple before the scam is exposed.

Adoption fraud thrives, in part, because there aren't enough babies to satisfy the demand of would-be parents. These parents are usually in a slightly desperate frame of mind—they've most likely been through an endless series of fertility tests and given impossible odds of ever conceiving a child. They won't take no for an answer, so they begin to pursue other possibilities, no matter how long the odds. Hiring a surrogate mother is one option, but the price can be astronomical—anywhere from $60,000 to $80,000, and that's no guarantee that conception will occur. There are adoption agencies, but fees there can run as high as $30,000, and the waiting list can stretch for as long as five years. That leaves the parents looking for other options … and con artists are stepping forward to supply them.

Take the case of "Kate" (real name withheld), a 21-year-old Los Angeles woman who, along with her 21-year-old boyfriend, promised her unborn child to six different couples and one single mother. In each case, Kate showed the prospective parents ultrasound photos of the baby and asked them to suggest names. Then came the pinch: Kate asked each for monthly payments to help with rent and medical expenses. One couple started paying $1,250 per month; all told, Kate took $16,000 from her seven victims. The scam was exposed when one would-be adoptive mother thought it was highly suspect that an eight-months pregnant woman would refuse to see a doctor, and her lawyer started checking with other adoption attorneys in L.A. Soon, it became clear that Kate had other women on the hook. "It was devastating," said one of the victims. "I can't think of a more personal affront." Kate had her three existing children taken away, and was charged with adoption fraud and grand theft.

Many consider adoption fraud the cruelest con going. "The saddest thing about it is it traffics in human emotions," said Jane Gorman, a California adoption lawyer in an interview with an AP reporter. "Adoption for almost everybody is the end of the line for an almost desperate need to have a family. They've gone through expensive and often difficult fertility treatments which have failed. They find a birth mother who's willing to have them and they start picturing the unborn baby in their nursery."

Sometimes the con artist isn't the birth mother herself, but a person who bills herself as an "adoption facilitator." Now, not all adoption facilitators are running scams, but there is a reason that 20 states have banned them. Facilitators are risky because, unlike traditional adoption agencies, they're not licensed by the state, and the opportunity for fraud is great. *Philadelphia Magazine* writer Roxanne Patel profiled about one particularly vile adoption facilitator named Sonya Furlow who had scammed over 44 families across the country out of $215,000. Furlow used the same M.O. when meeting with prospective clients: She would almost always show up late, dressed in hospital scrubs, explaining that she had just rushed away from the delivery of a baby destined for another happy client. Her fee ranged from $1,500 to $12,000, and in return would-be parents would be matched up with the birth mother of their choice (Furlow supplied health records and short bios for each), and be allowed to check in with the birth mother over the phone. But it was all a scam. The babies didn't exist.

It's a Scam
Be wary of private "adoption facilitators." They're illegal in 20 states and aren't regulated by state agencies.

The "birth mothers" were actually some of Furlow's Southwest Philadelphia neighbors, who read their lines from a script. And invariably, at the last moment, the "birth mother" would change her mind. Furlow would hem and haw and promise to do everything in her power to find another baby, but after that, the couple would never hear from her again.

The adoption process is already fraught with worry and expenses—you don't need the extra worry that you might be the victim of a cruel con game. Here are some tell-tale signs you might be dealing with a con artist birth mother:

- **She wants cash up-front.** It'll sound like the money is for an awfully good cause—food, clothes, rent, medical expenses for the woman who is going to bear your child. But there's nothing to prevent her from taking the money and running. Money should only be given to your attorney, or a qualified adoption professional. Besides, some states have laws about how much money is allowed to change hands during an adoption.

> **Grifter Speak**
>
> She doesn't want to give up the baby. I can't believe this is happening—I had no warning. I promise you, Michelle, I'll find you a baby. I'll call you every day until I find you a baby.
>
> —Convicted adoption scammer Sonya Furlow to a teary-eyed would-be adoptive mother

- **She asks for a plane ticket.** According to adoption fraud experts, this is a routine scam. You lay out the cash to fly her to you, expecting a bouncing baby boy in her arms, but you never see her again. She's cashed in the ticket, and you're left with an empty nursery.

- **She limits the ways you can contact her.** You should always have a verifiable phone number and physical address for the birth mother. Don't settle for an e-mail address or pager number. Also, be wary if the birth mother limits the amount of information she gives you. If she's always promising you proof of pregnancy or legal documents but never seems to deliver—"Oh, I've just been so run down and tired, being pregnant and all …"—it might be a scam.

- **She wants to handle it without lawyers.** This just means she doesn't want someone else—unencumbered by the emotional weight of the agreement—looking over the details. A legit birth mother will want someone watching her back as much as you do.

- **She made it too easy.** Alarm bells should be ringing if your first phone conversation goes something like this: "Hello, Mr. and Mrs. Kerr. How's it going? You like kids? You do? Cool. She's all yours!" A concerned birth mother will want to make sure you are truly the best parents for her unborn child; a scamming birth mother will want to make a match quickly and speed along the financials.

- **She changes her story.** One minute, she's telling you how glad she is that you'll be raising her child. The next, she'll say that she hopes Junior grows up to be an architect, just like your husband. The only problem: Your husband is an actuary.

This might be a sign that your birth mother is talking to multiple couples, and planning to swindle all of you.

Let Me Scam You, Sweetheart

In the late 1800s, hundreds of American men fell victim to sex swindlers who ran something called the *badger game*. Here's how it worked: A hapless ne'er-do-well would meet a nice young lady in a saloon, who would use her beguiling ways to lure him back to her boudoir. (Okay, okay—maybe that young lady wouldn't need to be all *that* beguiling.) At any rate, the two would end up in a bedroom and start to engage in activities quite unbecoming a Victorian lady. Just in the nick of time, however, the door would burst open, and in would rush the young lady's father. Said father would not be amused. Said father would threaten to throw the louse in prison. Said father would demand some kind of restitution that—while it may not quite restore his daughter's good name—just might salve the bitter sting of familial embarrassment. Such restitution would usually be in the form of money. Lots of money. Then the father would wisk his daughter away, only to have to break in another door and rescue his daughter from a similar fate. And so on.

Grifter Speak

Badger Game A scam in which sex is used as a lure, and then an angry husband/parent shows up, demanding money.

Panel Game A scam in which sex is used as a lure, and then a thief sneaks into the room through a hidden panel and steals money and jewelry from the preoccupied victim.

The master of the classic badger game was a downtown New York city gangster named Shang Draper, who used the badger game to con nearly a 100 men a month in the 1870s. Draper owned the saloon at Sixth Avenue and 29th Street where men would get hooked; he also owned the boudoir house at Prince and Wooster where the men would get stung. Rich fellows were favored targets, but Draper's gang wouldn't turn down less-prosperous men, either. For swells with only an average-sized wallet, Draper would play the *panel game*. Same lure; different sting. Instead of an angry husband or father, the unwitting victim would go to bed with his new friend, and a thief would emerge from a hidden panel in the room. When the victim was finished, he'd discover his wallet and jewelry missing.

Con-trary to Popular Belief

Another popular sex swindle of the 1800s was the Murphy Game. No, it wasn't named after the popular bed—instead, a charming pimp named Murphy, who had a knack for describing beautiful young ladies of ill repute. You want the chance to spend the afternoon with such a knockout? Easy. Just give Murphy your dough—that way, the cops can't pinch you for giving money to a prostitute—and go upstairs to Room 473 and have yourself some fun. Of course, once Murphy's victims handed over the money, they were none too happy to discover that Room 473 didn't exist. And their smooth pal Murphy would be long gone by then.

Today's sex swindlers keep the spirit of the badger game alive and well, but now it's the men who are laying the traps. Eva Chmielik, a 49-year-old real estate and insurance agent in Southern California, ran into a so-called "lothario con man" in 1999. Chmielik was recovering from both a divorce and painful spinal surgery when she met Hannan Brandys through an online dating service. Online, Brandys sounded like a dream. He was a globe-trotting businessman with an elegant French accent who had lived in India, South Africa, England, and France. "I like the arts, classical music, history and current affairs," he wrote in an e-mail. "I'm gentle, considerate and correct in my behavior."

Offline, Brandys was no slouch, either. He drove a new SUV and took Chmielik to four star restaurants. "He was fatherly, he was protective," Chmielik told the *Orange County Register* in 2002. "He was helpful with you all your needs." But Brandys had some needs, too. He convinced Chmielik to invest in his computer business—he claimed to buy PC parts and accessories and ship them off to his brother in Israel at a huge profit—and promised her 5 percent interest a month. Chmielik gave him $10,000, and as promised, Brandys started paying the interest. Since the extra money really came in handy, Chmielik upped her investment to $35,000, using money from a mutual fund she shared with her dad. Not surprisingly, the relationship soon ended, and Brandys refused to give back Chmielik's $45,000 investment. And then he disappeared.

After Chmielik came forward—something victims of lothario con men rarely do—she discovered that Brandys had done this at least twice before. One of his victims, a 43-year-old woman who now lives in Utah, says that Brandys absconded with a cool quarter of a million bucks from her retirement savings. The con left her homeless and in the hospital from the shock. "This has been the most traumatic year of my life," she told the *Register*. "It's hard to function." In early 2002, Brandys was charged with three counts of felony grand theft, but by then he had already fled the United States to avoid deportation.

There are an increasing number of these lothario cons every year. Two factors give them the edge. Internet and dating services allow smooth-talking scammers to practically pre-screen their victims before making a move. Plus, there is a larger and larger pool of victims, since more women today are building their own careers and fortunes than ever before. Lothario con men can also count on relatively few victims coming forward, because it's embarrassing to admit you had both your heart broken and your bank account raided by the same slime ball. Few of these slimy studs are ever prosecuted; Brandys was a rare exception.

How can you protect yourself from dashing middle-aged men with French accents? In some cases, knowing the profile helps: males, middle-aged or younger with an exotic background (former rock guitarist, stock car driver, ex-U.S. president) who is now involved in some kind of business opportunity and who meet their quarry through a personal ad, Internet dating service, or a "random encounter" in public. In some cases, the con artist will actually scan the newspaper obits to find a suitable victim, find some excuse to "accidentally" bump into her, claim infatuation, then move in for the kill.

Another favorite trick of sweetheart con artists: "the held-up fortune." This is where Prince Charming claims to be worth thousands/millions/billions. But sadly, he's a little light in the wallet because his money is tied up in his business/another country/Fort Knox. So until he's liquid again, he asks if you wouldn't mind spotting him dinner/a late-model SUV/a 15-room country estate in the Hamptons.

Grifter Speak

You don't look a day over 50.

—Sweetheart scammer Michael David Rogers, 41, talking to a 68-year-old widower. She would later loan him $15,000.

This is how one 45-year-old con artist named Ping Lui scammed $130,000 out of seven women over 18 months. Lui would read personals in the World Journal, a New York City-based Chinese-language newspaper, and look for women who owned small businesses. He would find a reason to meet them, then claim to be a multimillionaire whose assets were temporarily frozen. The women would loan Lui money, but the repayment checks would bounce, and by then he'd have moved on to his next true love.

40 Acres and a Fraud

The idea of slave reparations—in which the U.S. government would give money or tax credits to the descendants of American slaves—is a hotly-debated topic. At this point in history, however, they do not exist, although many con men would like African-American families to believe otherwise.

It's relatively simple: the con man approaches an African-American family and offers to help them file for a "black tax refund" with the IRS. The alleged refund is substantial: anywhere from $40,000 to $80,000. The con man will even show his victims a copy of a check from the U.S. Treasury, just to prove the refund is real. But he'll also caution his victims not to call the IRS, because they'll deny it exists—just imagine if every African American family in the country filed for it! That's why, the con man will say, he's only approaching upstanding families with this offer. For a small preparation fee—say, $500—the con man will attach Form 2439 to the family's tax return, and the family can expect their check in a matter of weeks.

The only problem: The check never arrives, and by that time the con man has moved to another town to bilk more African American families. And that Form 2439? It's not a slave reparation tax credit form. It's the notice that company shareholders use to file for refunds on overpaid taxes. What makes this con so effective is that convincing nugget of truth—the very real notion of slave reparations. What makes this con so cruel is that it often targets families who are desperately looking for extra money.

The irony is that sometimes the victims actually *benefit* from this scam. Big time. While IRS says it has caught over 80,000 bogus claims in time—claims that would have cost the government $3 billion—a number of them are actually processed and paid out. That's what happened to Virginia resident Crystal Foster, who on her 2000 tax return claimed an income of just $3,429, but asked for a slave tax credit of $507,534.95. She explained that she had overpaid taxes on long-term capital gains, but didn't include the name of the source of those gains. According to the *Washington Post*, the IRS sent Foster a letter asking for that source. Foster wrote back: "Black Capital Investments fund of the U.S. Department of the Treasury." (This fund does not exist.) Then the IRS sent Foster … a check for $507,534.94.

Con-trary to Popular Belief

It's true that after the Civil War, Congress voted to provide reparations for slaves in the form of those infamous 40 acres and a mule. (This would become the name of director Spike Lee's production company.) But few remember that President Andrew Johnson vetoed the bill.

In 1993, *Essence* magazine calculated the updated value of 40 acres and a mule, and came up with a figure: $43,000.

Immediately after the IRS came to its senses, it sued for the return of the 500 grand. By then, Foster had already given away $100,000 to her father—a paid tax preparer!—and slapped down $40,900 for a shiny new Mercedes Benz. (So much for the mule.) A federal judge ordered Foster to return the money, but her lawyer appealed, saying that "[Foster filed her taxes based on a strong belief, which she still holds, that she is owed money based on slavery reparations."

The slave reparations con seems to sink and surface every couple of years. It was big back in 1994—when the IRS received 20,000 phony claims—hit another peak in 1996, faded away, and came back with a vengeance in 2001. The latest twist on this scam: Fliers posted in black churches and senior centers that ask for birth dates and Social Security numbers because "anyone born before 1928 is owed money, thanks to the Slave Reparation Act." In this case, the scammers aren't that interested in a measly $500 fee; they want those birth dates and SS numbers to perpetrate identity theft. (For more on this, see Chapter 5.)

> **It's a Scam**
>
> Tempted to claim a slave reparation tax credit? Don't. The IRS is getting better at detecting false claims, and starting April 15, 2002, you'll be hit with a $500 fine if you're caught.

If you've been approached by someone who claims to be able to get you a slave reparation tax credit, call the IRS at 1-800-829-1040. (Those last four digits are cute, aren't they? I guess 1-800 BLOOD-SUCKERS was already in use.)

The Least You Need to Know

- Sometimes, a con artist is a member of your own family. Think long and hard before lending money to or going into business with a relative.

- Adoption scams are considered the vilest of con games.

- Never jump into a "sure-fire" business opportunity pitched by someone you're dating—always bring it to an impartial third party first.

- Don't be suckered by the slave reparation tax credit—there's no such thing.

Chapter 9

Step Right Up: Gambling and Carnival Cons

In This Chapter

◆ The truth behind three-card monte

◆ Carnival cons

◆ How con artists try to take Vegas for a ride

Years ago, right before I left for my honeymoon in Las Vegas, my boss gave me $100. It wasn't a wedding present. You see, he had this system: if anyone he knew was going to Vegas, he gave them $100 and specific instructions to play it all on one hand of baccarat. Out of the five people he'd given money so far, he said, four people had come back with it doubled. It was a great return on his money, he explained, and it outperformed any money market.

Still, this worried me. I'm not a gambler. I have no particular passion or talent for card games, and besides, I work too hard for my bankroll to blow it at the crap tables. While it's true that I chose to take my new bride to Las Vegas on our honeymoon, we planned to do nothing more than pump a few quarters into a few slot machines. (Well, okay, we planned to do more than that—but this is a family publication.) Still, I couldn't exactly tell my boss to keep his $100. Our first night in Vegas, I found a baccarat table at the New York, New York Casino and decided to get it over with. The rules can be complex, but it's actually one of the easiest games to play as an outsider. Simply put, you bet on either the bank, or the player. Basically, it's 50/50 odds. My boss told me to follow the results on the screen, and then slap down the Ben Franklin whenever it "felt right." I watched that screen carefully.

It felt right. I slapped down the Franklin.

I lost.

Boy, did I feel like a sucker. And I was playing a perfectly legit game. Imagine if the game had been crooked? (I was already embarrassed to tell my boss I lost his $100 in 0.4 seconds.) The sad truth is, wherever you find gamblers, you're going to find con artists. If you enjoy games of chance, you'd better keep your eyes peeled. Sometimes, games of "skill" and "luck" are heavily stacked in favor of the house—and here I'm thinking of street corner card dealers and small town carnivals—but more often, lone operators enter a game to fleece casinos and try to hit the jackpot by any means necessary. In this chapter, I'll walk you through three levels of gambling—the corner, the carnie, and the casino—and describe how con artists try to manipulate the odds at each level.

Follow the Queen: The Truth Behind Three-Card Monte

In Great Britain, it's known as "Find the Lady." The French call it "Bonneteau." Here in the states, it goes by a slightly more rough-and-tumble name: three-card *monte*. The rules are simple: There are three cards, slightly arched at the middle so they'll be easy to grab. One of those cards is a Queen; the other two are not. The dealer shows you the Queen, then starts moving the cards around. Your job, as the player, is to keep your eyes on that Queen no matter what. If you can guess which is the Queen after the dealer shuffles the cards, you win the pot.

The thing is: no player ever wins.

Oh sure, the dealer might let you win one or two games, just to keep you hooked. More likely, he'll allow one of his friends to win a game or two, just to convince you that you could make some money here. But let me assure you: You won't. This is not a game of skill, nor a game of chance for that matter. "It really is an art form, but it's also a scam," said magician Joseph Kerr to *The New York Times*. "Even if you somehow pick the right card, you can't win."

To complicate matters, you're not just facing off against the dealer. There is usually a whole gang on the scene, ready to back him up. The dealer is also known as the *broad tosser*, or just tosser. Nearby are *shills*, accomplices who hang out and play a game or two to make people believe that the game can be won. The *wall man* keeps an eye peeled for police; if he sees any, he'll signal the tosser to fold up the game quickly. Also on hand is the *muscle man*, who is there to calm down any marks—sometimes called *punters*—who see fit to whine about losing. Finally, the tosser may employ *ropers*, whose job it is to bring business in off the street.

Grifter Speak

Monte   a Spanish word that means "heap" or "mountain." In three-card monte, the word refers to the slightly-bent playing cards. (Also, any dealer who tells you it's possible to win at three-card monte is giving you a heap of you-know-what.)

Broad Tosser   slang for a three-card monte operator. A "broad" is 19th century slang for a certain type of playing card. It's not as misogynistic as you might suspect—back then, some playing cards were made wider than others.

Usually, the tosser is talented enough to keep that Queen hidden away from the punters, either by sleight-of-hand moves or distractions. ("Hey look—is that Gwyneth Paltrow over there?") One common trick is to hold both a red Queen and a black card in the same hand, Queen up front. The tosser pretends to the throw the Queen down to the table, but is actually releasing the black card behind. From the get-go, the punter is following the wrong card. Another trick is to have the shill sneak and put a bend in the Queen when the tosser isn't looking, but in full view of the punter. The punter watches the shill win a few games, and then decides to take advantage of the bent card. However, when the punter steps up to the table, the tosser will smooth out the bend in the Queen card. The advantage disappears, and the tosser proceeds to fleece the punter.

The tosser is also prepared if a punter just so happens to guess correctly. One of his shills may "accidentally" knock over the table, rendering the current game void, or the tosser may accept a simultaneous bet from a shill, cutting the punter out of the game. The tosser can also pretend to see a plainclothes detective, and suddenly decide the game is over. If all else fails, the muscle man is there on the scene to shoo the punter away. As my grandmother always said: It's smarter to lose $20 on the table than to lose four teeth on the sidewalk. (Okay, maybe she didn't exactly put it that way, but the sentiment was there.)

Because three-card monte is such a scam, many areas have banned the game, which is why it is usually played on a light and easily-transportable folding table. Gangs take the risk because the profit margin can be huge. According to *The New York Times*, a veteran tosser can set up shop on a busy Manhattan street corner and expect to make $200 in his first five minutes.

Carnival Ruse Lines

What's more wholesome and innocent than a small-town American carnival in late summer? Pretty much everything. Carnivals are notorious breeding grounds for small-time scams of all shapes and sizes. (As I mentioned back in Chapter 1, the very word "mark" comes from the carnival world; people who fell for rigged games were marked with a piece of chalk, so other game operators could pick a sucker right out of the crowd.) Some might argue that carnivals are designed to use sleight-of-hand and spectacle to separate a mark from his hard-earned bucks—and that's part of the entertainment value—but the scams go deeper than you think. Somebody call Oliver Stone.

Take the innocent dart-and-balloon game. The rules are simple: $1 buys you three darts, which you use to try to pop one balloon on a board full of them. Beneath each balloon is a tag, usually marked S (for small), M (medium), or L (large). This indicates the size of the prize you've won. But if you're at a crooked carnival, it doesn't matter how amazing your aim, because the game is stacked against you. The darts are usually dull, which make it difficult to puncture a balloon, even if you jab at it *Psycho*-style. Pay careful attention to the balloons with tags marked "L"—they're most likely saggy and underinflated, which also makes them difficult to pop. (You'd have a better chance at puncturing Anna Nicole Smith's butt with a Nerf lawn dart.) But even if you do manage to puncture a saggy balloon with a dull-edged dart, you'll most likely win what carnival operators call *slum*—cheap prizes that cost only a nickel or a dime to manufacture. Think about it. You gave the operator $1 for three darts. Even if you could get all three darts to pop balloons, the operator is still 85 cents richer. Or, the prizes may not even be marked S, M, or L, so you have no way of knowing what you're shooting for. The booth itself may display portable CD players or huge stuffed animals, but a crooked operator won't actually put any of those prizes on the

> **Con-trary to Popular Belief**
>
> You used to be able to throw a rock in Manhattan and hit a three-card monte tosser, then watch two others come to his aid. But it's a dying form, thanks to increasing efforts to police "quality of life" crimes and the Disneyfication of tourist hangouts like Times Square.

tags. All you have a chance of winning is a cheap plastic comb. (Then again, if you have a lot of hair, maybe this is a good thing. Enjoy!)

Same goes for those shoot-the-basket games. Sure, it looks awfully easy. The hoop is only five feet away, and it's at eye level. But you could be Kobe Bryant and still miss your shots—that's because your ability to make the basket depends on the angle of the basket. If it's tilted even lightly forward or backward, your shot will be off, and the ball will bounce right back out of the basket. More devious operators will adjust the angle of the basket with a hidden switch, right in the middle of your throws. So even if you compensate for the tilt, your next shot will be off. The game can also be thrown by overinflating the basketball, which will make it bounce like crazy, or simply by raising the required number of wins to earn a prize. Three balls cost $2. Let's say you have to make 12 shots to win a huge stuffed animal. You plunk down six bucks, and you brilliantly make every single shot sing through that hoop. You can almost feel the NBA scouts crawling out of the woodwork, ready to wave contracts in your face. The operator hands you a giant stuffed armadillo. Little do you know that the stuffed animal cost the operator only $2 to manufacture.

> **Don't Be a Sucker**
>
> You can be scammed at a carnival even before you step up to your first game. Shortchange artists are notorious for manning the ticket booths at carnivals; for more on their tricks, see Chapter 3.

That's not all. Know that game where you take a softball and try to knock a cute stuffed cat off a ledge? (Clearly, this game was invented by dogs.) This can be rigged by making the fall space—the clearance behind the rack—too narrow for the stunned cat to fall through. And as the operator will tell you, the cat has to fall completely off the rack for you to win. Crooked operators might even make that space adjustable, thanks to a moving wall. If someone accuses the game of being fixed, the operator can sneakily move the wall, step out front, grab a softball, then pick off three felines with a single softball. Another way to fix the game: hidden supports that prop the cats back up.

My great aunt Betty was always fond of this next game: the bulldozer. (The fact that my great aunt Betty resembled a construction worker is only a coincidence.) You've seen these before—big piles of shiny quarters precariously balanced on a flat surface, mirrors everywhere, and a thick mechanical arm poised to push those quarters over the edge and into your pocket. Well, Aunt Betty thought this was the best thing going. She pump in a quarter, watch the bulldozer push those quarters even closer to the edge, only to stop short just in the nick of time. She'd pump in another quarter, and the bulldozer would do its stuff. Those quarters were ready to fall, damnit. Any second now. *Really.* Aunt Betty is gone now, and she never did figure out that the bulldozer was never going to push those quarters over the edge. For one thing, the edge had a raised lip, which kept the quarters herded back like cattle. And the bull-dozer itself was designed to push the quarters not forward, but to the sides, back into feeder slots to be returned to the operator. I like to think that somewhere up in Heaven, Aunt Betty pumped in her quarter and finally got the Bulldozer to do what she wanted.

Grifter Speak

Flat Game   The carnival word for a game of skill or chance that may or may not involve skill or chance. These games can flatten your wallet.

Flattie   The guy who operates a flat game.

Gaffed   When a flat game is tilted heavily in favor of the carnival operator.

Flash   Expensive-looking prizes that will attract suckers.

Slum   The cheap prizes you'll receive on the off-chance that you *do* win.

Plush   Stuffed animal prizes.

Live One   A player with money.

Lot Lice   Carnival-goers who stroll around but never play games of chance..

Another easily-rigged carnival game is the red star. This appeals to the Charlton Heston in all of us. You give the operator a buck, and he hands you a submachine gun that shoots BBs. Then he shows you a small card with a red star printed in the middle. Your mission? Blast away at the card until there's no star left—not even a single trace of red. You step up to your mark and open fire. But if the game is crooked, you'll never have a shot. The card itself may be designed to shred, not break apart completely. Just when you think you've sent that red star screaming to hell, the operator will unclip the card, smooth out the rough spots, and show you the red you missed. You resist the temptation to pop a BB into the operator's fleshy buttocks.

The gaffed games go on and on and on. In the peach basket toss, you're supposed to throw a softball into a tilted basket. It stays in, you win; it pops out, you lose. The operator shows you how to do it, and lands one perfect. It looks easy. But he has a trick up his sleeve: When he pitches, there's already another softball inside the basket, which absorbs the shock of the thrown softball. When you pitch, the basket will be empty, and it will be next to impossible to get the ball to stay inside. In cover the spot, you're given five cut-out circles and instructed to drop them on the playing board so they completely cover another circle. Once again, the operator shows you how. But he doesn't tell you that the circles he uses are actually capable of covering the area; the five circles he gives you aren't.

Once again, maybe you don't consider all of the above scams. Maybe you think it's just part of the experience. I disagree. If I want to be entertained, I'll go see the bearded lady and offer her a Gillette Mach 3. If I want to test my skills—however limited they might be—I want the match to be fair. When I find myself at a crooked carnival, I stick with the only sure bet on the midway: the funnel cake.

> **CAUTION**
>
> **Don't Be a Sucker**
>
> Want a shot in hell at winning a carnival game? Stick to the ones where you're competing against other people, not the game operator. Law enforcement officials say those types of games are less likely to be gaffed. (Of course, no game is gaff-proof.)

Player Takes All: Scamming Casinos

Q: Where can you find a virtual river of money?

A: Behind the cushions of Bill Gates' sofa.

Q: No, wise guy. Somewhere else.

A: Bill Gates' sock drawer?

Okay, enough with the guessing game. The river of cash I'm thinking of flows through the desert gaming community known as Las Vegas, which was founded by gangster Benjamin "Bugsy" Siegel in the 1940s as a playground for mobsters and suckers and washed-up lounge singers and freaky-ass magicians with goofy white tigers. Since its founding, other areas have followed in Vegas's footsteps: Atlantic City, southern states with riverboat gambling, and Indian reservation resorts. ("Win Big, Paleface!") More and more states push to legalize gambling in some form or another, which simply means more rivers of cash to attract the thirsty con artist.

The oldest way to pull a casino con is to use *marked cards*. This is when you devise some kind of pattern system on the backside of playing cards to let you know who's holding what. For example, maybe your deck features an old-fashioned illustration of a guy riding a bicycle. If the front tire has ten spokes it could denote a ten card. A cloud formation behind his head might mean a spade, a heart, a club, or a diamond. However, professionally-marked cards are never that obvious. These will have slight variations in design that will tell the con artist at a glance what his opponent is holding. Cheats have used White-Out to mark cards, since the correction fluid will only show if the cards are tipped at a certain angle. Some card and magic shops even sell marked decks—for entertainment purposes only, of course. The con artist, however, knows it's not hard to find a marked deck. His concern is getting a marked deck into the game.

My favorite marked deck story comes from Andy Bellin's *Poker Nation* (2001). Bugsy Siegel—the guy who basically invented Las Vegas—had his own personal poker game going at the Flamingo Hotel. Cheating at Bugsy's table? Not an option. But reportedly, one gambler named Jimmy Altman did manage to sneak a marked deck into the game. The operation required three accomplices, and a whole lot of chutzpah. First, one accomplice walked into the Flamingo gift shop and purchased every single deck of cards they had. A short while later, Altman himself entered the shop and tried to buy a pack, but was told they were sold out. Altman shrugged his shoulders, then went upstairs to join Bugsy's game. A few minutes later, the second accomplice walked into the gift shop, also looking for cards. Sorry, sold out, the cashier said. This second accomplice, however, threw a huge fit, cursing and yelling at the cashier before storming out. Meanwhile, upstairs, Altman kept looking at his cards funny, as if trying to detect a flaw. It was subtle, but like a well-placed yawn, every one else at the table started looking at the cards funny, too. At the same time, Altman's third accomplice made his move. He walked into the gift shop claiming to be a playing card salesman. The frazzled cashier practically fell over himself purchasing every deck the salesman had to offer. Of course, every single deck was marked. A short while later, Altman had managed to raise enough concern over the cards that when he suggested they change the deck, everyone agreed. Altman suggested someone run down to the gift shop to buy a deck. Bingo. The marked deck made it into the game, and according to Bellin, Altman took Bugsy's table for a ride to the tune of nearly a million bucks.

Another casino scam is *card counting*, any system where a player keeps mental count of the cards in play. This is most useful if you are Dustin Hoffman's character from *Rain Man*. (Definitely King of Spades. Definitely. Definitely. Uh-Oh. Vinnie the Legbreaker. Definitely Vinnie the Legbreaker.) There are dozens of techniques and books on how to count cards, and the funny thing is, they're not technically illegal. Sure, casinos hate it when they get a card counter, but by law there's not much they do about it, other than send in a *bust-out dealer*—a special dealer casinos employ to get rid of troublemakers.

Then there are *card mechanics*, who develop the amazing ability to manipulate a deck of cards from start to finish of a poker hand. Some mechanics are so skilled, they can not only give themselves a straight flush, but make sure two other players have full house so they'll be inclined to raise the pot to ridiculous levels. Master mechanics only need to manipulate the deck once per evening, so they're less likely to be caught—unlike the poor slob who's caught with a marked deck, or caught shorting the pot by $2 on every single bet.

Andy Bellin describes the four steps of manipulating the deck in *Poker Nation*. First, you have to gain access to the deck at some point in the game. Secondly, you have to find the cards you want to use in the deck—this is called "rabbit hunting." With games that involve many cards face-up on the table—like Texas Hold 'Em, the professional player's poker of choice, it can be relatively easy to spot what you want. Third, you have to place the cards you want in the order you want. According to Bellin, those first three steps are the easiest. Now comes the clincher: beating the shuffle. Every child who's ever played a hand of Go Fish knows the peculiar joy of taking a deck of cards and then shuffling them into chaos. A shuffle is how fate is introduced into any card game; let the gods decide the order of the cards. But a good mechanic knows how to beat the gods. One way is to do an *overhand tumble*: you take cards out from the middle of the deck, then put them on the bottom. This is strictly amateur hour, though: any serious player will spot this in a second. Another way, more professional method is the *jab shuffle*, where you cut the deck in half, push the two halves together to supposedly intermix them, but then push them past each other so they stay in the exact same order when you join the two halves again. Some games try to stop card mechanics by using a plastic bottom card called a *shoe*, but that only stops cheaters who bottom deal. Pro mechanics know how to deal from the middle of the deck without getting caught.

> **Con-trary to Popular Belief**
>
> Blackjack cheating gangs are so successful, some legitimate business men actually invest money with them, because they know the returns will be extremely lucrative, according to *Cigar Aficionado* magazine..

Lone-wolf card cheats are common, but sometimes a con artist will work as part of team—sometimes even with a casino dealer. If the dealer is on the take, a casino is in big trouble. Here are just three ways an inside man can steal thousands from the house:

♦ **The Cooler**   A fixed deck of cards—marked by bent edges, or ink, or grease—is called a cooler. Coolers are prepared ahead of time, then slipped into play by a crooked dealer. "I've seen people take $300,000 out of a casino in one night by playing blackjack with a cooler," said one casino security consultant in *Cigar Aficionado* magazine. Usually, a payoff also goes to the security camera operator, who points his camera elsewhere while the cooler is in play.

♦ **Pushing Back the Odds**   Instead of going through the pesky trouble of having to rig a game or somehow finagle the cards, all a crooked dealer has to do is ignore his accomplice's losses. ("Whoops—you lost again. Heck, let's do it over!) Even if the dealer only helps the player once in a while, it still dramatically boosts his odds against the house. Casino detectives look for this scam by surveillance camera.

♦ **The Chip Cup** This scam requires a little device known as a "chip cup." Basically, it's designed to look like a stack of five $5 chips. But only the top chip is real; the four chips beneath are actually the outsides of a hollow cylinder. When a con artist with a chip cup slides it to his accomplice dealer and asks for change, the dealer then loads four $100 chips into the empty slots. The con artist walks out with $400, embezzled from right under the casino's nose.

But who needs a dealer on the take when you can use an accomplice who won't rat on you? Some casino cheats today use miniature computers to pull their scams. A tiny camera hidden in a coat sleeve can be pointed at the game table. The image is sent to a wearable computer hidden in a fanny pack to be analyzed. Then, the computer uses tiny jolts to tell the con artist when to hit and when to stick. Some cheating gangs have even used cameras and satellite transmissions to identify certain cards in a deck, then signal their players by remote on how to proceed. And you thought George Clooney came up with one humdinger of a caper in *Ocean's 11*.

Grifter Speak _____

Bluff your way into any high-stakes table with some professional gamblers' slang:

♦ **action**   the amount of money on the line throughout a game

♦ **cold deck or cooler**   a marked deck that is slipped in during a game

♦ **croupier**   the guy who spins the roulette wheel

♦ **hit**   in blackjack, this means "deal me another card"

♦ **hole card**   in blackjack and stud poker, the card that is face down.

♦ **juice**   another term for marked cards

♦ **mechanic**   a skilled con artist who knows how to manipulate a deck of cards

♦ **natural**   a winning hand in blackjack that consists of only two cards: an ace, and a Jack, Queen, or King.

♦ **paper player**   a con artist who uses marked cards

♦ **stacking**   how a mechanic organizes a deck of cards

♦ **upcard**   in blackjack, the card that the dealer turns face-up

Still, casinos know how to look for these kinds of scams and pour millions into security teams specially trained to prevent them. The stakes are higher these days, too. Cheat a casino in the 1960s and get caught, and you used to end up in that casino's "Black Book," which bans you from their playing tables for life. (You may also end up tangling with a guy named Vinnie Knuckles, who will be keenly interested in your kneecaps.) Cheat a casino today, and you'll strike GOLD—a computer database full of mug shots, fingerprints, and rap sheets of Vegas cheaters. And forget about taking your business elsewhere; pull a scam at the Belaggio, and the Mirage and the MGM Grand and the Luxor will know about it, too. You'll be left with nothing to do but visit those goofy white tigers.

The Least You Need to Know

- ◆ Nobody's ever won a hand of three-card monte against the will of the dealer—the game can be fixed in many ways.

- ◆ Carnival games are routinely gaffed to make them impossible to win.

- ◆ Casino cheats count cards, use marked cards, or sometimes even use accomplices to swindle their way to a jackpot.

Part 3

Kites, Claims, and Cons: Business and Institutional Frauds

Your average street hustler can probably sucker enough people to make a decent living. But for the big con dollar, most con artists prefer to pick on slightly larger targets: insurance companies, banks, businesses, even the federal government. Think about it: how much money do you carry in your wallet or have in your checking account?

In this section, I'll walk you through some of the biggest and most common business and institutional scams—everything from con artists who fake certain professions for personal benefit, to phony check passers, to insurance fakers, to tax scofflaws, to people who still try to pull so-called Ponzi schemes. (More on this Ponzi jerk later.) But business scams can work the other way, too. If you've even read one newspaper in 2002, you've probably come across the words *Enron* or *WorldCom.* Dress it up all you want, but the guys behind Enron and WorldCom were pulling good old fashioned con games. You'll read about those games later in this section.

Chapter 10

Impostor Cons

In This Chapter

- How con artists use impersonations to perpetrate crimes
- All you need is a uniform: posing as authority figures
- The star-studded world of celebrity impostors
- Extremely weird impostors

I'd like to take this opportunity to come clean with you. Before I became a writer and editor, I was involved in a completely different career: music. This is not something I exactly like to brag about, but I was the keyboard player in an obscure early 1980s band called A Flock of Seagulls. We had a modest hit called "I Ran"—which everyone assumed was about the country, but really wasn't—and then our lead singer got rid of his goofy flattop haircut, and it was downhill from there. I stumbled into journalism, and before I knew it, I was looking at New Wave music in the rear view mirror.

Now before you write me, asking for an autograph, let me come clean again: I never did play keyboards for A Flock of Seagulls. (If I had, do you think I would admit it?) But you can see how easy it would be to make you think I did. After all, my name is on the spine of a book, and people tend to believe what they read in print. If I were a sneaky, conniving kind of guy, I might be able to convince people to give me money to stage A Flock of Seagulls reunion, or sell a bunch of bogus A Flock of Seagulls memorabilia. I might even be able to convince women to go to bed with me. (Then again, maybe not. I'd probably have to say I played keyboards for Naked Eyes or Kajagoogoo for that to happen.) Welcome to mysterious world of impersonation crimes, which can be seen as the flip side to identity theft. Whereas identity thieves hide behind credit reports and swiped Social Security numbers, impostors go boldly where no con artists have gone before—into the very skin of their victim. That means free goods, services, information, money, credit, travel and more … just by pretending to be someone else!

You're Bogus, Dude

Steven Chin Leung was in trouble. He tried to snag a U.S. passport with a bogus Social Security number in Hawaii but ended up getting arrested for the federal fraud in New York City. He posted bail, and was released from prison to await his hearing in Federal District Court. A short while later, he started consulting for Cantor Fitzgerald in the World Trade Center. Tragically, he was at Cantor Fitzgerald on September 11, when hijacked planes crashed into the towers, collapsing the buildings and killing thousands.

At least, that's what Leung wanted the world to believe.

Actually, everything after (and including) the bit about Leung consulting for Cantor Fitzgerald was a lie. After September 11, Leung called his lawyer and pretended to be his own brother, and reported that he was missing after the attacks. Federal marshals didn't exactly believe the story, and eventually they discovered that the supposedly-dead Leung was using a series of rented mailboxes in Manhattan. After staking one out, they arrested Leung on February 12, 2002. Leung admitted his plot in court in front of a Federal judge, who asked: "You were hoping that if the prosecution and the court believed you had been killed in the World Trade Center attack the criminal charges would be dismissed?"

"Yes, your honor," said Leung, according to *The New York Times*.

Leung's con game is the latest variation of perhaps the oldest trick in the book: pretending you're someone else to gain some kind of benefit. For Leung, the benefit would have been avoiding a Federal fraud charge.

Impostor con games involve a little bit of acting, a little bit of information, and a whole lot of confidence. Take Leung's case, for example: He impersonated his brother (acting), tried capitalize on a disaster (information), and actually thought he would get away with it (confidence).

Sometimes, though, impostor con games also involve a willingness to change your personal appearance. Radically. A 34-year-old woman in Gainesville, Florida, shaved her head bald and rolled around in a wheelchair to make people believe she was stricken with cancer. Concerned friends and neighbors held a yard sale and a concert to help raise money—a total of $6,436—for her medical bills, which she pocketed. Other county residents sent contributions in excess of $10,000, which she also pocketed. After the ruse was revealed, the woman was ordered to return the money, write letters of apology, undergo psychiatric treatment, and perform 200 hours of community service.

But faking cancer or lying on the phone is small-time con. To pull a successful, big money impostor con, you have to live the life—fully immersing yourself in the role you're mimicking. Perhaps the most successful impostor con man in recent history is a guy named Christopher Rocancourt, who became infamous in 2000 for posing as a scion of the Rockefeller family in the Hamptons and scamming over $1 million from his wealthy victims, mostly by convincing them to loan him money or invest in stocks he'd hand-picked. And the Hamptons were only the latest stop in the 33-year-old's tour de con—he'd been accused of pulling cons in Miami, Beverly Hills, and Hong Kong.

While romping around East Hampton—with his Playmate centerfold wife, Pia Reyes, along for the ride—Rocancourt was fond of quoting the philosopher Kierkegaard and dispensing little nuggets of financial wisdom. However, Rocancourt didn't do all of his homework. One East Hampton resident, a painter named Gines Serran-Pagan, was suspicious of Rocancourt's story, and invited him to a dinner party in July 2000. "I wanted in on his game," said Serran-Pagan to *The New York Times*. The painter's suspicions were partially confirmed when he handed Rocancourt a glass of wine, and the con man proclaimed it to be "vintage wine."

"I knew he wasn't a Rockefeller," said Serran-Pagan. "As a con man, I'll give him an 8. "Rocancourt's wine faux pas was just the first mistake. His second was skipping on a $19,000 bed and breakfast tab, which led to his arrest. Rocancourt jumped bail, and even taunted his pursuers—which included the FBI, the U.S. Marshals Office, and the East Hampton Police Department—from afar, saying that "If they

Grifter Speak

I would not consider myself a criminal—I steal with my mind. If I take things, if that is your definition of a criminal, then I am a criminal.

—Impostor con man Christopher Rocancourt, speaking from an undisclosed location to *The New York Times*.

catch me, I will make no deal. I will do my time." As it turns out, Rocancourt was caught just months later, and this time faced serious theft and fraud charges.

Tip to wannabe impostor con men: Study the wine list.

Respect My Authori-tah!

What is it about a man in uniform? Put on a set of standard issues, and whether they come from a police department, a fire battalion, a hospital or an Army unit, people will immediately lend you a certain degree of respect. (Why do you think the Village People were so freakishly popular back in the late 1970s?)

Con artists and other criminals know and exploit this tendency. Although he wasn't a con artist per se, infamous bank robber Willie Sutton used uniforms to pull many of his heists. "A uniform provided automatic entrée," wrote Sutton. "Ring the bell and you could walk right in." Once, Sutton disguised himself as a Western Union delivery man and knocked over the M. Rosenthal and Sons jewelry store in the heart of Times Square and walked away with over $150,000 worth of gems and jewelry. Not a bad haul, considering all it took was a $20 uniform.

Career opportunities for con artists are limitless. With the right amount of bluffing and the appropriate look, scammers can be pretend to be a …

Doctor: Gerald Barnes loved the practice of medicine. But legally, that's all it was— practice—because Barnes never earned a medical degree. The San Francisco-based impostor wasn't your typical scam artist; he seemed genuinely interested in helping people. Barnes ran clinics that treated poor people, and led volunteer medical missions to Mexico. He even gave San Francisco-area FBI agents their physical exams. The scam lasted an amazing 20 years—and five arrests. Yep, that's right. Barnes was arrested and sent to jail for being a bogus doc five times, but each time he was paroled and didn't wait long before practicing medicine again. The charges against him included illegally practicing medicine, mail fraud, grand theft, and involuntary manslaughter. (The latter can be a nasty side effect of visiting a doctor who doesn't have an M.D.) "He keeps getting caught, but he keeps doing it," said one deputy U.S. marshal to the *San Francisco Chronicle*. "You could see how he could get away with it. He's a Marcus Welby type of guy."

So how exactly do you go about faking an M.D.? Gerald Barnes started with a name change. The bogus doc was born Gerald Barnbaum, and worked as a pharmacist in Illinois until the state took away his license for Medicaid fraud. That didn't stop him. Barnbaum checked a directory of California doctors, and found what he was looking for—an orthopedic surgeon named Gerald Barnes. Barnbaum legally changed his last name to Barnes, then wrote the Medical Board of California and requested a copy of Dr. Gerald Barnes' medical license. The Medical Board complied, and a 20-year con began.

Barnes isn't the only one. One Michigan quack faked his way through 200 surgeries—including amputations—over a 10-year bogus career. How did his scam remain undiscovered for so long? Medical authorities were stumped. (Insert rim shot and cymbal crash here.)

Con-trary to Popular Belief

Perhaps the greatest impostor of them all is Frank W. Abagnale, who made big bucks pretending to be a pilot, a doctor, a lawyer, and a college professor among other poses (and the basis of the 2002 Steven Spielberg-Tom Hanks flick, *Catch Me If You Can*.) You can read more about him later in this book, in the Con Man "Hall of Shame."

Lawyer: Why anyone would want to impersonate bottom-feeding scum bags without souls is beyond me, but con artists love to pretend they're lawyers. (Just kidding, guys. No, really. Put down the briefcase.) In 1998, a lawyer named Eugene Garrett agreed to represent a credit union teller named Princess Phifer and her 24-year-old son, who had been injured in an auto accident. Phifer had given him over $10,000—some of it even borrowed from her church—when her insurance company notified her that Garrett wasn't really a lawyer. Her $10,000 was gone, and not even an injunction from a judge could get the scam artist to pay her back.

Cop: Impersonating a cop is a con artist classic. What other uniform is meant to inspire more trust? (Except if you live in South Central Los Angeles.) The cop impersonation swindle you should watch out for is the classic badge player scam, a.k.a. the bank examiner scheme, which I discussed in Chapter 1. Remember: Never give a cop money or discuss money with anyone you don't know, no matter what kind of uniform they're wearing.

Firefighter: Now here's a scam artist you'll want to smack around. A few days after the September 11 terrorist attacks, 34-year-old ex-convict Jerome Brandl got a bright idea. He

Grifter Speak

"I am the cops."

—A Louisiana man who, after stealing an FBI badge and demanding an "FBI discount" at a motel, proceeded to harass guests and drive his car like a maniac around the motel parking lot. Motel employees threatened to call the cops, and the would-be impostor replied with the above statement. (Later, the real thing showed up to arrest this rocket scientist.)

broke into a firehouse on Manhattan's Upper East Side, then promptly reported to Engine 39, Ladder 16, claiming to be a volunteer fireman from Milwaukee. Brandl went to Ground Zero, answered a few calls, was given free room and meals at Engine 39 in exchange for his help with the continuing rescue efforts. But then he started acting strangely, according to other firefighters at Engine 39. Brandl preferred to hang around the station house all day, eating food and watching TV. "He seemed more interested in spending time at the firehouse," said Lt. James McGlynn to the *New York Daily News*. "It proved he wasn't sincere." After eight days, Brandl was kicked out, yet he enjoyed a free Mets ball game on September 21—the first after the attacks—and there scammed a woman out of her camcorder, $500 in cash, then later $800, when he used her bank card to crack open her checking account. (Are you hating this guy yet, or what?) Brandl then attended another free game, this time a Monday Night Football match, that honored 9-11 emergency workers. He was finally arrested in Pennsylvania in late November 2001 after he stole a car, and he was charged with grand larceny, scheming to defraud, and criminal impersonation. Needless to say, the firefighters at Engine 39 were eager to see Brandl receive more free room and board—at the nearest available prison.

Subway Conductor: People tend to instinctively avoid people who talk too much about trains and their inner workings. (It's almost as bad as being caught on a bus next to a comic book fan.) But for one 19-year-old con artist in Queens, NY, a geeky fascination with subway cars and their operations paid off for him. He would dress up like a conductor and walk into a conductor's locker room and start talking shop with the other conductors. Only a fellow motorman, they reasoned, would have a reason to know this stuff. But when the real conductors left to do their runs, the conductor would rifle through the lockers and steal wallets and other gear. "He knows everything about the transit system," said Sgt. Scott Guginsky of the Queens Transit Robbery Squad to a reporter from *Newsday*. "He would be a valuable employee to the Transit Authority, if he took the test." Instead, the bogus motorman was arrested in the Hillside/Midland Avenue station after a month-long spree in July 2001 that included 8 break-ins. The same man clearly had a subway fetish; he had served jail time for impersonating a transit worker three years previous. God help his cellmate.

Rear Admiral: In January 1999, the Rotary Club of South Sioux City, Nebraska was treated to the thrilling war tales of Rear Admiral Richard Tracy Spencer, who fought hard as a Navy Seal and was later awarded the Medal of Honor. Too bad the Rotary Club was being told a tall tale. Spencer had been impersonating a Navy man for nearly 20 years, forging letters and wearing military decorations to impress various people. He was arrested in 2000 and charged with one count of wearing unauthorized military decorations (kids, don't try this at home) and one count of forging a federal agency seal.

Con-trary to Popular Belief

In the March 1953 issue of horror comic *Tales from the Crypt*, two con men receive their comeuppance in "Oil's Well That Ends Well." The scammers roll into a small Midwestern town, claiming to be oil speculators, and—lo and behold— they find a huge deposit of oil beneath the town park. They convince the mayor to give them $60,000 in drilling fees, so that the town can reap the financial benefits of their oil well for years to come. Their getaway plan? One of the con men fakes his own death, and is buried in the local cemetery, then awaits his partner to dig him up. As it turns out, there is oil in town, right beneath the cemetery, and it bursts through the coffin. The con man nearly drowns in oil, but is saved at the last minute by his partner. Unfortunately, the partner's cigarette drops out of his mouth, and … well, there's an oil boom after all.

Say, You Look Like Somebody Famous ...

Human genetics are a funny thing. Depending on a combination of factors known only to God and Stephen J. Hawking, your genes can make you handsome or goon- ish, tall or short, fat or thin, blue-eyed or green-eyed. And once in a while, by some quirk of genetic dice-rolling, your genes can make you look like someone else on the planet. Someone famous.

Like Robert DeNiro, for instance. DeNiro is one of the most memorable actors in the world—those soulful, deep-set eyes, that chiseled Roman nose, that baseball bat, smashing your head like an overripe melon. (Sorry. I've watched *The Untouchables* too many times.) He has the kind of face that says, *Nobody messes with Bobby D*. But in 2001, someone did. It was a 51-year-old former firefighter named Joseph Manuella. He had served as the actor's movie double in *The Fan* (1996) and *Great Expectations* (1998), and enjoyed a nice living impersonating DeNiro at birthday parties and wed- dings, earning around $1,500 for each performance. But then Manuella, according to investigators, started immersing himself too deeply in the role. Manuella would show up at exclusive parties in the Hamptons, pretending to be Bobby D., and luring star- struck young ladies into his arms, according to a report in *The New York Daily News*. Manuella also had a credit card in DeNiro's name, and used his likeness to enjoy hotel discounts and free meals at swank Manhattan eateries. After his stints as DeNiro, Manuella would return to his small home in Glen Rock, New Jersey to live a decid- edly un-DeNiro-like life with his wife, an officer in the Air Force.

Even the best roles, however, have to end sometime. Reportedly, the real DeNiro caught wind of Manuella's dead-on impersonation after the impostor tried to put together his own movie deal. "Bobby was outraged that someone was taking advantage of people by pretending to be him," said Tom Harvey, DeNiro's lawyer. "Then we went to work."

But instead of baseball bats and the business end of a .45 automatic, Bobby D., Harvey, and a private investigator helped state police arrange a trap. Manuella was asked to come to a Holiday Inn to play DeNiro at a private party. A limo was dispatched to bring Manuella to the hotel, and when he arrived, he was greeted by state investigator Andrew Werner. "What's this all about?" Manuella asked, and was answered by handcuffs snapping around his wrists. Manuella was charged with two counts of criminal impersonation. If you ask me, he got off easy. I mean, *nobody* messes with Bobby D.

Although he's not nearly as famous as DeNiro, the bass player for 70s rock band The Eagles has also been plagued by an impersonator. "God I want to get this guy," Randy Meisner told the *San Francisco Chronicle* in 1997. "It's been eight years of this."

> **Grifter Speak**
>
> What's all this about?
> —Robert DeNiro impersonator Joseph Manuella, using his best Robert DeNiro voice while speaking to a state police investigator who was there to arrest him. If he was really on the ball, Manuella would have said: "You talkin' to me? Are you talkin' to me? You must be, because I don't see anybody else around."

> **Don't Be a Sucker**
>
> Sure, we're all star struck from time to time, but be wary when dealing with famous people who suddenly need to borrow money, or want to discuss anything financial, for that matter. You really think Madonna needs to borrow $20 to catch a cab ride back to her apartment at the Dakota? (Hint: She lives in London!)

"This" would be a con artist named Lewis Morgan representing himself as the rocker to casino managers and innocent bystanders across the country. They're both about the same age, but don't look much alike. "I consider myself ugly," said Meisner, "but this guy is pretty darn ugly." Nevertheless, Morgan knew enough about Meisner and the rock industry to scam free guitars, lodging, meals, and clothing from unsuspecting booking agents and fans … especially the ladies. In 1990, one woman from L.A. believed Morgan's puppy-dog eyed story about losing his wallet, and she ended up burning through $2,700 on her credit card to pay for dinners, rental cars, and eventually a plane ticket back to New York, where Morgan claimed he was doing a promotional tour with the other Eagles. Later, after Morgan was "Already Gone," the woman went home and looked carefully at one of her Eagles albums. She came to the bitter realization that the man with whom she'd become romantically entangled was not actually Randy Meisner. This was not an isolated incident, either. Once, the real Randy Meisner was approached by an angry woman with an ice pick who wanted to kill him. Lewis Morgan had struck again.

The scam lasted for the better part of the 1990s until police finally nabbed the duping Desperado. They didn't "Take It To the Limit," but they did charge him with fraud and grand theft, which resulted in a two-year hitch at the "Sad Café" (a.k.a. jail) and an undisclosed sum of restitution for Meisner. The real Meisner, for his part, was left with anything but a "Peaceful, Easy Feeling." He was snubbed for the Eagles' huge 1994 reunion tour, and wonders if his impersonator was to blame for some of the bad blood with his old bandmates.

As for Morgan's motives in impersonating a lesser-known member of the Eagles, well … "I Can't Tell You Why."

Then there's the case of Steven Spielberg's nephew, Jonathan. Precocious kid. Even though he was only 16, he drove a BMW with a vanity plate reading SPLBERG around Fairfax County, Virginia, and thought nothing of parking in the spot reserved for his principal at Paul VI High School, the Catholic school he attended. Or should I say, *didn't* attend—absenteeism was a chronic problem for young Spielberg. In spring 2000, school officials at Paul VI decided it was time for a close encounter with the elder Spielberg to discuss the matter. But when the school called one of the most powerful men in Hollywood, they learned that Spielberg didn't have a nephew named Jonathan. Spielberg's security consultants alerted police, and soon the wayward younger Spielberg was picked up.

Con-trary to Popular Belief

Steven Spielberg is apparently a popular target of con artists. One of the most infamous is Abraham Abdallah, who had a credit card in Spielberg's name when he was arrested in March 2001. Abdallah started with a copy of *Forbes* magazine's "400 Richest People" issue, and then used the Internet to glean enough personal details of celebrities and execs to steal their credit card numbers.

Then again, maybe Spielberg is asking for it. In December 2002, Spielberg released his latest directorial effort, *Catch Me If You Can*, a film about real-life con artist Frank Abagnale, starring Tom Hanks.

Turns out, Spielberg *was* the kid's legal name. But he had changed it two and half years previous from Anoushirvan D. Fakhran, the name given to him when he had been born in Tehran, Iran over 27 years ago. (At least that explained how a 16-year-old kid knew how to handle a BMW.) To get into Paul VI, Spielberg had faxed a phony transcript from the "Beverly Hills Private School for Actors" and claimed that he was researching a film role. Paul VI admitted him and even waived tuition. In July 2000, Spielberg was convicted of forgery, and ordered to receive counseling, perform

100 hours of community service, and avoid contact with anyone under 18. "He's not to be palling around with teenagers," said the County Circuit judge. Jonathan Spielberg's story has yet to be optioned by Dreamworks SKG.

My favorite recent celebrity impersonation however, involves an R&B singer. He's not a particular favorite of mine—in fact, I'm not even sure I could hum any of his songs. But it's his name that thrills me. The fact that someone would actually impersonate a singer with this name just makes my day.

The singer's name? Ginuwine. Wait, wait. It gets better. One of Ginuwine's bigger hits? A song entitled "Can You Tell It's Me?"

Ginuwine's impersonator was a 24-year-old guy named Ronrico Madison, a native of St. Paul, Minnesota. Madison would call concert promoters to book performances, and asked for a deposit to be wired to his account. One Jacksonville, Florida, promoter, Sanday Mushatt of N-Da-House Entertainment, lost $5,000 this way. Another promoter in Ohio got suckered for $10,000, and a casting agent in Minnesota ended up paying a $2,000 hotel bill. All told, Madison pocketed $25,000 before police nabbed him December 2001, and he was charged with two very real counts of wire and mail fraud. Mushatt found out about the scam when a relative saw a reference to a Ginuwine Impostor on the Internet. "I told him, 'We know you're not the real Ginuwine,'" Mushatt told *The New York Daily News*.

Con-trary to Popular Belief

R&B singer Ginuwine's real name is "Elgin Lumpkin." (We're glad he stuck with the Ginuwine article.)

You really can't make up stuff like this, folks.

Double Takes: Weird Impostor Tales

Most times, the advantages of impersonating someone are clear: money, sex, power, fame, free meals at fancy restaurants. Other times, they're not so clear.

For example, why would a group of men carrying musical instruments impersonate an orchestra? We still don't know. But in August 2000, the *South China Morning Post* reported that a recent performance of the Moscow Philharmonic Orchestra in Hong Kong may not have featured the Moscow Philharmonic after all—but instead, a bogus orchestra of con artists. "It's a huge scandal in Moscow," said Dimitri Yablonsky, the Philharmonic's guest conductor. "Very upsetting." If the claim is true, then each audience member was bilked of $240 Hong Kong dollars (about $29 US). Then again, it wouldn't be the first fake thing to come out of Hong Kong.

It's a Scam

Don't look like any particular celebrity? No problem. All you have to do is claim that you belong to a famous group—one that has enough members to make checking your story difficult. In the 1990s, one San Francisco man passed himself off as a former San Francisco 49er. Steven Travis had used his alleged pigskin fame to convince people to loan him money and invest in various real estate projects. Travis would show them his two Super Bowl rings (both fakes) and photos of himself in 49er, Chicago Bears and Notre Dame uniforms (also fakes). Amazingly, he was able to convince people that he was a professional football player for nearly 10 years. Remember this, the next time a New York Yankee approaches you with a can't-miss business opportunity.

Would you go to prison for a friend? Pierre Carlton, a 32-year-old in Atlanta, Georgia, did just that. In 1999, Carlton agreed to serve a 20-month prison term in a minimum security prison for his buddy—and drug supplier—Dexter Mathis. In return, Mathis gave Carlton nearly a thousand bucks and the promise of free crack when he got out. It seemed like a good deal to Carlton. So on a hot June day, Carlton walked into the U.S. Marshal's office and turned himself in, claiming that he was Mathis. Apparently, nobody noticed that Carlton was about four inches shorter than Mathis, and that his face looked nothing like the mug shot of the man they'd arrested months earlier. *Details, schmetails.*

Carlton had a good time in prison. He earned a high school diploma, kicked his nasty crack habit with the help of prison counselors, and even became an avid reader. Fifteen months into his sentence, Carlton was sprung for good behavior, and told to report to an Atlanta halfway house. Oddly enough, this is where Carlton had second thoughts about the deal he'd made. Maybe the allure of free crack didn't do it for him anymore, but Carlton skipped the halfway house. Meanwhile, an FBI agent was investigating a bank robbery when he discovered a car with tags that could be traced to Dexter Mathis. Once Mathis was picked up, authorities realized that this wasn't the same guy who'd spent 15 months in prison earning his G.E.D. Mathis was charged with conspiracy, but his lawyer claimed that Mathis was only trying to help his buddy Carlton. "Mr. Carlton had a drug addiction," the lawyer explained to the Associated Press, "and Mr. Mathis educated him on the benefits of drug treatment in prison." Carlton, meanwhile, pleaded guilty to fraud charges and faced probation. (Hopefully, his time in jail taught him an important lesson … oh, never mind.)

Technology vs. Cons

Impostors may find it tough going in the twenty-first century, as biometric technology becomes more widely used. Biometric tech is that James Bond-type stuff you've seen in movies: laser scanners that can read your identity based on your eye, fingertip, hand, or face. It's nearly impossible to fake, unless you have your victim's eye, fingertip, hand, or face readily available. Certain airports are already using this technology, as well as many private companies.

Of course, con artists have always found ways around other technological barriers, and some experts believe it wouldn't be too tough to find your way around a fancy biometric system. "All an ID card with a biometric identifier will prove is that the same person who has that fingerprint or iris-scan obtained the card; it doesn't prove their actual identity," said Barry Steinhardt, associate director of the American Civil Liberties Union, to a Scripps-Howard reporter.

The Least You Need to Know

◆ Identity thieves steal their victim's financial lives; impostors try to actually *live* their victim's lives to gain some kind of benefit.

◆ A "badge game" is where a con artist impersonates a cop to steal your money, often outside of a bank branch.

◆ Be wary of celebrities who want to borrow money—they might be impostors.

◆ New technologies might make it hard for impostors to steal someone's identity, but then again, con artists have always found ways around technology before.

Workin' It: Business Bunco

In This Chapter

- ◆ Are your employees stealing from you?
- ◆ The best ways to detect in-house fraud
- ◆ How con artists give you the business
- ◆ Phony bill schemes

It's no coincidence that this is Chapter 11. Because that's where your business will end up if you let con artists have their way with you. Businesses, large and small, have always been very popular targets of swindlers. Why? Because businesses exist to make money, and money to con artists is like a bucket of blood to sharks—an instant attractor.

The sharks in business bunco schemes, however, come in all shapes and sizes. Some are outsiders who look for weaknesses—or create one—in your organization and then invent ways to exploit it. Some sharks, however, are already inside your organization, and know every single weakness and *exactly* how to exploit it. After all, they've been with your organization for years, and have already earned your trust. In this chapter, I'm going to show you how to spot both kinds of sharks, as well as the weaknesses they exploit.

A Little Extra Take-Home

You think you treat your employees fairly. You give them a competitive wage, generous amount of vacation time, a truckload of benefits, and even a fancy cappuccino machine in the staff kitchen. Still, it doesn't matter. Some employees will think you owe them more. And to receive more, they'll take matters into their own hands.

Most people lump employee theft under the umbrella of "embezzlement," but the modern term for stealing from a company is occupational fraud. Here's a handy definition, written by the Association of Certified Fraud Examiners (ACFE, the professional organization of scam busters that helps businesses investigate fraud): "The use of one's occupation for personal enrichment through the deliberate misuse or misapplication of the employing organization's resources or assets." Here's a simpler definition: when your employees steal from you. It's a serious problem that, according to some experts, costs companies up to 6 percent of their annual revenues. Nationwide, occupational fraud can add up to losses of about $600 billion. Obviously we're talking about a bit more than filching a few pens and paper clips from the supply closet.

Grifter Speak

You call it "what you deserve," but businesses call it **occupational fraud**. That's the technical term for using your job to swindle money out of your employer. And yes, even fudging your expense report counts.

According to the ACFE, occupational fraud comes in three distinct flavors: asset misappropriation, corruption, and fraudulent statements. In their most recent *Report to the Nation* (2002), the ACFE did an excellent job of neatly categorizing what can be murky terrain. Here's the rundown:

Asset Misappropriation

This is when your employees take your stream of revenue and divert some of it into their own pockets. The technical term for it is asset misappropriation, and it accounts for the overwhelming majority—as much as 85 percent—of occupational fraud cases. Most of those involve stealing cash. There are three basic ways employees can swipe cash from their employer (don't you just love how everything breaks down into threes?):

#1. Fraudulent Disbursements

Here, scamming employees might cook up a fictitious invoice for, say, a shipment of office supplies that was never actually ordered. The invoice is processed, a check is cut, and then mailed to this fictitious supply company. The check is then cashed by the scamming employee. "I have seen this scheme used where companies lose millions of dollars in a very short time," says ex-FBI agent Mike Connelley. "It is very effective, and sadly, very common in business." The average cost of these billing schemes to a company, according to the ACFE's 2002 report? $160,000.

Fraudulent disbursements also include shifty payroll schemes where Joe Sixpack invents a shadow employee—call him "Jim Keg Stand"—and the money ends up directly in Mr. Sixpack's account. Some crooked employees don't even have to go to that much trouble. If it's a small company, and the boss entrusts his monthly banking statements to his lone accounting officer, it's far too easy for that officer to write checks to himself. After all, who's going to catch him? The boss isn't even reading the monthly statements anymore. And as long as the officer doesn't get too greedy and write himself a particularly large check, which the bank might question—basically, anything over a grand— he's in the clear. It might be years (if ever), before the missing money is actually missed.

And oh, by the way—if you've ever fudged an expense report, you're technically guilty of fraudulent disbursement. People like you cost companies an average of $60,000 every year. (Now don't you feel guilty?)

> **Grifter Speak**
>
> **Lapping**   A fraudulent disbursement scheme that's structured like a pyramid scheme: an employee who works in accounts receivable takes a sizeable payment and pockets it. To cover it up, he then takes a later payment, and uses part of that to cover the first one. Then he uses a third to cover the second. And so on and so forth, until he is finally caught, or he reaches retirement age—whichever comes first.

#2. Skimming

In this one, employees help themselves to your revenue *before* it makes it into the accounting records. The simple version: You own a candy shop. Somebody buys a Chick-o-Stick for 15¢. Your employee pockets the nickel, and puts the dime in the drawer, but only rings up a 10¢ sale. Average cost to a company: $70,000.

#3. Cash Larceny

This is when employees help themselves to your revenue *after* it makes it into the accounting books. Your candy-shop employee rings up the 15¢ Chick-o-Stick sale, then later helps himself to it.

But cash isn't the only thing a crooked employee can steal. He might also try to boost some other assets, such as equipment (goodbye, Pentium laptop), inventory (goodbye, five dozen cases of widgets), or even company secrets, which he might be able to sell to a competitor. All of these fall under the heading of noncash misappropriations. (Clever, huh?) Most crooked employees stick with the cash schemes, but the noncash schemes tend to result in fatter paydays. The average cash scheme costs a company $80,000, but the average noncash scheme is more like $200,000.

Good Old Fashioned Corruption

In a word: kickbacks. When an employee trades on his position with the company to make a little coin for himself, that's corruption. It can be as simple as accepting an illegal tip (which doesn't necessarily cost you money, but it can cost your reputation), or as complex as a bid-rigging scheme (which can definitely cost you business—especially if losing bidders realize that someone on the inside is on the take). According to the Association of Certified Fraud Examiners' 2002 *Report to the Nation*, corruption accounts for about 12 percent of all occupational fraud cases. That's not many, but consider the average cost of a corruption scheme: $530,000.

Fraudulent Statements

This is when an employee falsifies a company's financial statements. (Also known as "cooking the books.") It might mean overstating revenues to the men upstairs, or downplaying expenses and liabilities. Think of this in terms of how you lied to your parents about your finances in high school. *Overstating revenues:* "What do you mean, Dad? Of course I still have that $5,000 saved for college. It's all there—want me to show you my bank passbook?" *Downplaying expenses and liabilities:* "Mom, you're not going to believe this, but school books went down in price this year. Plus, there's no science lab fee! Looks like I'll have more in my savings account, after all." Meanwhile, that money was funneled into important ventures, such as procuring Pink Floyd albums and imported bongs made with real Indian jade. If you were able to forge convincing financial documents (your savings account passbook, receipts for supplies, and lab fees), you were well on your way to a successful career in cooking company books someday. Your parents should have been proud.

> **Con-trary to Popular Belief**
>
> According to the Association of Certified Fraud Examiners, the average occupational fraud scheme lasts for 18 months before someone discovers it. (Hell, some employees don't stay with companies for 18 months!)

Fraudulent statements represent 5.1 percent of occupational fraud cases, but take a look at the average cost of these schemes to a business: $4,250,000. (Yes, that's four *million*.) That's a lot of Pink Floyd albums, my friend.

Inside Men, and How to Catch 'Em

So who's the most likely person to steal from your company? Is it Ritchie, the 20-something, shifty-eyed mailroom guy who creeps out all of the ladies in the steno pool and has a devil-may-care attitude toward personal hygiene? Or is it assistant vice president Danforth, who has three kids, a wife in the Junior League, and a shiny blue SUV in his suburban driveway?

Hold on to your Palm Pilot: According to recent statistics, it's probably that bastard Danforth.

The ACFE's 2002 report says that the typical fraudster is someone who has never done this before, and has been with the company for quite some time. It's also more likely to be someone you trust. Their study also showed that managers pulled cons roughly 40 percent of the time, while corporate underlings pulled them 60 percent of the time. Age plays a factor, but not in the way you might think. The Boomer crowd (employees 40 years and over) were 6 times more likely to defraud their company than the *Total Request Live* generation (employees 25 years and younger). Finally, the ACFE report said that you could trust the ladies more than the guys: Men were four times more likely to pull a con than women.

Con-trary to Popular Belief

The older the occupational fraudster, the bigger the bite.

So your typical business bunco artist? Just might be the 55-year-old C.F.O. who has been with the company for 20 years. But that's not enough to damn them. You should also look for other tell-tale signs—if your legal clerk is suddenly tooling around town in a shiny new Caddy and sporting gold chains thicker than a newborn's forearm. (Either that, or he's moonlighting as a pimp.) "Employees who steal generally have to spend the money somewhere," says ex-FBI agent Mike Connelley. "The business owner should always be conscious of the employee making $9 bucks an hour who suddenly pulls up to work in a brand new Lexus. That doesn't make sense."

The biggest sign, however, can be found in your suspect's human resources file. Look under the vacation column, and see how much time he's taken off over the past five years. Again, you might think that somebody who takes off weeks at a time—probably

Don't Be a Sucker

You're only as strong as you weakest link. And your weakest links—receptionists, assistants, interns—may unwittingly help someone scam your company, just by giving out information they shouldn't have. If you implement anti-fraud procedures in your office, make sure everyone, not just the company vice-presidents, is included in the training sessions.

snorting cocaine by the pound while he's jet skiing around Ibiza, the rat thief!—is your more likely suspect. Wrong-o, Daddy-o. You want to look for the employee who *never* takes time off. As Jack Nicholson so clearly demonstrated in *The Shining*, All Work and No Play Makes Jack A Dull Boy. In this case, All Work And No Play Makes Jack An Occupational Fraudster. Think about it: If he's running false billing schemes, or even sneaking away $1,000 bucks a month to a phantom employee, the last thing he's going to want to do is take a week off work. That would mean that someone else would be filling in for him, and that greatly increases the chances of discovery. If Jack never leaves the office, it's time to start asking Jack why.

Why do these valued, trusted employees suddenly stab their bosses in the back? Well, there are usually three factors.

♦ **The need.** The employee has a growing need for extra money. Maybe he's late with alimony, or owes Vinnie the Legbreaker 20 large from the last Super Bowl, or maybe something simple and stupid like a DVD movie addiction. (At $20 to $35 a pop, they can add up. Trust me.) Sometimes, a relative needs the money— maybe it's a son with an expensive medical condition, or a daughter with a drug problem.

♦ **The opportunity.** The employee is in a position to spot vulnerabilities in the company's financial armor, and knows exactly how to exploit them.

♦ **The rationale.** The employee either thinks you owe him anyway, for his decades of hard labor, or the employee thinks of his stealing as merely a loan, which he'll happily repay when he's on more solid financial footing.

All of these signs and motives, however, are generalities. You can't simply build a psychological profile of an employee and think you're going to catch him with his hand in the petty cash drawer. What are best ways to stamp out fraud in your company?

If you're a small business owner: Open the bank statements yourself. "That's the best single effective tip to assist in preventing fraud," says Mike Connelley. "The owner or spouse, should do it. Small businesses cannot afford the big security departments and internal auditors to do the detection work, but keep in mind what the embezzler wants—money. And all of it flows through the bank statement. By opening the bank statement, you can look at the general flow of funds in and out of the account and ask yourself, 'Who did I write checks to? What money should have been deposited this past month?'" If you know you pay Joe Sixpack $4,000 a month, and you start seeing odd checks made out to Joe Sixpack for $1,500, or $3,250, or even $8,900, you know something's wrong.

If you're running a larger business: Institute an anti-fraud program (checking out ACFE's website, www.cfenet.org, can start you on the path) in your company, and certainly encourage whistle-blowers. The ACFE found that 26 percent of fraud schemes were first uncovered thanks to tips from other employees. The idea is to make your employees comfortable with the idea of communicating with managers. You want to create a climate of open communication, not a Ministry of Evil where cubicle dwellers are so pissed-off at the company that they would like nothing better than to see Old Ironbutt take a shot in the wallet. Internal audits uncovered scams almost 19 percent of the time, and external audits did the trick in 11.5 percent of the cases. Don't count on the FBI or Secret Service to uncover the fraud for you—law enforcement only uncovered business scams 1.7 percent of the time. (In their defense, they do have other grievous crimes to investigate.)

CAUTION   Don't Be a Sucker _____

Corporate fraudsters are rarely caught, and even if they are, they usually receive nothing more than a slap on the wrist. In *The Art of the Steal*, ex-con man Frank W. Abagnale details a nifty way to get back at an employee who has stolen thousands of dollars from you. "There is one recourse," he writes. "It's rarely used, but it's my favorite. If someone steals $60,000 from you, you can file a 1099 on that employee with the government." In short, you're reporting that slimeball to the IRS for not paying taxes on his ill-gotten gains, and you get to write off as much as a third of it on your return. "It's always been my experience that the threat of a 1099 is far greater than the threat of a lawsuit or prosecution."

How Con Artists Give You the Business

Now that you know all of the ways your own trusted employees can stab you in the back and rob you blind—boy, your next office Christmas party is going to be fun, isn't it?—let's talk about some of the more common ways outside fraudsters can try to ruin your day. They are as varied as they are clever; the best way to prevent them is simply to know they exist.

Bankruptcy Schemes

Most people think of bankruptcy as a last-ditch effort to salvage what remains of your business, but it can also be a highly lucrative scam. To pull a bankruptcy scam, you have to set up a phony company, then order a small amount of supplies from a distributor. Let's say you go into business selling pianos. First, you order five Baby Grands, and pay for them right away. Then, you order 5 uprights, and again, pay immediately. Your piano distributor now starts to consider you as someone who pays for supplies right on time, making you an excellent credit risk. Your relationship continues, with you ordering more and more pianos and paying on time, and the distributor starts to give you discounts.

So finally you come back to the distributor, asking for a rush order of 100 pianos—you've got customers lined up for them—he'll think nothing of shipping them right out to you. Now it's time to have a "Grand Piano Blow-Out Sale of the Century." You unload those ivories at an obscene discount, and very quickly those 100 pianos are gone and you have thousands of dollars in your pocket. That's when you suddenly decide to go bankrupt, and list your piano distributor as one of your creditors. (Which it is.) You get to skip away with thick stacks of green, and you're even free to pull the same stunt again simply by setting up another phony company. And if you set the business up right, your personal credit will never suffer, since it's your fake company, and not you, who's doing the stiffing. (These kinds of scams are also referred to as "bust-out schemes.")

> **Grifter Speak**
>
> I've gone bankrupt at least thirty times and my credit is great!
>
> —Morris Shane, a.k.a. "King of the Bankruptcy Con," in Chuck Whitlock's *Scam School*.

Letter from the Government Swindles

Your business receives a letter from some official-sounding state agency, informing you that you are required by law to purchase signs stating minimum wage, occupancy levels, and so on. The agency asks for the immediate delivery of a check to cover printing, mailing, and administration fees. Well, part of that is true; businesses are often required to post legal signage. But you don't have to pay for them. They're available free from the government. This is as ridiculous as someone trying to sell you a 1040-EZ form.

A similar scam involves a letter from the "Yellow Pages," along with an invoice and a copy of your company's ad. Someone in your company might simply assume this is the yearly bill for running an ad and go ahead and pay it. Problem is, that's not the real "Yellow Pages," and instead of customers' fingers doing the walking, it's a piece of your hard-earned revenue.

The Cleaners

If you can't beat 'em, clean for 'em. That's how some con artists gain access to your company—either by temporarily signing on for real janitorial work, or by simply purchasing a janitor's uniform and forging a plastic security badge. Once inside your offices after 5 P.M., it's like Christmas in July. They have access to your laser-printing check machine. Your laptops and fax machines. Your artwork. Your business records. Sometimes, a clever janitor/scammer can even steal a photocopy machine and replace it with an inferior, broken unit. The sky's the limit.

The Gift Certificate Scam

Some malls issue holiday gift certificates, good for use at any store in the mall. It makes one-stop shopping all that much easier: Gift certificates are the gifts that keep on giving, and you don't have to worry about color or sizes. The only problem with gift certificates is that they're not exactly currency. They rarely include security features such as watermarks or holographs. In other words, they're pretty damn easy to counterfeit. Ditto with supermarket certificates. Sometimes a con artist will set up shop in front of a grocery store, and offer $100 gift certificates for only $50, all for simply answering a few simple survey questions. Many bargain hunters consider this a sweet deal, and happily fork over $50 for the chance to double their shopping buck. The sting comes, however, when the bargain hunter takes that certificate along for their next shopping trip and realizes it's worthless. According to Chuck Whitlock's *Scam School*, one Arizona con artist made $3,000 in just a few hours with this scam.

The 90# Scam

The phone rings. Your receptionist answers. The voice on the other end claims to be a customer rep from the local phone company, and asks the receptionist to help him test the line by punching in 9, then 0, then the pound key (#). She does and hangs up, not realizing that on some systems, 9, then 0, then the pound key (#) enables the caller to make any phone calls he wants on your business' dime—including four-hour gabfests to Thailand.

Receipt Swindles

Don't like your purchase? Keep the receipt, and return the product within 30 days for a full refund. Don't want to ever pay for your purchases? Then simply do your shopping, get a receipt, then go out to your car and dump your purchases into your trunk. Fold up the bags under your coat, walk back into the store, and repeat your order, filling those same bags along the way. When you're done, go to customer service and return everything for a complete refund. After all, you have the receipt, right? (Fortunately, an increasing number of stores include line-item bar codes on the receipts, matching up individual products with their UPC codes. But there are still many stores who don't bother.)

The Irate Customer Scam

"Dear Sirs: After sitting down to enjoy your Hale'n'Hearty Salmon Head Stew at your restaurant, I was suddenly taken ill. Seriously ill, as a matter of fact. I demand your return the entrée price of $7.99 immediately ..."

Any restaurant owner who receives that might reflexively reach for his checkbook and send out that $7.99 right away—after all, that's probably getting off cheaply, what with the risks of lawsuits these days. But you might reconsider. George Sarris, the 49-year-old owner of a seafood restaurant in Birmingham, Alabama received a similar letter, demanding $6.89. Then, according to an article in *Entrepreneur* magazine, Sarris began hearing tales of the same letter popping up all over Birmingham. As it turned out, it was from a con artist, who sent out dozens of these letters, counting on the fact that a good percentage of restaurant owners would simply reach for their checkbooks. "He didn't ask for a lot of money, so some people would probably send it, no questions asked," he told *Entrepreneur*. "If he sent out 1,000 letters and got half back, that's over $3,000."

Advance Fee Loans

The offer is tempting: You need more operating capital, and you're pitched a low interest loan, approved within 24 hours, all in exchange for a simple "advance fee." Once you pay this fee, however, you never hear from the lender again. This is a common scam, especially in real estate deals, but also in business loans. Legit lenders won't charge you an advance fee; the most they'll ask for is a small fee to cover ordering credit reports, or maybe a nominal processing fee. (For more, see Chapter 15.)

CAUTION

Don't Be a Sucker _____

Con artists love to target companies when they are at their weakest. Two such times are immediately after a company has moved and during the summer and winter holidays. There's usually a fair amount of confusion during a move, and it's conceivably easier to slip something past the accounts payable office. And summer and winter holidays are when regular employees tend to take vacation, and less-experienced workers fill in for them.

Oh, No—Mr. Bill!

A rule of thumb in my household: If a piece of mail has a little plastic window, it's never good news. But if you think you receive a ton of bills, it's nothing compared to what business owners receive. These poor guys really get walloped. Aside from the usual charges—rent, power, gas, water, phone, heat—there can be a host of other charges, depending on the business. Landscaping. Water cooler service. Copier toner. Computer support. Periodical delivery. Office supplies. Coffee filters. Even the most basic amenities can add up to a stack of monthly bills thicker than a Stephen King novel.

So who's to notice one extra bill slipped into the mix?

In what is perhaps the easiest, most brazen—and most common—business scam, a con artist will draw up a list of mid-sized corporations, then use a computer and laser printer to zap out a series of phony bills. They could be for anything; the more mundane the better. "Then they send these bills, hoping the corporation is so sloppy or busy that they won't check it and just send it through to accounts payable," explains ex-FBI agent Mike Connelley. "The check goes out, and the scammers get their money delivered to a rented box or mail drop address—with no way to trace it."

A con artist can do any number of things to make the bill seem legitimate. It doesn't take much to scope out some info on your company. Think about the guy who waters the plants. The bike messenger guy. The greasy-haired dude who replaces the tanks on the water

CAUTION

Don't Be a Sucker ____

If you own a business, never pay a bill on reflex. Check to make sure you're actually in a business arrangement with the company or individual sending the invoice, and instruct your employees in accounts payable to do the same.

cooler. That new college intern. These people are in and out of your office all the time, and you probably never give them a second thought. Maybe you should. If that water-cooler guy just makes a simple note of your photocopier make and model, he could easily whip off a fake invoice that seems genuine.

The Least You Need to Know

- ◆ Occupational fraud is when employees use their positions to steal.

- ◆ Surprisingly, occupation fraudsters tend to be long-term, trusted employees.

- ◆ Some con artists use bankruptcy schemes to earn thousands, all without ruining their personal credit histories.

- ◆ If you own a business, don't automatically pay any bill that lands on your desk—some con artists will send you invoices for stuff you didn't order.

12

Sign on the Dotted Line: Banking Fraud

In This Chapter

- How scammers order refills of someone else's checks
- Altered, forged, hot, and kited checks
- ATM scams
- Deposit and stop payment schemes

In my first book, *This Here's A Stick-Up*, I wrote about the many ways people try to liberate money from financial institutions. Most of the people in that book had names like "Machine Gun" and "Pretty Boy" and used tommy guns and six-shooters to accomplish their goals. But there are more ways to knock over a bank than sticking it up. (Nevertheless, stick-up stories are fun to read, and I heartily recommend *This Here's A Stick-Up*—only $16.95, and available at most reputable booksellers—for any heisting occasion. It also makes a great bar mitzvah gift!)

Those methods include check kiting, ATM scams, bogus deposit slips, counterfeiting, and loan swindles. And here's a surprising fact: They all pay a heck of a lot better than the average bank heist. In 2000, bank robbers walked away (collectively) with over $78 million. But according to industry experts, bogus checks alone are responsible for losses of almost $20 *billion* every year. And you don't even need a gun or a fancy nickname to pull a highly lucrative check scheme. This is bad news for anybody who has a checking account. In this chapter, I'll describe some of the most common banking swindles, and tell you how you can keep your money safe.

Checks and Your Balances

Checks are weird, if you think about it. First, there was gold. But that was too valuable to carry around with you, and too difficult to break down when trying purchase a sack of grain or something. So human beings invented money—slips of paper that represent the value of gold. For years, we used that to pay for things like sacks of grain. But then, money became too valuable to carry around with you. So human beings invented checks—slips of paper that represent the value of other slips of paper that represent the value of gold. (Or something like that.)

It's damn near impossible to counterfeit gold, although every alchemist from here to Toledo has tried. It's pretty darn tough to counterfeit U.S. currency. But checks? That's the funny part. They're not hard to duplicate at all. And today, checks are just as valuable as cash or gold.

Fraud expert Frank W. Abagnale used to be an expert check forger, passing $2.5 million in bad checks until he was finally caught by two New York City plainclothes detectives. Today, he teaches and advises companies on how to avoid guys like him, and in his fraud book, *The Art of the Steal*, he can't help but marvel at how absurdly easy it is to pass a fake check—or even better, someone else's check. "Years ago, when a forger came to a city, there was a great deal of preparation involved if he wanted to forge checks." There were apartments to rent, birth certificates to fake, driver's licenses to obtain, fraudulent accounts to open. But not today. "You can just buy your checks through TV Guide," Abagnale writes, "or over the telephone. Anybody can order anybody's checks. We've made it so easy for people to steal from us."

Who's to blame? Abagnale makes the interesting case that the check industry itself— the DeLuxe Corporation, in particular—stripped away all of the security controls that used to be standard, all for the sake of giving people the option of having cute little puppies or Teletubbies on their personal checks. (Once again, vanity provides opportunity for con artists.) To reorder 200 new vanity checks, all you need are the numbers at the bottom of one of these vanity checks. All con artist needs to do is receive a check, or just see one for a certain length of time. And as Abagnale points out, we receive and send personal checks to each other all the time. If you've ever bid on an eBay item and paid a complete stranger by personal check, you've opened the door. A con artist can take one look at your check, fill out a form—either online, or using one found in the Sunday newspaper coupon section—and can even request that the new checks be sent to a P.O. Box. You'll never know what happened until you notice your checking account has been completely drained.

Con-trary to Popular Belief

Every day an average of $27 million in bad checks are returned by banks and credit unions.

The solution, Abagnale says, is to never use those vanity check services, and always order checks right from your bank, which makes it difficult for anyone else to reorder your checks, and whose checks include built-in security features. But sadly, that's not the only way someone can use a check to steal money from banks.

Altered Checks

In this scheme, a con artist somehow gets his hot little hands on a legitimate check. Maybe it was written to him, for a $3.99 eBay item. Maybe it was written to someone else, for $9,000. Doesn't matter. Skilled forgers can use chemicals to strip away the dollar amount or payee name, and then use a laser printer, typewriter, or even a pen to write in what he wants. Suddenly, that $3.99 eBay check becomes a check for $9933.99, and that other $9,000 check that was written to the "Trevor Co." suddenly becomes a check to "Trevor Connelley," which is cashed when a con artist presents fake I.D. for "Trevor Connelley" at the *drawee* bank.

There's not much you can do to prevent these schemes, other than make sure you don't make it easy for con artists by leaving blank spaces near the name of the payee or the dollar amount. The Check Fraud Working Group—a collaboration of the FBI, Justice Department, U.S. Treasury Department, Secret Service, and other financial watchdogs—recommends that you report stolen checks to your bank immediately, but the problem is you often don't even realize your check has been filched until it is too late. Instead, the onus is on financial institutions to be more vigilant when paying out on a check. Tellers need to be trained to spot signs of erasure, or mismatching signatures.

Sometimes, con artists can try to alter a bunch of checks at the same time. On April 10, 2000, a 28-year-old former taxi driver walked into a bank in Savannah, Georgia, and used a phony Florida driver's license to open two personal bank accounts. Around the same time, he also opened a business checking account under another false name. A little over a month later, all kinds of mail was stolen from roadside boxes all over

Savannah. The FBI alleges that the Bulgarian-born cabbie took a bunch of personal and corporate checks and altered them, making his personal alias and phony business name the payee (depending on the type of check), then deposited them into his three accounts. Then, between June 5 and June 14, 2000, the cabbie went on a shopping spree, using checks from his bogus accounts to buy fax machines and computers. He returned the office equipment for cash, and then skipped town.

FBI agents found a van he'd rented all the way up in New Jersey, and presume he's fled the country. Although no one is releasing exactly how much the Bulgarian cabbie was thought to have stolen, he has been charged with 81 counts of financial institution fraud, and that covers a lot of checks.

Grifter Speak

Drawee   Most often the financial institution responsible for paying out the money represented by a check.

Drawer   The person who writes a check, and who is a customer of the drawee (financial institution).

Payee   The person who is to receive funds from the drawee.

Presentment   When the payee presents the check to the drawee. (Say that three times fast!)

In short: The con artist is always trying to be the payee, and has various methods of tinkering with presentment. Who pays? The drawee and drawer.

Forged Checks

If computers and laser printers can be used to counterfeit American dollars, do you think it requires a graduate degree in nuclear biology to cook up a fake check? No way. Fortunately, banks have built an increasing number of high-tech safeguards into every check. There are laser locks, which use a chemical to bind toner—the "ink" used by laser printers—to the paper for good. You also have secure-number fonts— fonts that print check amounts that cannot be altered or expanded. (These tend to look like the opening titles from a 1970s-era blaxploitation flick: chunky and funky.) There are secret printing techniques where the word VOID will appear if someone tries to copy or scan the face of the check.

Unfortunately, not every bank uses all of these nifty features on your checks. It takes money to protect money; if you're concerned about your checks being forged, ask your bank what kinds of safeguards are implemented. Frank Abagnale's *The Art of the*

Steal goes into terrific detail about these security features—after all, he spent the early part of his career trying to beat them—and says that he helped one particular bank cut its annual fraud losses from $3 million a year to only $120,000 year, thanks to security features.

Hot Checks

A wise old man once told me: "Never write a check with your mouth that your ass can't cash." (Come to think of it, that wasn't a wise old man. That was my father-in-law. And it was my wedding day. And he was holding a pistol.) Bank scammers ignore this advice—they love to write checks that the accounts can't cover. This happens in two ways: either the account has insufficient funds to cover the check, or the check is being drawn on an old/outdated account. Either way, the check is accepted, the scammer receives the goods that he used the check to purchase, and the sting happens later.

The most usual red flag that a hot check is being passed is the register number. Extremely low register numbers on checks made out for large amounts should be immediately suspect. I found this out the hard way a couple of years ago. I had just moved to a new city and opened a brand new checking account there. Then, a month later, I tried to buy a home computer for $1,800 using one of my new checks. I was shot down, merely because I was using a check with the register number "118." It was too low—a sure sign that the account is new and could be a bogus account set up by a scammer. Smart retailers will automatically call to check on any check with a register number between 100 and 200. (Some businesses even set the bar higher, at 400 or 500.)

Of course, there is a way around this. When I called my bank to tell them what happened, they said it was easy to fix. They could just send the next batch of checks starting at a higher number, like 700 or 800. Some scammers know this, and request the higher numbers. Or they keep ordering checks until they have that coveted 800.

> **Grifter Speak**
>
> Please Don't Pay Me! I Am A Counterfeit Check!
>
> —the words scribbled on a $1,000 fake check by NBC's *Dateline* for a show on check fraud. And the check? It was cashed anyway.

> **It's a Scam**
>
> Someone trying to buy a $34,000 SUV with a check that has a register number under 200? That has the word "scam" written all over it. Low register numbers means the account is new, and might just be a shell account with a minimum deposit.

Kited Checks

The name of the game in these scams? "Float." That's banking lingo for the lag time when a check is deposited into account, and the money is actually available to be withdrawn. (Kites float; get it?) So the scam artist takes $200, opens a checking account at Bank A. He receives a handy new set of checks, then immediately writes a check for $500 and opens another checking account at Bank B. He receives another set of checks, and writes one for $1,000 at Bank C. By the time he gets to Bank J, our scam artist may be looking at $50,000 in one account, thanks to a measly initial deposit of $200. The key? The float time. Before a check is revealed to be rubber, there is usually a two to four day "float" period. It takes a while for banks to catch up, and by the time that happens, the money has already floated away.

Corn Chex

A fat-free, cholesterol free, oven-toasted cereal with 12 essential vitamins and minerals and a light, crispy texture. For more, see *The Complete Idiot's Guide to Breakfast Cereals*.

ATM Bombs

ATM machines are just as weird as checks. Sure, they're handy—I find myself tapping them at least every couple of days. But think about it: They're just big metal boxes full of money. All you need to get the money inside is a little plastic card with a magnetic strip on it and four little numbers. It's all about convenience; banks don't want to employ tellers to work 24 hours a day, seven days a week, and with so much good stuff to buy out there, people need access to their money. (Sometimes I think ATMs were invented solely for people who were out drinking late, and needed to find a way to get more cash right away to keep on drinking. If you don't believe me, check out how many bars now offer mini-ATMS right there next to the jukebox.)

Convenience however, can bite back. The very thing that makes your cash so accessible to you is what makes it so accessible to swindlers.

The most common ATM scheme operates on the same principle as kited checks—the float. It's even better with ATM machines, because you don't have to deal with any potentially-suspicious bank tellers. Simply open a checking account under a bogus name for the minimum amount—say, $200—and ask for an ATM card. Then, deposit a nice fat bogus check to yourself. Make it $1,000. Heck, you don't even have to go through the trouble of forging a check. Put a blank piece of paper in the ATM envelope. Immediately, the $1,000 will be credited to your account. And a good chunk of it will be readily available for immediate withdrawal. (Convenient, isn't it?) Find an ATM with a nice big maximum withdrawal number—$500, perhaps—and you've more than doubled your money. (Actually, you can probably hit another ATM and get your original $200 back, too.) Repeat as needed.

Another ATM swindle pinches you, not the bank. Using a 79-cent tube of Krazy Glue and a laser-printed note, scammers can earn $300 in one shot. Here's how it works: first, they make up a professional-looking notice on a computer:

ATTENTION VALUED CUSTOMERS

The minimum withdrawal for this ATM is $300. We

apologize for the inconvenience.

Thank you for using Moore Savings and Loan for all

of your banking needs.

They find an after-hours ATM, then tape it to the front of the machine. Then, they take their 79-cent tube of Krazy Glue and seal the metal jaws of that little metal cage where the money spits out. Finally, they go off somewhere to have a smoke, and to keep on eye on the ATM machine.

You amble along. You need $20 for a late-night sixer—the game's on tonight, and a couple of buddies are getting together to watch the Dallas Cowboys get their butts handed to them. You tap the ATM, then notice the sign. Crap, you think. You really need to get going. Fortunately, you know you have plenty of money in your account, and hell, you'll just tap once now for $300, and be good for a week or so. So you withdraw $300, and see the money spit out into the cage.

But wait a second … the cage won't open. What the !!!?? It seems to be … this sounds crazy, but *glued* shut. With your 300 bucks inside! You're hopping mad. The bank's closed. Where's the nearest phone? You're calling the bank. This is ridiculous. You leave the enclosed ATM space to go to the phone down the block.

Meanwhile, the scammer enters the ATM space, pries open the cage with a crowbar, and takes your $300. He uses part of it to buy a sixer. After all, the Cowboys are on tonight. He can't wait to see them hand the Eagles their own butts.

> **CAUTION**
>
> **Don't Be a Sucker** _____
>
> If you see a printed sign on an ATM machine about "minimum withdrawals," don't stick your card in. This is a common ATM scam in which customers are tricked into withdrawing large amounts of money, then losing it when the money fails to spit out. By the time they find help, the perpetrator has taken your money and run.

Give 'Em the Slip: Deposit Swindles

It's a busy day, and you need to deposit a check. So you dart into your bank branch during your lunch hour, whip a deposit slip out from its little shelf on the customer counter, and start filling in your account number and name and address. Then you take it to the next available teller, or into one of those nifty little teller-less deposit envelopes, and go off to buy your ham and provolone on rye at the nearest deli. No big deal. Happens every day.

Can you spot the scam opportunity in the previous paragraph?

No, it's not those nifty teller-less deposit envelopes. And no, it's not that ham and provolone on rye (unless you're in midtown Manhattan, forced to pay $8.99 for a sandwich like that, which is a scam in itself).

It's the deposit slip. You never think twice about grabbing one from the stack, thinking that, heck, I'm in a bank, and the bank officers put those slips there. What could be safer? Well, some bank scammers are fond of taking their own deposit slips—the ones with the magnetic strip on the bottom encoded with their account numbers—and placing a stack of them on the customer counter. All day long, unsuspecting people like you pick up one of *their* deposit slips, fill it out, and inadvertently deposit your check into the scammer's account.

Granted, this is not the most sophisticated of swindles. It doesn't last more than one day, typically, because it's not hard for the bank to figure out where the money actually went. But if a clever scammer has already set up a dummy account, and then walked into the bank shortly before closing to withdraw all of the money he's made all day, then what's the difference? You're out a couple hundred bucks, and the scammer is walking away with the day's proceeds. Frank Abagnale, when he was still using his fraud powers for evil purposes, once made $40,000 this way.

Another deposit slip swindle, called the *less-cash deposit*, depends on a scammer obtaining someone else's deposit slip. Oddly enough, it happens all the time—some people don't think twice about writing their e-mail address on the back of an old slip and handing it to a colleague. The most common way swindlers get your deposit slips, however, is when you simply thrown them away. We've all done it. We've used up all of the checks in a booklet, and have made nearly as many deposits, so we simply toss the booklet away whole. Any scammer who searches trash bins and finds a discarded check booklet thinks he's hit the lottery. Because, in a way, he has.

All the scammer has to do now is come up with a bogus check. Could be one he's altered or forged. It doesn't really matter. He writes a check to you for, say, $1,000. Now comes the twist: Deposit slips have this handy little line called "less deposit received." (Take a moment to look at one of your own checking deposit slips. See it?) The scammer writes "$400" in that line, then takes the bogus check and your deposit slip to the next available teller. The teller doesn't think anything's wrong; after all, the scammer has a deposit slip, and there is more money being deposited than withdrawn. So the teller doesn't bother to ask for I.D., and simply hands the scammer $400. That's four big ones, all from something you forgot to tear up when you threw it away.

Grifter Speak

Less-Cash Deposit Scheme When a scammer uses a discarded deposit slip to present a bogus check to a bank, then asks for a certain amount of money back (less-cash) right away.

Don't Be a Sucker

When you're throwing away any kind of financial paperwork—and that includes bank deposit slips—get medieval on it. Shred, burn, fold, spindle, mutilate the beejesus out of it. Pack it up into a box, and drive it to the nearest atomic blast test range.

Hold On! The Stop Payment Scheme

Here's a particularly diabolical swindle that takes advantage of a little-known banking rule: the 180 day rule. Let's say you receive a check from a large company—a refund check, or a freelance business payment. If you're decent and honest, you deposit the check and later spend the money on something wholesome like granola or a Save the South African Tree Sloth contribution.

If you're not exactly decent or honest, here's what you do. You call the company. Tell 'em the check never showed up. The company apologizes, and promises to put a stop-check order on the first one, and send you another one posthaste. Yeah, thanks a lot, I'd appreciate that, you say. You put the first check in a safe place, and wait for the second one to show up. It does, and you cash it right away. Then, you wait 183, 184 days. You deposit the first check. It clears.

What happened? Most people don't realize that "stop-check" orders last only 180 days unless you tell the bank to extend them. After 180 days, the order is gone, and that first check is suddenly viable again. If you own a small business and place "stop-check" orders, even once in a while, ask your bank to automatically extend all orders to the maximum accepted length of time. Waiting six months for a payday is one thing. But few scammers want to sit around for a couple of years just for an extra couple hundred bucks.

> **Don't Be a Sucker** _____
>
> One very popular check scheme involves your good friends, the IRS. Whenever you cry blood and finally sit down to write that fat check to the IRS, make sure it goes to the "Internal Revenue Service," not the IRS. Scammers can easily make that "I" into an "M," then add the words "Smith" afterward. Suddenly, you're paying $17,500 to "MRS. Smith"—a phony name attached to a very real con artist.

The Least You Need to Know

- ◆ Avoid "vanity" checks—anybody can reorder them and raid your account.

- ◆ Fraudsters take advantage of the "float" time—the amount of time it takes for funds to clear—to pull many scams.

- ◆ Never throw away blank deposit slips. Scammers can use them to cash out portions of bogus checks.

- ◆ Extend stop-payment orders to the maximum length of time allowed by your bank; some con artists try to double-dip with your checks.

Chapter 13

Investment Swindles and Business Manipulations

In This Chapter

- How pyramid schemes (don't) work
- The legend of Charles Ponzi
- The most popular investment scams
- Enron and managed earnings scams

As I mentioned early in this book, most con artists can only be successful if you willingly hand them your money. Now think about one of the few times in your life when you hand someone a large amount of money—an *obscene* amount of money. No, not when you buy a carton of cigarettes in Manhattan. The obscene amount I'm thinking of is when you hand someone a check for an investment.

Investment scams have been around as long as there have been investments. For every fortune made thanks to stock market wizardry, another fortune is lost thanks to sneaky fraud tricks. Sure, eventually a company's bottom line suffers thanks to internal shenanigans, but investment fraud almost always ends up hurting ordinary people like you and me. (Well, me, if I actually *had* any money to invest.) In this chapter, I'm going to explain the three Ps of investment fraud—pyramid, Ponzi, and phone schemes—and also try to make sense of some of the headline-grabbing corporate fraud stories of the year 2002.

The Not-So-Great Pyramids

The investment scam most people are familiar with is the classic pyramid scheme. Here's how it works: Someone approaches you with a sure-fire investment plan. All you have to do is kick in, say, $100. To make your money back right away, all you have to do is recruit two more people into the plan, each of them paying $100. You pocket $50 from each, and the other $100 goes to the "kitty" (or top of the pyramid). Then your recruits recruit two people, and their recruits recruit two more people, and so on and so forth, *ad infinitum, ad nausea, quid pro quo*.

At a certain point, the person at the top collects the kitty, and then the very next person who joined the plan is in line to collect the next kitty, and so on and so forth. Theoretically, as long as people below you on the plan keep recruiting more people, you'll eventually rise up the ranks and get your shot at the top of the pyramid.

Notice I said *theoretically*. Unfortunately, this never happens.

You see, how quickly you get your investment return depends on which level you entered the plan. Let's take this little pyramid structure for example:

First level	1 person
Second level	2 people
Third level	4 people
Fourth level	8 people

Now say you enter at the fourth level, along with seven others. There are seven people ahead of you. Not so bad, right? Wrong. For you to make it to the top, you have to climb three levels. That means three levels of the pyramid have to be created below you:

Fourth level	8 people
Fifth level	16 people
Sixth level	32 people
Seventh level	64 people

Add it up—16 plus 32 plus 64 equals—that's right, at least 112 people have to enter the scheme before you make it to the top. And what are you and your fellow schemers going to tell those people right below you on the pyramid? The truth? That their chances of making it to the top depend on … [quick number crunching here] … 1,920 more people joining the scheme?

No. Of course you can't tell them the truth, because no one in their right mind would hand over $10, let alone $100, when faced with long odds like that. So, you do what every person involved in a pyramid scheme does: lie your ass off. Tell them that they're getting in at the beginning, that they're one rung away from the promised land. Once they've joined, who cares if they discover the truth? They'll just have to recruit even more people with the same lies you used to cover their own butts.

Con-trary to Popular Belief _____

For a pyramid scheme to reach the Thirteenth level, it would require the participation of everyone in the United States. Heck, we all can't get together and pick a President. How are we all supposed to agree to kick in $100?

Unfortunately, it's not always clear from the start that you've agreed to enter a pyramid scheme. Sometimes, you may actually think you're getting involved in an altruistic enterprise. So it is with a recent scheme called "Women Helping Women." The idea seems so wholesome and homespun: 15 women gather together for a dinner party, of sorts. Eight people are designated as "appetizers," four are "soup and salad," two are "entrees," and finally one lucky attendee is "dessert." Each "appetizer" is required to bring $5,000, which is collected and given to "dessert." The soup and salad crowd, as well as all the other "dishes" except dessert, also have to fork over money, which dessert pockets. For an appetizer to move up to "soup and salad" level, she has to bring in eight more appetizers, and so on. The goal? Why, to empower women and to give them a sense of financial security they might not find otherwise. Apparently, $40,000 buys a whole lot of empowerment.

CAUTION

Don't Be a Sucker _____

Even if you know how a pyramid scheme works, and somebody assures you that you'll be in on the action from the start, don't fall for it. Con artists always tell you're in at the beginning. What other hook can they use to make you cough up some dough?

Of course, this is a pyramid scheme, no matter how noble it may sound. (One element of some Women Helping Women meetings is a canned food drive, meant to help needy folks in their area.) However, it's pretty far from noble. The group should actually call itself "Women Screwing Women"—but that might attract an altogether different group of attendees. Even if all participants are in it for the right reasons, you can't escape the fact that the pyramid will eventually collapse from its own weight, and a lot of women are going to lose their $5,000.

It's a Scam

Watch out for those chain letters that promise big bucks via the mail. They seem harmless—simply send $5 to the eight people on the list, then send the letter to eight more people, and watch the bucks start to roll in as your name starts climbing the list. Once again: This is a classic pyramid scheme, destined to collapse under its own weight. Kiss that $40 goodbye.

A Pyramid, or Multi-Level Marketing?

There is another business model that seems like a pyramid scheme, but is actually a completely legitimate enterprise. It's called multi-level marketing, and that's when a company recruits independent distributors to move their products. Ever have an Aunt who dealt Tupperware or vitamins? That's multi-level marketing. In a sense, your friendly neighborhood crack dealer could be thought of as engaging in a multi-level marketing opportunity.

What makes multi-level marketing different from pyramid schemes is that there's actually marketing—i.e., the selling of products—going on. Sure, you may have to lay out some money in advance to receive inventory, but your success doesn't depend on recruiting new people to sell the products. If it does, it's probably a scam. Some pyramid schemes, however, disguise themselves as multi-level marketing. There will be some lame product offered up, maybe a new kind of anti-baldness cream, or something. You will be asked to lay out a lot of money up-front to purchase huge amounts of the stuff, but with the promise of big returns on your initial investment. They'll introduce you to person after person who made thousands of dollars selling this stuff. The best part: You don't even have to be a good salesman! That's right—just find eight other people to take on your inventory, and collect your half!

It's a Scam

There's a simple way to determine if a particular business opportunity is multi-level marketing or a pyramid scheme. If your objective is to sell a product—Tupperware, vitamins, or Spider-Man pajamas—then it's probably multi-level marketing. But if your objective is to bring in fresh recruits every so often, then it's probably a pyramid scam.

In other words: Rope eight more suckers in, like someone roped you in. That, my friend, is classic pyramid scheme.

Perhaps the scariest thing about pyramid schemes is that you may be criminally liable for participating in one, even if you didn't start it. It's probably the only crime I can think of that spreads like the Ebola virus: The victims become the perpetrators, and so on and so forth, until there's no one left standing. Think a business opportunity sounds a little fishy? Call your local Better Business Bureau or State Attorney General and run the plan by them. They'll tell you if it's on the up-and-up, or on the down low.

Heyyyyyyyy! Ponzi!

A man named Charles Ponzi took the pyramid scheme and brought it to a whole new … uh, level. Ponzi was an Italian immigrant who came to America looking to make a quick buck. He stumbled upon an oddity with international reply coupons—basically, the international version of prepaid postage. Seems you could buy them in Italy for one price, then sell them in the United States for almost double. Ponzi started making some green this way, but it wasn't exactly the quick buck he'd been hoping for.

Ponzi decided he needed to expand his operations. He sought out investors in Boston, and explained his little scheme. He also promised that their money would doubled in three months. It sounded terrific to the investors, and soon Ponzi had people shoving fistfuls of cash in his face. Ponzi worked his coupon magic—thanks to a friend in Italy who sent him stacks of international reply coupons—and soon, those original investors had what they were promised: double their money back in less than three months. Word spread, and that's when the scam that would come to be known as a Ponzi scheme was born.

You see, the problem with Ponzi's coupon plan was that there were only so many international reply coupons you could buy in Italy and resell in the United States. With an increasing number of investors clamoring for a piece of the action, Ponzi came up with what he thought was a brilliant solution: Simply take money from new investors and give some of it to the old investors, no coupon-buying necessary. As long as new investors kept rolling in—and why wouldn't they, with the amazing returns original investors were receiving?—the scheme could go on indefinitely. Ponzi opened up satellite offices across the country, and on some days raked in money by the millions.

Of course, this was simply a pyramid scheme without the framework of a pyramid. There were only two levels: Ponzi's level, and then everybody else. Sure, some investors got rich at first, but it was doomed to collapse … and collapse it did, just six months after the scheme began. *The Boston Post* started poking around, and the negative publicity put the kibosh on the flow of fresh blood. Without new and constant infusions of money, Ponzi's empire imploded. By the time he was carted off to federal prison for mail fraud, Ponzi owed over $15 million to some 40,000 angry investors.

A Ponzi scheme, in short, is any business model where you rob Peter to pay Paul, just for the appearance of profitability. The biggest Ponzi scheme in recent history involved a company called Cash 4 Titles, and it hooked all kinds of prominent people—sports figures, business leaders, and government officials. Cash 4 Titles offered car loans to people who really couldn't afford them—loans with insanely high interest rates, such as 36 percent. The collateral? The very title of the car the "customers" purchase. If the customer paid up, Cash 4 Titles stood to make a fat buck from the exorbitant interest. If not, Cash 4 Titles repo'd the car. It was a win-win situation, and it attracted plenty of investors. *The Wall Street Journal* profiled Cash 4 Titles in a story about auto-title loans, and soon there were 30 satellite offices throughout the South, Midwest, and Southwest. The high-profile investors included several professional football players, such as Philadelphia Eagle Duce Staley and former Green Bay Packer Robert Brooks.

But as it turned out, Cash 4 Titles wasn't quite raking in the money it said it would, and it started paying original investors with money brought in by new investors, according to an investigation—and subsequent shutdown—by the Securities Exchange Commission (SEC). All told, over 2,025 people invested in Cash 4 Titles and collectively lost $200 million, much of which was hidden in offshore accounts. (Aside from the Ponzi-like scheme Cash 4 Titles also came under the influence of organized crime figures, who used the operation to launder drug money.) Those 2,000 or so investors have filed suits, but the SEC says they'll be lucky to get back pennies for every dollar they lost.

> **Con-trary to Popular Belief**
>
> Actually, Ponzi wasn't the first to pull this financial stunt. That credit goes to William "520 Percent" Miller, who predates Ponzi by 20 years. For more, check out Miller's short bio in Part 4.

> **Con-trary to Popular Belief**
>
> Want to know an increasingly favorite target of investment scammers? Professional football players? According to an article in *U.S. News and World Report* published in February 2002, at least 78 NFL players were defrauded out of $42 million, mostly through shady investments. (Tell Junior to stick to ice hockey or basketball.)

Turning Up the Heat: Boiler Rooms and E-Mail Pitches

There are plenty of other scams aside from pyramid and Ponzi-type schemes. The most common investing scams find their victims thanks to two devices you probably have in your home right now: a telephone and a computer connected to the Internet. And surprise, surprise, just like with many other scams, senior citizens are favorite targets. How do they find their targets? Why, funny you ask.

Telemarketing Boiler Rooms

Ever see the 2000 Vin Diesel flick *Boiler Room?* Don't worry—nobody else did either. But it was about the high-pressure world of stock brokers using cold calls to try to sell initial public offerings (IPOs) to rich folks. (The high-pressure room where they place these calls is known as a "boiler room.") Cold-calling is a perfectly legitimate stock broker strategy; many young brokers at large firms are encouraged to hit the phones hard. (Often, their jobs are on the line unless they can come up with a certain dollar figure a month; at some firms, that figure is $1 million.) But some investment scammers hit the phones hard to make a buck from unsuspecting marks, who don't know that the investment—and all of its promised returns—is bogus. According to some experts, these illegal "boiler rooms" are raking in $1 million a month.

Scamming cold callers will use certain catch phrases, such as "risk-free" or "guaranteed return." Then they'll crank up the ticking clock, making it sound like you have to jump on this investment rightthisverysecond, otherwise you'll be missing out on the "investment deal of a lifetime." Don't buy it. No investment is ever "risk-free" or "guaranteed"; just look at what the stock market did 2001–2002. Cold callers who feed you lines like these are like drug dealers who tell you "it's not addictive." They're feeding you a line.

One recent investment scam making the rounds is the **promissory note scam.** Like many investment scams, the perfect mark is a senior citizen, mostly because they tend to have a lot of dough socked away in savings. Here's how it goes down: A crooked life insurance agent calls one of his elderly clients and explains that he knows a company that needs some capital to help their business grow. Typically, it's a well-known company that the mark is familiar with. The agent explains that

Don't Be a Sucker

Never give your personal or financial info to a cold caller offering an "investment deal of a lifetime." If you are interested, check 'em out by contacting the Securities Exchange Commission at www.sec.gov.

the company is looking for investors to buy promissory notes—notes that will mature quickly (usually in nine months) and pay 10 to 20 percent, guaranteed. There's not a better offer anywhere, the agent will explain. What better way to safely and securely watch your money grow? After all, the life insurance company is guaranteeing your investment. Why not write me a check right now, and leave your heirs something *really* substantial? In fact, why not cash in your life insurance policy and roll it into this investment?

Here's what the agent isn't telling the mark: The promissory note isn't really guaranteed by the life insurance company; the crooked agent is working this deal on his own. (And getting handsomely compensated for his trouble.) Plus, the company that allegedly needs all of this working capital doesn't need it at all. The whole thing was made up. The mark writes a check, receives a worthless note, and it's good-bye savings.

I can't stress this enough: Whenever you're presented with an investment deal that sounds as sweet as Willy Wonka, check it out. Call or log on to the Securities Exchange Commission website (www.sec.gov) or talk it over with your financial advisor.

Internet Offers

Despite the fact that any 12-year-old with an AOL account can easily create his own web page, people still tend to believe what they see on the Internet. (For other web scams, see Chapter 5.) Investment scammers know this, and pitch all kinds of "risk-free!" and "guaranteed!" deals via e-mail, hoping that at least a few of the people they're spamming will bite.

Other scammers use slightly different methods to pull a web-based investment scam. The most notorious recent case involved a 15-year-old kid from Cedar Grove, New Jersey named Jonathan Lebed. First, Lebed snapped up stock in a bunch of minor companies. Then he hit some high-profile Internet message boards and left anonymous notes claiming that a particular stock was going to "explode this week!" Enough people saw those notes and took a chance, buying stock in those companies. The stock swelled, and Lebed quickly sold, making approximately $800,000 in the process. (What has your 15-year-old done for you lately?) The SEC sued Lebed for stock manipulation.

The point is, don't believe "hot tips" you read on the Internet. Sure, they might be coming from a disgruntled insider. But more likely, they're coming from a scam artist—or in the case of Lebed, somebody who isn't even old enough to shave yet.

Other investment scams use the Internet to lend the schemes an air of believability. One Australian con artist convinced 300 people to invest a total of $10 million in companies based in the Dominion of Melchizedek. Go ahead. Check your Rand-McNally Atlas. (I'll wait.) You're not going to find the "Dominion of Melchizedek," namely because it doesn't exist. It was solely the invention of an American swindler, who created it as a front for a multitude of scams. If you're near a computer, go log on to www.melchizedek.com, and you can tour the entire nation, made up of Pacific islands. Fairly realistic, huh? That's what those 300 investors thought, too. Again: Don't believe investment advice you see on the Internet. After all, the web was created by people who grew up playing Dungeons & Dragons and not dating very much. There's going to be some freaky stuff out there in cyberspace.

> **CAUTION**
>
> ### Don't Be a Sucker
>
> Never invest in something over the phone or the Internet without checking on the company first. Forget the lure of the web; would you hand a check for $1,000 to a complete stranger in the middle of a parking lot? Of course not. Then why do the same with a stranger you can't even see?

Enron for Your Life: Managed Earnings Scams

In early 2002, the media was obsessed with Enron. Come to think of it, even *Playboy* was obsessed with Enron. (That magazine, however, was interested in uncovering something other than corporate fraud.) Every other day it seemed as if there was another screeching bombshell from the Enron scandal, and then there was the WorldCom scandal, and then Adelphia, and Tyco …

The only problem: I don't think many people really understood what kind of fraud was actually being perpetrated. I know I sure didn't—not at first. Each scandal-ridden company seemed to use a different kind of swindle. All of them seemed to be sort of like investment scams, but not quite.

All of these different corporate scams fall under the heading of *managed earnings scams.* "Managed earnings is a nice way of saying that the company is very careful in how much (or how little) they show each quarter in earnings and losses," says ex-FBI agent Mike Connelley. How do you make money from quarterly reports? By giving yourself a truckload of stock options. Most top officers at any company are given stock options in the company. If you can illegally manipulate the value of your own stock, you can make yourself richer in no time simply by buying when the stock is low, and selling when it suddenly skyrockets (through your illegal manipulations).

My favorite explanation of managed earnings scams comes from *The New York Times* columnist Paul Krugman, who contributed a story called "Flavors of Fraud" on June 28, 2002. Krugman takes a simple business—an ice cream parlor—and pretends that it employed the same scams that Enron, Dynegy, Aldelphia, and World Com did. For example, an ice cream parlor using an Enron-type scam would enter into agreement to supply one ice cream cone per day to each customer for 30 years. (That's a lot of licking.) Now to appear wildly profitable to its investors, the parlor would say it cost far less to make each ice cream cone (say, 45¢ instead of 90¢). And when reporting one year's profits, the parlor would actually list the potential profits for the next 30 years (and not tell their investors what they were doing). The bottom line? That little ice cream parlor would—on paper—appear to have opened an extremely lucrative operation. Stocks would surge, the owners would profit, and the investors would be completely hoodwinked.

Grifter Speak

Managed earnings scams   when corporations try to illegally boost their stock by tampering with earnings statements in a variety of ways.

Now a Dynegy-type scam is a little different. In this one, the ice cream parlor admits to its investors that business isn't looking too creamy-rich at present. But it tells its investors that it soon will be. And to prove it, the parlor shows them tons of orders for future cones. The truth is, however, that the parlor has entered into a backdoor agreement with another ice cream joint down the street to buy 100 cones from each other everyday. The sales aren't real, but both stores look awfully busy. Stocks surge, owners profit, and the investors, again, are hoodwinked.

An **A**delphia-type scam depends on the ice cream parlor telling investors that it's the number of customers—not profit—that matters. So the parlor simply makes pretend that it has hundreds of customers, lined up around the block, waiting for a scoop of fudge ripple. (Repeat after me: Stocks surge, owners profit, investors hoodwinked.) And in a WorldCom-type scam, the ice cream parlor pretends that everyday costs (sugar cones, milk, chocolate jimmies) are actually equipment purchases, which gives the appearance of a robust, profitable business.

Partly, we have the go-go Dot.Com era of the 1990s to blame for this mess. During the Internet boom, industry analysts would watch corporate earnings reports like hawks, looking for any deviations from how the stocks were expected to perform. If the company performed the way analysts predicted or better, whamm-o! The stocks would go through the roof. If not … well, hope you brought your parachute. So in reaction to the analysts, some companies decided to make the corporate earnings reports dance exactly the way they wanted. "Officers, managers, and key employees would carefully choreograph the earning to fit the market expectation," explained ex-FBI agent Mike Connelley, who now investigates corporate fraud. "The issue is: When does simple, legitimate 'management of earnings' become criminal action?"

The fact that the C.E.O. is spending $1.5 million in company money on his pet Yorkie's first birthday party might be a hint that something's a bit shifty in the accounting department.

The Least You Need to Know

- Pyramid schemes always collapse, except for the people at the very top—and despite what con artists will tell you, you'll never end up at the top.

- Charles Ponzi is credited with coming up with the "rob Peter to pay Paul" idea in investing.

- The most common investment schemes are pitched by phone or e-mail, and often target senior citizens.

- The corporate scandals of 2002 boil down to one act: misrepresenting financial statements to investors.

Chapter 14

Lawyers, Guns, and Money: Tax and Insurance Scams

In This Chapter

- ◆ Beating the IRS at their own games
- ◆ A kinder, gentler IRS?
- ◆ The many, *many* types of insurance fraud
- ◆ Making a killing—literally—from insurance

A father of a friend of mine used to grumble: "All I gotta do is live, die, and pay taxes." (He'd grumble this until his wife showed up with a chore list, and then he'd grumble: "All I gotta do is live, die, pay taxes, mow the lawn, and pick up the dry cleaning.")

Nevertheless, my friend's father was on to something. You can't do much about death—but living and taxes are the real tricky ones. Predictably, some people do their best to avoid them. Either they pretend they're not living so they can really live it up, or they hide their money where the IRS can't find it.

These cons are the two white-collar crimes that pinch hard-working citizens the most: insurance fraud and tax evasion. According to Conning Corporation, an insurance investment research firm, insurance fraud in 2001 cost the average American household more than $5,000 a year in terms of higher premiums. Sure, these are institutional rackets, but when the institutions get squeezed, they turn around and squeeze the rest of us. So forget Enron (unless you're an investor). The institutional scams you should worry about are the ones you'll find in this chapter, because you end up footing the bill.

Enter Taxman

George Washington didn't pay his income taxes. Abe Lincoln did, but William McKinley, Theodore Roosevelt, and William Howard Taft didn't. That's because the very idea of an "income tax" didn't exist until Lincoln introduced it in 1862 to pay Civil War expenses. Ten years later, the tax was repealed. In 1894, Congress got the bright idea to bring it back, but the Supreme Court shot it down as unconstitutional in 1895. But Congress wasn't going to give up that easily. In 1913 Congress ratified the Sixteenth Amendment (arguably the least popular amendment because it's the one that outlawed booze). In short: The Sixteenth allowed the government to collect an income tax. At the time, the pinch wasn't too bad—just 1 percent for all incomes over $3,000, and a 6 percent surtax for any lucky Americans who were pulling in over $500,000 a year. The percentages gradually increased over the years and after World War II paycheck withholding and quarterly payments were invented. In the 1950s, the Bureau of Internal Revenue became the service we all love to loathe, the Internal Revenue Service (IRS for short).

Some people, however, like to pretend like it's still the heady tax-free days of 1912. They try to hide money from the government, or convince the IRS that they actually don't owe anything.

Con-trary to Popular Belief _____

Joseph Nunan, former head of the IRS in the mid-1940s, once won $1,800 after betting that Harry Truman would win reelection in 1948. Nunan, however, failed to claim his winnings and was later convicted of tax evasion.

(Source: A confidential history of the IRS Criminal Investigation Division, meant for internal use only, but unearthed by the Associated Press in 1988.)

The "Federal Taxation Is Unconstitutional" Scam

As you know, the Supreme Court ruled that an "income tax" was unconstitutional in 1895. Some tax evaders will try to hold that century-old factoid up as proof that their employers should not withhold any taxes from their wages. What they fail to mention is that Congress has passed one or two laws since 1895, among them the Sixteenth Amendment, which made it perfectly legal for the U.S. Government to ask for its share. Like it or hate it, it's the law. And if an employer buys the lie and doesn't withhold taxes, he's in trouble, too.

Fraudulent Tax-Busting Services

Sure, there's money to be made avoiding taxes. But there is also money to be made counseling other people to avoid taxes. Some con artists offer "untax" programs, where for only $49.95, you will receive tapes and books that explain how to avoid paying federal and state taxes forever. Send in your check, however, and you won't be seeing any tapes or books. If you do, they'll be filled with the same kind of baloney that other scammers try to sell in the form of "tax-busting secrets." The rich always skip out on taxes, the sales pitch goes, so why shouldn't you? Simply pay my $99.95 fee, and I'll tell you how to skip paying taxes, too. (As it turns out, there are no secrets—and you'll be $99.95 poorer.)

Or better yet, goes another tax scam sales pitch, give me your Social Security number, and I'll file a phony W-2 form that'll boost your tax withholding. I get a small fee, but you get the benefit of a nice fat return! The problem is, it's easy for the IRS to catch these kinds of scams, and you'll be on the hook for the back taxes and penalties (plus, some scammer now has your Social Security number). Yet another scam pitch encourages you to set up a bogus home business, and thereby be able to claim all of your personal expenses (rent, heat, phone, groceries, and so on) as "business expenses." The only problem: You have to be able to demonstrate profit from this "home business" to the IRS, otherwise, you'll get nailed.

In short, never trust any person/service/website that promises to help you squirm around paying federal and state taxes. Leave that kind of stuff to your accountant. (Just kidding, IRS. Really. As Walter Matthau put it in *Grumpy Old Men*, "My accountant is straighter than a grizzly's dick.")

Under-the-Table Payments

In college, I used to play keyboards. I'd make a legitimate buck every Sunday morning playing the organ at St. Jerome's Parish—with federal and state taxes dutifully withheld from my $50 paycheck. But Friday and Saturday nights, I'd occasionally play in a bar band at certain nightspots I won't name in this book. The owner of the nightclub would give our five-piece band $350—that's $70 for each of us. It'd be in cash. There wouldn't be any pay stubs, or receipt of any kind. In other words, it was under the table. (And right now, I'm praying to God there is a statute of limitations for this sort of thing.) The nightclub owner was guilty of penny-ante tax evasion, but some large companies try to pull the same thing, too—paying their employees under the table so neither employer nor employee has to worry about reporting anything to Uncle Sam.

Exaggerated/False Returns

Here's the form of tax evasion you're probably most familiar with. No, not you *personally*. I know you'd never do anything such as try to claim an extra dependent, or try to write-off ridiculous items for a home business. But some people do. And some even file false returns, hoping for a fat refund check before anyone at the IRS notices it went out. One of the biggest false return swindles happened in California in 1998, when five men invented a bunch of returns for homeless people, children, and fictional entities and filed them. Collectively, the returns sought $9 million in refunds. Some checks were actually sent before the IRS caught on.

Fraudulent Tax Shelters and Offshore Havens

Here's the form of tax evasion you're probably most familiar with if you're wildly rich. This is where crooked accountants and financial advisors use loopholes—including foreign banks and credit cards—to hide money away from the IRS. I'm not going to detail many of these because, quite frankly, I never took accounting in high school, and many of these schemes go way beyond my limited financial imagination. (Hell, I can't even figure out how to hide $20 from my wife, let alone the world's toughest tax collection agency.) You can find a host of grisly details at www.irs.gov by clicking on the "Tax Frauds and Scams" link.

But I will mention two recent shelter/haven-type scams that I can actually under- stand. One of them is using offshore credit cards—you know, MasterCards that origi- nate from Belize, Bermuda, the Bahamas, Antigua, Switzerland, and so on—and using them to pay for all kinds of goods and services, including plane tickets, car rentals, jewelry, computer gear, and even groceries. Such offshore purchases have allowed people to evade billions of dollars in taxes, according to the Justice Department's Tax Division. But as you'll read in the next section, the IRS has set their sights on this particular evasion scam. In 2002, the agency filed a "John Doe" summons with federal court in Miami to force MasterCard International to cough up the identities of all of these offshore account users. In short: If you've been cheating Uncle Sam by using foreign plastic, your tax-evading days are numbered.

Another is a trust scam, in which fraudsters promise that—for a fee ranging from $5,000 to $70,000—your money will be safe and free from taxation in their overseas trust corporation. But many of these "trusts" aren't trusts after all—and thus, not free from taxation. (A real trust puts control of the assets in the hands of a board of trustees, not the individuals.) Both the government and the people putting their money in these phony "trusts" end up getting stung.

It's a Scam

Another increasingly popular tax scam covered elsewhere in this book is the so-called Slave Reparation Scam, in which descendents of slaves file for non-existent tax credits. For more, see Chapter 8.

There are also a number of Internet and e-mail scams in which con artists claim to be from the IRS and ask for personal information, including your Social Security number and mother's maiden name. For more, see Chapter 5.

The IRS: Not as Bad You Think?

In September 2002, the world as we know it changed. The IRS publicly announced that it would stop picking on you.

You, me, and the rest of the small fry taxpayers. Instead, the IRS intends to use more of its investigative muscle to go after those high-income guys who use complicated schemes (like the tax shelter/haven/offshore schemes) to avoid paying taxes. That means the IRS is less likely to go over your 1040-EZ with an electron microscope, and more likely to smoke out tax scammers who use credit cards from foreign banks. "The real world is such that we have limited resources," said IRS Commissioner Charles Rossotti to the Associated Press. "We are trying to figure out, where is the most threat to the system?"

It's a matter of sheer numbers. The tax gap—the difference between the amount of tax we all owe and the amount of tax that is actually paid—is about $207 billion every year. A huge chunk of that tax gap is thanks to tax evaders. So it actually makes sense to go after the big fish. Sure, the IRS might be able to pummel a couple of grand in back taxes out of you or me, but that's not even a drop in the bucket compared to the return they'd get if they catch a multi-million dollar evader.

CAUTION

Don't Be a Sucker

We, the taxpayers, cough up 39 cents to help pay the IRS for every $100 they collect. Don't let some other rat skip out ponying up his share. To report tax crimes, call 1-800-829-1040 or log on to www.irs.ustreas.gov.

Of course, the IRS stresses that it's "not giving anybody a free ride"—you will still be expected to pay your taxes in full and on time. But the agency is trying to alter the perception that it audits mostly middle-class taxpayers instead of the rich fat cats with all of the fancy tax breaks cooked up by overpaid accountants. "The really big point is that we're trying to maintain the faith that the honest taxpayer has in the system," said Rossotti. "We know that when people abuse the system, it tends to reduce that faith."

Con-trary to Popular Belief

In 1998, Chinese tax officials unearthed the largest evasion scam in the country's history, something to the tune of 6.3 billion yuan ($760 million) and involving over 200 companies and 65,536 fake receipts. But the four men responsible—one of them a tax official—didn't have to pay back a single yuan in back taxes. Instead, the four men were sentenced to death. (Let's hope the IRS didn't hear about this case.)

Dude, Where's My Wreck: Insurance Rackets

Insurance is a lot like gambling, only on a much larger scale. Instead of chips, cards, and dice, the playing pieces are your body, your car, your house, maybe even your wife. With insurance, you are betting that at some point, you will die. Or you'll wreck your car. Or your house will get flattened by a tornado. Or your wife will wreck your car, and then be in your house when it is flattened by a tornado. The insurance company is betting you won't. If you "win"—e.g., you die—the insurance company must pay out. If the insurance company "wins"—e.g., you don't die—it continues to take your money.

Yeah, it's grim. If this was how other gambling operations worked, Las Vegas would be shuttered in a week.

But just like with other games of chance (see Chapter 9 for more), con artists try to beat the system and trick insurance companies into paying out, even though the con artist hasn't died. Or had his car wrecked. His home flattened. His wife deep-sixed. There are hundreds of ways to pull insurance scams, and con artists at this very minute are probably busy thinking up new ones. In this section, I'll describe some of the most common.

Fake Car Accidents

You remember riding in bumper cars as a kid, don't you—where the object was to crash your little car into other little cars? The difference between bumper cars and faked car wrecks is that bumper cars don't result in multi-thousand dollar payouts from insurance companies. And bumper cars don't result in real injury or death for innocent people. Still, this is how some scammers choose to make a buck. They'll pull up ahead of a large truck, then slam on their brakes, hoping that the truck behind them won't have enough time to brake or swerve out of the way. Freight and delivery trucks are always insured; as long as the scammer survives, he's probably looking at a nice fat payday. That, sadly, is what happened in Long Beach, California in 1997. A pair of fraudsters pulled on to the Long Beach freeway, raced up in front of a tractor trailer, then slammed on their brakes. Behind the tractor trailer was Juan and Marie Lopez, along with their two-year-old daughter Joanna. And behind them was a gravel truck. All four vehicles collided, but only the Lopez car burst in the flames, burning the young family alive. As the result of an investigation, the two con artists who caused the accident were sentenced to 11 years in state prison.

Some accident-fakers work alone or in pairs; others belong to tightly-organized crime rings. One of the largest such rings operated in Los Angeles in the mid-1990s and was run by a group of 45 doctors, lawyers, and other medical professionals. (Yes, you read that correctly—the doctors and lawyers were behind the whole thing.) The ring hired recruiters—known as "cappers"—to find people who would be willing to be involved in accidents on L.A. streets and freeways. The capper, along with his recruit as a passenger, would drive into traffic in a rusty wreck of a car, then either ram another car from behind or speed in front of another car and slam on the brakes. From 1992 to 1996, at least 100 accidents like these were faked. (One woman who claimed she'd been recruited by the ring gave a deposition in which she said she took part in over

Con-trary to Popular Belief

About $200 billion is paid out every year in property/casualty claims. Industry experts estimate that about 25 percent of those payments are for fraudulent claims.

Grifter Speak

El Toro y La Vaca
Spanish for "the bull and the cow," this refers to the method of driving in front of a vehicle, then slamming on the brakes, for sole purpose of causing an accident. The bull is the insured car; the cow is the car full of potential "victims." Also known as the "swoop and squat." The accident-causing car is also known as the "swoop vehicle."

5,000 staged accidents. That's a lot of time in a lot of neck braces.) Allstate conducted a four-state investigation of the ring, and finally smashed it apart in 1997, when it sued the 45 doctors and lawyers for $107 million statutory damages.

Another such ring, this one operating in Riverside and San Bernadino counties in California, recruited college students to report false auto accidents. Each student was given $1,200 to file a false report; passengers posing as victims would be given $300 per "accident." The ring collected $2.5 million in fraudulent payouts before the father of one of the students tipped off the insurance company, who in turn alerted the Riverside D.A.'s office and the state department of insurance. Still another ring operated in central New Jersey in 1997 to 1999, but instead of using college kids they used real children, some of them as young as seven years old. The ring of 28 people faked almost 100 accidents in that two-year period and collected $2 million in insurance. "The children were held out as injured and sent for treatment," said one investigator to *The New York Times*. "And in every one of those cases where there was an actual crash, there was the potential of real injury to those children."

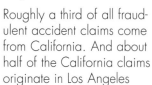

Con-trary to Popular Belief

Roughly a third of all fraudulent accident claims come from California. And about half of the California claims originate in Los Angeles County. In most of the country, 29 bodily injury claims are filed for every 100 car accidents. In L.A., the rate is 99.6 injury claims per 100 accidents. Someone want to tell me why Randy Newman loves L.A. so much?

Faked wrecks are not the only way con artists try to squeeze money out of car insurance companies. Someone may have a real accident, then lie about their injuries. This kind of scam, along with the phony neck brace handed out by crooked personal injury lawyers, has become a cliché. Still, it happens all of the time. The Rand Institute for Civil Justice estimates that one-third of auto accident victims exaggerate their injuries, which means that the rest of us suckers have to pay an additional $30 billion each year in car insurance.

It's a Scam

Are you in a car accident and not sure if someone's pulling a scam or not? Here are some tell-tale signs of a car wreck scam: (1) the vehicle is rented, full of people, and either just recently insured or with insurance that is about to expire and (2) the person making the claim gives a P.O. box or hotel room as their primary address. If you suspect fraud, contact your insurance company's fraud division or your state's department of insurance.

Property Damage Scams

As comedian George Carlin once noted, "people have increasing amounts of stuff." They buy stuff to help them save time so they're able to work harder to buy even more stuff. They buy other stuff to house the stuff they've got. And they spend money on insurance policies to protect that stuff. But what happens when you have all of this stuff, but no money to buy more stuff? Ask a con artist, and he'll tell you it's simple. Destroy the stuff, and collect the insurance policy to get money to buy more stuff.

One of the most common property scams involves the old fraud favorite: the automobile. Making a car disappear isn't terribly tough; you could just hand the keys to an accomplice, who then drives your car 100 miles away and into a gravel pit. The next day, you report it as stolen, and then later collect the insurance. Or you could drive it to your friendly neighborhood chop shop and have them dismantle it for you. Or, if you're somewhat sentimental, you can destroy the vehicle identification number (VIN), put the old rust bucket in storage for 10 years, collect the insurance, then pull it out again when the heat has died down. Sadly, these fake claims are all too easy to pull. And we all wonder why our car insurance rates keep climbing and climbing.

But property scams aren't limited to cars. Boats can be insured, too. In 2001, a Beverly Hills lawyer was caught in the act of attempting to sink his 76-foot luxury yacht off the coast of Naples. When Italian authorities pulled up to the vessel—which had not been successfully sunk—the lawyer quickly explained that he had been held hostage by shifty-looking Russian gangsters, who had originally wanted to steal his yacht for drug-running, but later decided that the craft wouldn't be fast enough to outrun coast guard ships, and tried to sink it. The Italian authorities didn't buy the cover story, and later it turned out that this incident was simply the latest in a number of scams this lawyer had tried. There were three other sunken/destroyed boats in his past (one 43-footer stolen by Peruvian coffee dealers, a 57-footer sunk after an accident off the coast of Italy, and a 47-footer that assassins blew up off the coast of Southern California), as well as claims for stolen art and bogus medical claims—a total of over $2 million in fraudulent insurance claims. In this latest attempt, the lawyer purchased that 76-footer for $1.9 million, then illegally inflated its value to $3.5 million, and then tried to sink it to collect on that larger value. Now the lawyer is on a slow boat to old age, in the form of an 80-year jail sentence for a variety of criminal charges.

The scams don't need to be that grand, though. One California software distributor decided to take advantage of a natural disaster—the Northridge Earthquake of 1994—and claim that Mother Nature destroyed a great deal of his inventory. He told his employees to physically destroy software packages, either by jumping up and down on them, or mangling them with their bare hands. The guy claimed $5 million in damages, and actually received close to a million of it before one of his employees came clean with insurance investigators.

Arson

Always be suspicious of someone walking away from their home, carrying a can of gasoline and whistling, "It's Going to Be a Hot Time in the Old Town Tonight." Some might consider torching a failing business easier than filing for Chapter 11, but it's also risky as hell. Fire investigators are skilled at tracing the origin of a fire, and unless the building has been completely obliterated, there's always a chance they'll pinpoint the smoking … er, match.

Homes aren't any easier. A Korean construction worker who lived in Philadelphia had fallen on hard times, and decided that the only way out was to set fire to his home. First, the man collected a bunch of gas-soaked rags in the basement, planning on spreading them throughout the house so no part of the house would be left standing. Then, he poured gas behind his stove. The idea was to pour a trail away to a safe distance, where he and his family could drop a match and watch the house explode. However, he'd forgotten about the stove's pilot light. The pilot ignited the gas vapors and caused a massive explosion. The man panicked and immediately raced to pull his wife and two sons to safety. Somehow, the house remained standing, even though the basement—full of those gas-soaked rags—was a mess.

At first, the man's insurance company paid the would-be hero $124,000 for fire and smoke damage to his house. But the fraud didn't last long, as investigators traced the cause of the fire, and took into account the man's financial difficulties. In late 2000, the man was convicted of insurance fraud, despite his protests that the house was hexed and that he was only following Korean customs by destroying the building and releasing the negative energy inside.

It's a Scam

Some tell-tale signs of arson are

- Items of value (computers, artwork, accounting records) have been removed from the house/building.
- The owner has recently called his property insurance company to ask, "Gee, uh, how much would I get if, oh I don't know, let's just say my store went up in flames?"
- The owner is on shaky financial ground.

Health Insurance Fraud (Individual or Corporate)

This is when your doctor (or health care organization) decides he's not quite making enough from you (or your health insurance company). Who knows? Maybe the price of golf clubs shot up last year. Anyway, a scamming doctor will order all kinds of unnecessary tests and treatments for you, then sit back and file insurance claims like crazy. One orthopedic surgeon in Massachusetts routinely put his patients through all kinds of ridiculous tests, and that included one poor sap who had to sit through 74 X-rays and 112 steroid injections over a three-year period.

In other chilling cases, rings of medical insurance kidnappers have been known to operate in certain areas—most notably South Florida. The crime is freakish: A "recruiter" will abduct children and take them to an unlicensed dentist, who will then perform drilling, fillings, and removals, whether the kids need it or not. The shady dentist then continues to file for reimbursement from the kid's Medicaid account until it runs dry. And when I say "kidnapping," I do mean kidnapping. One "recruiter" used to drive her van through an inner city neighborhood of South Florida, looking for kids who were easy to round up, or she could lure with promises of toys or fast food. But sometimes, she would approach the children's mother, and offer to take the kids for free dental care.

There are all kinds of medical scams. Some medical practices will have a less-experienced doc do the medical work, but bill it under a more-experienced doc's name, enabling them to charge more. And some scams don't even require the doctor and patient to meet—bills are submitted for visits when the patient was actually on vacation!

The corporate variety of health insurance fraud is rare, but sometimes you do see health insurance companies who decide to stick it to Medicare and file for hundreds of unnecessary tests and phony expenses. One of the largest medical fraud settlements in history, Columbia/HCA Healthcare agreed to pay $754 million after it was caught overbilling Medicare for years. Let's not forget: Medicare is funded by your taxpayer dollars, and it's meant to help the elderly and children, two segments of the population who need it the most. "Fraud and mismanagement are threatening to destroy the Medicare system," writes fraud buster Chuck Whitlock in his book *Scam School*. "In another decade it may no longer exist."

Faked Deaths

Want to cash in a life insurance policy? Easy. Simply die of natural or accidental causes. You can't kill yourself, because insurance companies frown on that kind of behavior (and insert clauses to that effect in your policy). Scam artists who want to collect life insurance but don't want to go through all of the trouble of dying are left with only one choice: faking their death.

The horrible attacks of September 11, 2001 seem to have inspired a bunch of con artists seeking to pull the ultimate faked death claim. Take the case of one Georgia couple. Not long after the collapse the towers, the husband called his insurance carrier, Minnesota Life, and explained that his wife had been in one of the World Trade Center towers. (She was in town to make a cosmetics deal and had an appointment on one of the upper floors.) There was a $200,000 policy on the wife, and the husband hoped that something positive could come of his beloved's death—namely, taking the insurance payout and putting it toward the $270,000 mortgage on their home.

The husband dutifully filed claims, showing officials an appointment book that clearly showed his wife at the World Trade Center on the morning of 9/11. He applied for Red Cross survivor funds and asked for an urn of ashes from the disaster site. According to a story at the Coalition Against Insurance Fraud website, Mayor Rudy Giuliani even sent the husband a letter of consolation.

The thing is, the wife wasn't dead at all. Nor did she make any attempt to hide, or leave the small Georgia town where they lived. The couple simply assumed that the disaster was on such a large scale that their insurance company wouldn't have the resources—or perhaps, the nerve—to investigate the claim. But Minnesota Life certainly did, and after a few quick phone calls to officials in Georgia, determined that the woman was certainly among the living. "It's my understanding that she was continuing in her daily walk of life," said a local sheriff to newspaper reporters. The couple was charged with insurance fraud, and faces 10 years in prison. If you're going to fake your death, here's a tip: It might help to actually pretend you're dead.

Sometimes the supposed victim isn't even in on the scam. According to a story in *Forbes* magazine, a Nebraska woman purchased 78 life insurance policies on her ex-husband, then claimed he got squished in an earthquake in Mexico. Then she tried to collect $11 million from the various companies. All of this was news to the ex-husband, who refused to play along. "He's such a jerk," the woman said from her jail cell. "If it weren't for him, I wouldn't be in here." (Then again, if it weren't for her, he wouldn't have been involved in that horrible earthquake in Mexico.)

Con-trary to Popular Belief

For another World Trade Center faked death tale, see "You're Bogus, Dude" in Chapter 10. The goal in this case wasn't insurance fraud, but something equally shifty.

Insurance investigators try to sniff out fraud in a couple of ways. One is the policy itself. Is it relatively new (under two years old)? Has the policy holder suddenly upped the coverage—from say, $5,000 to $500,000? And is that half a million bucks worth of coverage pinned to a loser who's never cleared more than $12,000 a year busing tables at the local greasy spoon? Maybe Earl Bob has suddenly earned a new-found respect among his family members, but to life insurance companies, these are all tell-tale signs that something isn't on the up-and-up. The other red flag is the death certificate itself, especially if it's been photocopied. That means that the original is still out there somewhere, and can be easily photocopied again and again—which, in turn, means that it might have been copied and sent to multiple life insurance companies.

For con artists pulling a faked death scam, it's largely a game of forging documents as well as beating the clock. According to the law, insurance companies have only two years to challenge a suspicious claim (there's a statute of limitations); after that, the case is, er, *dead* to them.

> **It's a Scam**
>
> Whatever you do, try not to die in a foreign country. Insurance companies look at death certificates from overseas as automatically suspect. That's because it's easier to fake a foreign document, and harder to investigators to link a fraudster with that foreign document.

> **Don't Be a Sucker**
>
> The National Insurance Crime Bureau is a not-for-profit agency that helps insurance companies (and state insurance departments) investigate possible fraud. To report a suspected insurance crime when you don't know the specific insurance company that may be at risk, call 1-800-TEL-NICB or log on to www.nicb.org.

Murder, She Underwrote

I've made a big deal in this book about how most con artists shy away from violence. There are a few exceptions, and this is one of them.

Murder for insurance is classic *film noir* stuff—where the henpecked loser teams up with the dizzy brunette from the steno pool to murder the loser's wife, collect the insurance money, then lam off to Mexico. Or the two-timing wife teams up with the garden boy to murder the husband, collect the insurance money, and then open up a diner in Tallahassee. But it does happen for real.

In 2000, one Oklahoma City man decided to kill his wife, and decided to use her own medical treatments against her. She had a small liver complication, which required small doses of medicine. But her husband convinced her that doctors prescribed injections of insulin, and started upping the doses. Soon, she had 100 times the normal amount of insulin racing through her system. The wife went into severe insulin shock, and none of the doctors could figure out why. The husband kept family at bay, claiming that his wife didn't want to see any them in her condition. Doctors wanted to keep an eye on the woman, but the husband insisted she come home to private care. And indeed, the husband had arranged for a private nurse to help. But he didn't tell anybody that the nurse was actually his secret lover.

A few days later, the husband and his girlfriend prepared for the wife's death. They went out and purchased a $17,500 RV, explaining to the salesman that he was expecting a fat family inheritance soon. Then it came time to do the deed. The husband injected the final insulin dose, while the girlfriend/nurse pressed a hand over the dying woman's face. Immediately the girlfriend arranged for a quick embalming, which would destroy all traces of the insulin, and then headed over to a bridal salon to pick out wedding dresses. By the time the new couple had a frilly white dress in a bag, the now ex-wife hadn't been dead nine hours yet, according to local police. The scheme was unraveled, thanks to the wife's family members, who couldn't believe the husband's incredulous stories about sudden illness. Cops separated the two killers, and soon, they individually confessed, each blaming the other for the plot. The husband received life in prison, and the love/nurse has 40 years in jail to plan her wedding.

Con-trary to Popular Belief

Double Indemnity (1944) is a murder-for-money noir masterpiece. Insurance salesman Walter Neff (Fred MacMurray) pays a visit to sexy housewife Phyllis Dietrichson (Barbara Stanwyck). Sparks fly, and the next thing you know, Neff and Dietrichson are arranging for Mr. Dietrichson (Tom Powers) to have a little accident, which would result in the payout of double the $50,000 indemnity clause. Mr. D. goes bye-bye, and insurance investigator Barton Keyes (Edward G. Robinson) starts poking around, convinced the accident was awfully suspicious. Double-crosses and verbal sparring matches abound. A must-see, especially if you find yourself up late at night, looking at your husband's chest rise up and down, and realize how easy it would be to grab one of those knitting needles and plunge it directly into his ...

Husband/wife murder plots are the cliché, but there are other forms of murder for insurance. One grisly way is to find a soon-to-be-dead body, then take out a life insurance policy for that body. Where does one find soon-to-be-dead bodies? Why, in the alleys of any major American city. That's right—some insurance fraudsters take out policies on homeless people, drug addicts and alcoholics, hoping for (or inducing) a quick death and a quick payout. A few years ago, two brothers from Alabama took this idea and set up a virtual drug addict death mill. First, they established a home where supposedly strung-out and destitute people could work for food and shelter.

However, the brothers didn't supply much in the way of work, or food for that matter. But there were plenty of drugs and bottles of booze available—one witness saw a case of whiskey on the premises. It was a fairly odd supply to have on hand for a shelter full of alcoholics. Then again, that was the whole idea: Coax the addicts and boozers into a quick death, which meant a quicker payout. Sometimes food was even withheld, in hopes that hunger would speed up the process.

Meanwhile, a retired insurance agent helped the brothers set up more than 100 policies on about 40 victims. (One alcoholic alone had nine policies worth $125,000 taken out on him.) Many of them were small—no more than $50,000—because they didn't require the addict to take a medical exam to qualify. By the time the death mill was exposed, seven addicts were dead. Both brothers were sent to prison, but one of them killed himself in his cell in February 2001. No word on whether his brother thought to take out a policy on him or not.

The Least You Need to Know

- Insurance and tax scams are the two white collar crimes that cost ordinary citizens the most.

- The IRS is now focusing on wealthy folks who avoid paying taxes, and leaving the modest taxpayer alone.

- There are dozens of insurance scams, and the most popular involves stolen or wrecked automobiles.

- People still do kill other people for the insurance money.

Chapter 15

This Land Is My Land: Home and Real Estate Scams

In This Chapter

- ◆ How advance fee schemes work
- ◆ The pitfalls of refinancing your home
- ◆ Do you really need aluminum siding?
- ◆ Time-share scams

Unless you routinely buy yachts or Learjets, the largest purchase you'll ever make is a home purchase. Owning a home is the singular goal of most American families, and not just because it'll keep the rain off your kids' heads. A home is a symbol of wealth and security, and owning a modest chunk of land is at the very heart of the American Dream, infused with the DNA of the Manifest Destiny. Once again, con artists are there to ruin it for us, trying to turn our own dreams against us.

The most infamous real estate scam in American history was probably the Florida land boom of the 1950s, where unsuspecting people were sweet-talked into purchasing huge lots in Florida only to discover that their piece of the American Dream was actually a swamp filled with slime and mosquitoes in the middle of the Everglades. (Some might say that the purchase of Manhattan island from the Lenape Indians for the equivalent of $24 was the greatest real estate scam in American history; I'll let you be the judge.) These days, you probably won't run into some swindler trying to sell you Brooklyn—or its famous bridge, for that matter—but that doesn't mean con artists have stopped trying to swindle home owners. In this chapter, we'll walk through the various modern-day real estate scams, including advance fee frauds, assessor's kickbacks, refinancing cons, home equity rip-offs, time-share scams, and home repair schemes.

Stealing Home: A Modern Real Estate Swindle

Scammers have come a long way since the lowdown, creepy stunt of selling an innocent chump swamp land in the Everglades. Today, the scams are even *more* lowdown and creepy.

A jaw-dropping property scam went down in my hometown of Philadelphia in the late 1990s, as reported by *The Philadelphia Daily News* (which, incidentally, did an excellent job of reporting the scam, with front-page headlines blaring: WHO STOLE HER HOME?). In essence, a 35-year-old ex-con managed to steal at least 36 Philly row homes, then resell them to unsuspecting buyers. When the real owners would show up to look at their property, they'd find another family living inside—or sometimes, padlocks on the doors.

How do you steal a home? Well, the scamster—along with at least 20 accomplices—had his own system. First, he'd pay a scout to drive around inner-city neighborhoods, looking for homes "that appeared neglected ... homes in disrepair or homes with accumulated mail or uncut lawns," according to a grand jury report. His scout would receive $100 for each promising address. Then, the scamster took that list to the city's Recorder of Deeds, and ordered a copy of the Deed for each one. (They're public record; anybody can walk in and ask for a copy.) The scamster then had three accomplices create forgeries of the deeds, naming still more accomplices as the owners of the property. Next, the scamster took those forged deeds to crooked notary publics, who stamped them with their seal of approval. Finally, back to City Hall to file the deeds, and presto—a home is stolen.

All that was left was the pesky matter of selling the properties to new owners. That wasn't difficult. According to the *Daily News*, the homes were offered at ridiculously low prices—usually under $10,000. Meanwhile, the real property owners were left with a rather nasty surprise waiting for them at ... well, at what used to be their home. The damages weren't just limited to property. One home belonged to the mother of a Rutgers University professor. The mother passed away, and when the house was stolen, all of her heirlooms and possessions were stolen along with it. Another woman—just out of the hospital after a prolonged illness—discovered all of her possessions lined up on the sidewalk, ready to be picked up by the city's sanitation department.

The scamster kept raking in the bucks for three years until he finally was sent to prison on an unrelated charge in 1999. It was the investigative efforts of the *Daily News* and the Philadelphia District Attorney's office that finally brought the swindle to the attention of the public.

> ### Con-trary to Popular Belief
>
> One of the great real estate frauds was perpetrated in the late nineteenth century by the U.S. Government's own General Land Office. The office was created to protect the 40 million acres of public land set aside as forest reserves; unfortunately, agents in the office immediately began to sell huge chunks of land, which would eventually end up in the hands of lumber companies, who didn't give two hoots about preserving forests. The resulting investigation by the Secret Service resulted in 33 convictions, which included a U.S. Senator and a U.S. Congressman. This land is my land, indeed.

More Money, More Problems: Financing Scams

Even if you do manage to purchase a home and avoid the swindlers, you're not out of the woods yet. Con artists have all kinds of ways of tricking home owners into surrendering large piles of cash, and many of them involve refinancing offers. The following scams are a few of the more prevalent.

Advance Fee Scheme

The offer sounds great: You see an ad from a mortgage broker who offers to refinance your mortgage at a much lower interest rate than you're currently paying, in 24 hours or less, and with no closing costs—all this, despite your murky credit history. The only requirement? That you give that broker a "good faith" gesture in the form of an *advance fee*. Usually it's a percentage of the mortgage. Pay it, and your application will be processed immediately.

Hold on to your checkbook. (Come on. So far, we've been through 14 chapters together. By this point, do you think there are any too-good-to-be-true offers that are indeed good and true?) Legit mortgage brokers never charge an "advance fee." At the most, they'll need a small fee to purchase a credit report, or maybe do a property appraisal. But nobody who's on the up-and-up will ask for 1 percent of the total loan. And if you're foolish enough to pay the advance fee, you'll wait the 24 hours ... and then hear nothing. Your calls will not be returned—that, or you'll get the runaround. "These swindlers gather as much money in advance fees as they can and move on," explains one fraud investigator.

Grifter Speak

Advance Fee Scheme

The scheme where someone offers a loan or mortgage with an incredibly desirable interest rate, but requires an "up-front" payment, usually 1 percent of the total loan. Once the mark makes the payment, the swindler disappears, taking this advance fee with him.

This scheme is most closely linked with real estate deals and refinancing mortgages, but it can also be used with consumers looking for consolidation loans, or even small businesses looking for a quick infusion of capital.

Assessor's Kickbacks

Ah, the power of the mighty tax assessor—able to slash property taxes with a single stroke of his pen. If you own a home, you already know how property taxes work. A county tax assessor will evaluate your property for its value, and then use that figure to estimate how much you'll pay every year in property taxes. For example, a $500,000, five-bedroom mini-mansion owner will pay much more in property taxes than someone who owns a $50,000 row home.

Imagine if a tax assessor could be persuaded to ... oh, I don't know, *undervalue* a certain property, maybe? Undervaluing a property would of course mean lower property taxes. Maybe the tax savings would be so great, the lucky property owner might be compelled to give that friendly tax assessor a little monetary gift.

Well, if you owned property in Manhattan between 1965 and 2000, you didn't have to imagine. Tax assessor kickbacks were a multi-million dollar reality. In February 2002, a third of Manhattan's property assessors were charged with stealing millions of dollars worth of bribes in exchange for undervaluing over 500 properties, according to *New York Newsday*. Tons of business owners made out like bandits, as did those 18 property assessors, apparently. One U.S. Attorney called the 35-year scheme a "virtual racketeering enterprise." The bite was significant, too: Investigators estimate that the scam cost New York City over $160 million lost tax revenues in just a five year period. (Goodness knows how much was lost since the 1960s.)

Yeah, you read that correctly—it was a 35-year scam, passed on down through the generations. How could it fester for so long? Barry Mawn, head of the FBI's New York office, told *Newsday:* "Everybody was getting a piece of the pie. They were protecting one another, it was kept very quiet, and everybody was benefiting."

But these kinds of kickbacks schemes do more than hurt local government. Don't forget—taxes are what keep cities and counties operating. If someone doesn't pay his or her fair share, the rest of us will be forced to make up for it.

Equity Purchaser Fraud

Equity Purchaser Fraud is when an owner has received a notice of default, and an "expert advisor" comes along, claiming to be able to help—but only sinks the owner deeper in debt. Take the example of one 79-year-old woman who lived in the Bronx. She was way behind in payments and facing eviction until one day a guardian angel in the form of a real-estate broker appeared. He offered an amazing service: If the woman could give him low monthly payments, he could hold off foreclosure until he could refinance the property at a lower interest rate. The woman eagerly took him up on his offer, and over the next 11 months, dutifully paid the broker a total of $24,000. Along the way, the broker sent her detailed receipts, and eventually, a letter saying that victory was theirs—the house was successfully refinanced.

The woman was thrilled, until she received another letter. This one came from her bank. They didn't know anything about any refinancing arrangement. Oh, and by the way, it said, you have 30 days to vacate the premises. Turns out, the broker was simply pocketing the money, and making a grand show of receipts and refinancing documents.

Kicking people when they're down seems to be a con artist's favorite pastime. People in desperate financial situations will do almost anything to get out of them, and the con artist takes advantage of their clouded judgment in scams like these. Other similar scams use more direct approaches. One California fraudster offered to help 30 South L.A. residents refinance their properties. Only later did some of them discover that, among the countless "refinancing papers" they'd signed, was one that signed over the deed of their homes to the fraudster—no one had explained that part of the deal. (Sure, banks do the same thing, but most banks aren't sitting around, rubbing their hands together, just waiting for you to start missing payments.) A few late mortgage payments later, and the fraudster was able to legally swoop in, evict them, and take over their property.

The Fix Is In: Home Repair Schemes

Houses fall apart. Happens to the best of 'em, and unless you're handy with a hammer and dry wall, you'll probably have to call in the professionals. Now there are plenty of honest, hardworkin', and creative contractors out there. But mixed in among them are the unscrupulous guys—either contractors who don't give a hoot how the job turns out and just want to collect your money, or outright con artists who use the *con*struction game as another way to a fast-and-easy payday. Either way, you're the one who will end up hemorrhaging cash. (And your hardwood floors will *still* squeak.)

One common trick is the building supply bait-and-switch. Let's say Joe Bob's Building Co. gives you an outstanding deal on a new storm door and matching storm windows. You agree to the amazing low price, then sign on the dotted line. Joe Bob starts work in a few days, but there's a problem. You see, the supplies he normally uses are out of stock, and it could take months to get them in. He'd be happy to wait, but you see, the doors and windows have already been removed, and it's, like, late November. So, Joe Bob is awfully sorry, but he's going to have to use slightly more expensive supplies to finish the job. Only "slightly more expensive" is putting it mildly: The cost can double. Or Joe Bob might not even take the blame himself. He may tell you that your house is an odd design, so the replacement parts need to be custom-fit. And custom-fitting can be expensive. If you try to cancel, he'll tell you it's too late—the parts are already ordered. Meanwhile, the chilly winter air is blowing through your house, and your kids are busy thawing out the pet ferret in the toaster oven.

> **CAUTION**
>
> ### Don't Be a Sucker
>
> Watch out for salesmen hawking unbelievable refinancing scams—especially ones that promise a refinancing plan no matter your credit history. Stick with your bank or another legitimate lending institution. If you're suspicious of a particular lender/broker, contact your local Better Business Bureau.

The most common scam, however, is good old fashioned shoddy work. The crooked contractor will rush through the work—in some cases, barely do the work at all—and demand payment. Sometimes, the home owner forks over the dough, and by the time the mistakes are noticed, the contractor has long skipped town. But the crooked contractor is often prepared in the event that a home owner notices the crappy workmanship halfway through the job. They'll often sneak in an extra page in the pile of papers you signed when you hired him, and that extra page, in essence, says that you agree that the work has been completed to your satisfaction. Your signature on that page makes it all that more difficult to fight.

Another diabolical scam is the lien trick. This is where contractors build in a special provision in their contracts: If you don't pay, the contractor reserves the right to place a lien on your property. And that pretty much means that you'll run into all kinds of trouble someday down the road when you try to sell the place, or it might even mean foreclosure. So if you see that the eaves don't look quite right, or your dog Skippy has already punched through the cheap paper-thin dry wall in the den, and you refuse to complete payment to the contractor, he has the upper hand, after all. Technically, a contractor is allowed by law to place a lien on property if he is not paid. *Technically.* (Legit contractors will only do this as a last resort.) But some con artists, particularly creeps who target senior citizens, build this lien trick into their contracts fully expecting to eventually foreclose on their victim. Some contracts are even worded so that if the victim fails to make just one payment, the property suddenly belongs to the contractor.

Don't Get Screwed

Writer—and homeowner—Jill Feldman detailed a step-by-step guide to hiring honest contractors in a recent issue of *Philadelphia Magazine* called (appropriately enough) "Don't Get Hammered By Your Contractor." I've included some of her best tips here:

♦ When hiring a contractor, make sure they give you a permanent, physical address—not some fly-by-night P.O. box. That way, if you have a gripe, you'll actually be able to find them.

♦ Ask for proof that the contractor is licensed in your area, and that they carry workman's comp for all employees. You have the right to ask to see the actual certificates, and to check the dates to make sure they're current.

♦ Make sure they're up to date with the latest local building codes. Feldman gives a great test question for all Philly-area builders: "What do all new homes built in Philadelphia now need on the first floor? Answer: Windows big enough to accommodate a fully clothed fireman."

♦ Check out the history of the contractor by calling your local Better Business Bureau. (To find yours, log onto www.mybbb.org.) According to one BBB rep, if the contractor has had two or more complaints lodged against him—and more importantly, has ignored them—then he'll be slapped with an "unsatisfactory" label. You could also check with your local building-trades organization to check a particular contractor's rep.

♦ Finally, ask for examples of other work they've done—specific addresses—and go and take a look for yourself. Knock on the door and ask the owners if they were happy with Joe Bob's Building Co. You'll most likely get a completely honest answer … unless, of course, the occupants are somehow related to Joe Bob.

It's a Rental: Time-Share Scams

It's not everyday someone calls you up and offers you a free weekend getaway, just for taking the time to look at a piece of land. Wait a second … it *does* feel like every day, doesn't it? I seem to get these calls every couple of weeks, offering me weekends in the Catskills, or in the Pocono Mountains, or in Florida, or maybe even Puerto Rico. All expenses paid. Just for listening to a measly little sales pitch about a *time-share* property. Harmless enough, right?

I've never taken these callers up on their offers, because I know what would happen: One "little sales pitch" would turn into three days of hard selling, with talk of appreciating values and "gettin' in while the gettin's good" and watching other guests clamor to plunk down their deposits as if this was the last time-share left on Earth. The truth is, most of these weekend time-share getaways are all about trying to sell undesirable locations. Usually, you don't even see what you're supposed to be time-sharing, and some of your fellow guests are actually shills for the time-share company, meant to make you feel as if you're missing out on the deal of a lifetime. And the drinks are probably watered down, to boot.

It's easy to avoid those cheesy phone solicitations if you know that most of them are scams. What's not so easy to avoid are those offers that come from trusted members of your community. That's what happened to a bunch of church-goers in upper Manhattan in the mid-1990s. Members of St. Elizabeth's Church in Washington Heights were approached by one of the church deacons, 57-year-old Odalis Rosado, who described an incredible time-share deal at a resort in the Caribbean. Not only was the Playa Bonita resort luxurious—with multiple pools and open countryside perfect for horseback riding—but it had the implicit backing of the Pope and the Vatican. "It's true," Rosado would say, "Each investment is backed by Rome."

Now the Holy Pontiff is involved in all manner of good works in all corners of the world, but hawking time-shares in the Caribbean ain't one of them. The parishioners at St. Elizabeth's learned that the hard

Don't Be a Sucker

Watch out for contractors who come with all kinds of financing plans, says the Better Business Bureau. Why? Well, for one thing, you're on thin ice if you ever decide to withhold payment for shoddy work—after all, you borrowed money from a lender who's in cahoots with the crooked contractor. That lender could pay the contractor anyway, then hold you responsible for the debt.

Grifter Speak

Time-sharing The practice of sharing ownership of a piece of property, with each owner reserving the right to use it for a predetermined period of time.

way. Over a six-year period, Rosado and a partner bilked $3 million out of buyers, with $1 million coming directly from St. Elizabeth's parishioners. (One woman paid $27,000 to Rosado, specifically because the investment was 100 percent backed by the "Pope and people from the church," according to a story in the *New York Daily News*.) In truth, the Playa Bonita had been abandoned—half-finished—back in 1992. But Rosado's victims had no way of knowing that, and put their trust in Rosado, who as a deacon, was a representative of the Catholic Church.

Sell, Sell, Sell!

The other kind of time-share scam targets people who already own time-shares. Let's imagine you time-share a sweet little pad down in Ft. Lauderdale, but you hardly ever have the time to use it. One day, someone calls up, offering to buy you out for nearly twice the original price you paid. You play it cool, but inside you're thinking: Yes! All you have to do, says the potential buyer, is agree to an appraisal. Sounds fair to you—after all, you would expect the same if you were in his shoes, wouldn't you? The potential buyer helpfully gives you the number for an agency that lists independent appraisers. You thank him, hang up, and call the agency, which recommends three or four names. You call one, and set it up. It'll cost you $500, but that's worth it, considering the profit you stand to make.

A week later, you receive a form in the mail: The appraiser has checked out your time-share, but he claims it's only worth one-third of what you originally paid for it. The potential buyer calls to offer you one-third, but you tell him to forget about it. Why on earth would sell for less than the original price? The buyer says fine, thanks anyway, and hangs up.

You hang up the phone. Maybe it doesn't hit you right away. But give it some time. Sooner or later, you'll realize you've been stung. And it was that "independent appraiser" who took

> **Grifter Speak**
>
> I've sold to tens of thousands of people, and I couldn't look one of them in face today and say, "I did you a good deal." We discriminate against people. We lie to people. Eventually, people get screwed.
>
> —one former time-share swindler, confessing in the *Orlando Sentinel Tribune*

> **Don't Be a Sucker**
>
> When you own a time-share, you're buying the right to use property—not the property itself. Thus, you should never have to pay anybody to appraise your time-share. Keep this in mind if someone calls offering to buy out your time-share but first requires an "independent appraisal."

your $500. What you didn't know is that the potential buyer gave you a number for a supposedly "independent agency," but it was actually in cahoots with the buyer.

This is exactly how one Boston-area ring conned $12 million out of approximately 20,000 time-share owners. The leader of this ring hired a team of telemarketers to blitz a list of time-sharers; meanwhile, he was busy establishing those fake "independent appraisers" under an umbrella organization called "Multi-State Listing Service," vague and bland enough to sound legit. When owners called Multi-State, they were given a list of four firms, but all of those were run by the fraud ring, too. The owners would be charged $400 or $500 per appraisal, then receive the sting: the lowball estimate. The majority of owners told the telemarketers to forget about selling. Surprisingly, though, some time-share owners decided to take the low offer anyway, and the ring would receive a nice time-share at an amazing discount.

In February 2001, a federal grand jury slapped the 10 members of the ring with fraud, conspiracy, and money laundering charges. "This was a very successful operation," a spokesperson from the local U.S. Attorney's office told the *Boston Globe*. "The whole point was fraud, and, unfortunately, they were pretty successful."

In a variation of this same scam, a crooked broker asks for a $200 to $500 listing fee to help sell your time-share. He also asks for some of that time to be reserved for his use—after all, he has to show the place to sell the time-share, right? But what happens is you never see that "listing fee" again, and the broker has rented out your space to another person and pocketed the proceeds.

The Least You Need to Know

- Beware the "advance fee" scam: Some scammers promise a sweet refinancing deal, then take an advance fee and run.

- Other refinancing deals can result in the loss of your property.

- Crooked contractors will try to put a lien on your house when you don't pay them for their shoddy/incomplete work.

- If you own a time-share, be wary of too-generous purchase offers—those offers might come from con men looking to make a buck with appraisals.

Part 4

The Con Man Hall of Shame

Usually, con artist don't want press. They prefer to lurk just below public consciousness, not raising any alarm bells or undue attention.

But con artists throughout history have been so skilled at their "craft," they couldn't help but become famous. Sometimes it's the ingenious scheme they've invented that makes them a household name (Hello, Chuck Ponzi!). Or the audaciousness of their scams (cough cough, *Crazy Eddie*, cough). Or the sheer force of personality (Joseph "Yellow Kid" Weil). Or maybe when Steven Spielberg and Tom Hanks decide to team up and film the story of your life—go ahead and take your bows, Frank W. Abagnale.

Here's a quick tour through the biggest names in American scams—that is, if they didn't use an alias. Sure, they've hoodwinked the best of us, but that doesn't mean we can't lend them a tiny bit of begrudging admiration. Hence the "Hall of Shame."

Chapter 16

Claims to Fame: Inventors and Inheritors

In This Chapter

- The greatest phony inventors and their bogus machines
- The story behind the infamous Drake inheritance scam
- The con man who scammed Chicago with chalk and water
- The con woman who used Andrew Carnegie to swindle banks

This doesn't happen much these days*, but one of the biggest con games of yesteryear was the phony invention. Con men promised all kinds of wild results—trains that could run from Philadelphia to New York on just a quart of tap water, machines that would print U.S. currency, and even a solution that would protect the exterior of a building for decades. The only difference between these men and other inventors such as Thomas Alva Edison? Uh, Edison's inventions actually worked. Other con artists kept their scams in the family. Not their family, of course—other, richer, more powerful

(* Then again, one of the biggest invention stories of 2001 was about the mysterious "IT," the invention that would change our lives forever. "IT" turned out to be a glorified scooter. Boy, what a load of IT.)

families: The Carnegies. The Rockefellers. And even some fictional rich, powerful families, such as the Edwardses and the Drakes.

What links these two seemingly different types of scams? Fame. Both require fame to attract investors, buyers, or would-be inheritors. In other words, invention and inheritance scams need the publicity. Without it, bogus inventors couldn't hope to attract a single dime, and scammers pulling inheritance schemes wouldn't have the pressure they need to squeeze their victims. In this chapter, I'll tell you about eight inventors and inheritors that grabbed headlines in their day.

John E. W. Keely's "Energy-Producing Machine"

Every time you pay $1.45 for a gallon of gas, don't you wish that somebody would have figured out how to power an SUV with water by now? Well, over 100 years ago, a former carnival pitchman named John Ernst Worrell Keely claimed to be able to do just that. Starting in 1874, Keely would lure wealthy investors—including bankers, lawyers, even the president of the Cunard steamship line—to his Philadelphia home to demonstrate his amazing "energy-producing machine." The machine itself was reportedly an amazing sight, an ornate sculpture of twisting brass tubes and wires and other mechanical whosits and geegaws. Keely would pour a quart of water into the machine, and right away the machine would begin pumping and bellowing, and a pressure gauge would read 50,000 pounds per square inch. "You, gentlemen," Keely would announce, "are looking at perpetual motion."

All of that pressure—all of that energy—just from a small amount of water! To demonstrate the machine's almighty power, Keely would use its force to blast apart chunks of iron and destroy thick planks of wood with steel bullets. It was an impressive—and loud—display. With this force, Keely claimed, it was possible to propel a 30-car train from Philadelphia to New York. All that distance, from a tiny amount of water.

How? Why, it was "the force of adhesive attraction," coupled with "polar currents of the Earth" and "molecular vibration" and "oscillation of the atom." Nobody really knew what Keely was talking about, but it certainly sounded—and looked—impressive enough.

Soon, the Keely Motor Corporation was formed, and money started pouring in. Keely kept the secrets of his machine close to his vest, but many scientists refused to believe that such results were possible. Thomas Edison called Keely "a damned fake," and Nikola Tesla said that "what [Keely] claims to be doing is impossible." *Scientific American*, in particular, blasted Keely's alleged discoveries, and one investor even employed a man to go undercover in Keely's lab to discover the secret. That spy reported that Keely's entire set-up was a scam, and the investor went to the press with the details. Still, people kept on believing in the former carnival man and his magical "energy-producing machine" until his death in November 1898. A month after his death, reporters from the *Philadelphia Press* forced their way into Keely's Philadelphia home on North 20th Street and tore the place apart. They finally discovered his secret, buried deep in the basement: a huge compressed air machine, pumping the air through a complex system of steel and brass tubes hidden throughout the ceilings and walls of the home. That's how he was able to show such incredible displays of pressure and destructive force; water had nothing to do with it. The scam lasted nearly 25 years, and with its perpetrator making the ultimate getaway. In a way, it's tough to blame investors who collectively lost a million dollars—the late nineteenth century was full of very real inventions that were equally astounding.

Con-trary to Popular Belief

Despite the fact that Keely was exposed as a fraud, there are still some people who believe he was on to something, and continue to study "sympathetic vibratory physics." Throughout websites and Internet discussion boards, they hold up Keely as a scientific pioneer, and claim that charges of fraud against him were in fact a fraud in themselves. "Keely's work was a direct threat to the power establishment at that time," reads one site. "It still is."

Harry Holland's "Magical Preserving Fluid"

They say you can't beat City Hall. That may be true. But you *can* paint it.

That was the offer from Harry S. Holland, a Chicago inventor who claimed to have concocted a "magical preserving fluid" that could protect any building from natural elements for decades, saving thousands on restoration and maintenance. The city of Chicago might not have listened to Holland's wild claim, except for the fact that he had a powerful patron: Chicago political boss Michael Cassius McDonald, who controlled the city's gambling, cops, media, transportation, and apparently, the maintenance of city buildings. (McDonald was also famous for the line, "There's a sucker born every minute!")

Grifter Speak

There's a sucker born every minute.

—a classic line credited to nineteenth century Chicago political boss Michael Cassius McDonald

So in 1886, with McDonald's influence, Holland was hired to supply his secret "preserving fluid" to the city for $128,250—a sum that, according to Jay Robert Nash in *Hustlers & Con Men*, bankrupted the city treasury. Workers coated the Chicago Court House (interesting target, no?) with this fluid, and the city fathers sat back and breathed a collective sigh of relief. After all, that was one less thing to worry about, right? Er, wrong. A storm blew in, and the heavy rains stripped all of the "preserving fluid" right from the walls of the court house. The fluid turned out to be nothing more than chalk and water, but by the time Chicago sent its police out to exact revenge, Holland had already skipped town. (Presumably, to take his ill-gotten gain and paint the town red.)

Fisher and Jernegan's "Gold Accumulator"

Charles E. Fisher was a scam artist from England who showed up along the Maine Coast one day with an invention he promised could change lives. "You see," said Fisher, "there is a huge amount of tiny gold flakes swirling about in the oceans, particularly near the Maine shoreline. All you need to collect the gold is a special machine." And Fisher had just the machine—a gold accumulator. Simply drop it into the ocean, wait one night, and lift it out again. The cage-like machine would be flaked with pieces of gold.

A Baptist minister from Connecticut named Prescott Ford Jernegan was an early believer in Fisher's "gold accumulator," and they traveled to Maine to help pitch the idea to local businessmen. Together, they demonstrated how easy it was to collect untold fortunes right from the Passamaquoddy Bay. Some folks were skeptical, however, and insisted on a controlled experiment. They wanted to select the site, and then guard it all night, just to make sure Fisher or Jernegan didn't have a chance to sneak down and plant some gold on the machine. Fisher and Jernegan happily agreed.

Don't Be a Sucker

Another classic gold swindle is the so-called "gold brick" game. This is when a shady figure offers to unload a bunch of gold bricks cheap—or a map, leading to buried gold bricks—but the bricks turn out to be next-to-worthless hunks of brass.

Of course, the Maine business leaders had no way of knowing that Fisher was an experienced deep sea diver. He simply dipped into the water further on down the shore, made his way to his gold accumulator, then replaced it with one already coated in gold flakes.

Thus, the Electrolytic Marine Salts Company was formed with $350,000 in stock from local businessmen. According to Carl Sifakis' book *Frauds, Deceptions and Swindles*, Fisher and Jernegan became rich when the new company's board of director gave them $200,000 each for their "services." Suddenly, Fisher remembered (you can almost hear the fingers snapping here)—he needed more supplies for the gold accumulator! Fisher quietly took his money and bolted. Much to the shock of the board of the Electrolytic Marine Salts Company, the gold accumulator stopped working. They went to Jernegan for answers, and by gum, he promised some answers, just as soon as he could locate Fisher. Jernegan set off in search of his partner, and wasn't heard from again until years later, when he was discovered living a life of luxury in the French countryside. Fisher, for his part, was never found again, although some angry investors liked to tell a story in which Fisher was caught doing the hibbity-dibbity with a tribal leader's wife in some obscure African country, and was sentenced to a grisly death. Clearly, the only thing Fisher's "gold accumulator" actually accumulated was a lot of ill will.

Victor "Count" Lustig's "Fabulous Money Box"

Well, at least this invention actually *did* make money. For Victor "The Count" Lustig, anyway.

Born in Prague in 1890, Lustig pulled scams in Europe before emigrating to America just after World War I. By the 1930s, he would become one of the most notorious swindlers in the United States—even once hooking Al Capone in a con game, and repeatedly selling the Eiffel Tower to scrap metal dealers—but The Count made his first thousands with an ingenious device he called the "Fabulous Money Box." It was a portable counterfeiting machine: Simply insert pieces of paper cut to the exact size of a $20 bill, wait 24 hours for the machine to work its magic, and then you would have 10 more $20 bills, all indistinguishable from the real thing. Lustig demonstrated his "fabulous" machine to his marks inside a luxurious hotel room, and quickly sold every money box he could make for $4,000 to $46,000, depending on the gullibility of the mark.

Of course, the money box—which cost about $15 in materials to make—was nothing of the sort. Lustig simply built a little trap-door beneath the box and filled it with real $20 bills. The blank slips of paper would disappear up into the guts of the machine, and the real money would come cranking out 24 hours later. In 1927, Lustig was caught and arrested in Crown Point, Indiana, after a curious purchaser popped open the money box and saw the trap door. But Lustig managed to saw through the bars at Crown Point—oddly enough, this was the same jail bank robber John Dillinger would escape from years later—and make his escape. Eventually, Lustig saw his money box scam as having limitations, and eventually got involved in real counterfeiting. (Yes, I used the phrase "real counterfeiting." Let's move on.) The Count, however, was out of his league, and in 1935 the U.S. Treasury Department succeeded in doing what no other law agency could do before: prosecuting and jailing The Count. He died 12 years in later in the U.S. Penitentiary at Leavenworth.

> ### Con-trary to Popular Belief
>
> In a battle of titans along the lines of *Godzilla Vs. King Kong*, Count Lustig once went head-to-head with Chicago kingpin Al "Scarface" Capone—and won. Lustig showed up at Capone's office one day, claiming that he could take $50,000 of Capone's money and double it in 60 days. Scarface cocked an eyebrow at The Count—he knew the guy was a con man—but decided to peel out 50 one-thousand dollar bills and see what happened. Two months later, Lustig returned, all apologies. Seems his plan hadn't worked out, and he was unable to double Capone's investment. "I'm just as sorry as you," explained Lustig. "I really could have used that money." Capone was livid, and probably about to reach for his baseball bat when Lustig surprised him by reaching into his pocket and removing the original $50,000. "Here you go," Lustig said. "Again, a thousand apologies." Capone was shocked—he wasn't being swindled after all. In fact, he felt bad for Lustig, who obviously in a rough patch. Capone was so moved, he handed Lustig back $5,000, just to help him along for a while. Which, of course, is what The Count had wanted all along.

Oscar Hartzell and "The Drake" Inheritance Scam

Oscar Hartzell was a 40-year-old farmer who had just lost his Texas cattle business to bankruptcy when he first heard of "The Drake." It was 1915. Hartzell's mother Emma had invested $6,000 in The Drake, and the business opportunity sounded like just the thing that could turn Oscar's misfortunes around. He was right about that at least. Hartzell was about to become swindled by a scam that he would eventually come to run himself for millions in profit, according to author Richard Rayner, who wrote a biography of Hartzell called *Drake's Fortune: The Fabulous True Story of The World's Greatest Confidence Man* (2002).

Hartzell did not invent The Drake—in fact, no one's really sure who first dreamed up the scheme. It was based on real-life Elizabethan Admiral Sir Francis Drake, an adventurer who became wildly rich after he helped England defeat the Spanish Armada in 1588 and collected his share of Spanish booty. Drake died without heirs, and at some point that inspired the idea that there were millions of dollars waiting to be collected by some heir, somewhere. By the time Hartzell and his mother had become involved in The Drake, it had already hoodwinked thousands of people in the American Midwest, all of whom purchased "shares" to help defray the legal expenses in the fight to free up the Drake fortune. The "shares" promised to pay out as much as a thousand to one (in other words, put in a buck and get back $1,000 when the legal battle ended). People happily handed over money by the wheelbarrow, all in hopes of being amply rewarded at the end.

For some reason—Rayner says it was pity—the con artist behind The Drake took 40-year-old Hartzell under her wing and employed him to run small errands. Eventually, after the con artist, her lawyer, and Hartzell moved to England to run the scam from afar, Hartzell came to realize that The Drake was indeed a fake, and he plotted to take it over for himself. By 1922, he had done just that, cutting out his former employers and writing letters to their "shareholders" stating that he'd taken over the legal fight for the Drake fortune.

> **Grifter Speak**
>
> When I get this money, and I expect to get it in the summer, I could buy the three states of Missouri, Kansas, and Iowa, every foot of land and every dollar's worth of property in them, and put a fence around the whole lot and then have more gold left over than all of you ever dreamed of."
>
> —con artist Oscar Hartzell, in a letter to his investors

Hartzell vastly improved what was already a very successful scam. He introduced drama into his letters—accusing his former employers of all kinds of evil doings—and even introduced a new wrinkle into the scheme: Hartzell's alleged discovery of a direct descendant of Sir Francis Drake named Colonel Drexel Drake. (In reality, there was no such person.) Despite continual promises that the legal battle would soon be over, and the billions of dollars would start flowing, Hartzell kept stalling, just as the best con men do. The scheme roared through the 1920s and even survived the Great Depression—the desperation caused by the Great Depression just fueled speculation. (Hartzell even had the cajones to claim that the impending release of the Drake fortune had *caused* the Depression, and not the Wall Street collapse.)

Hartzell was finally brought down thanks to a determined U.S. postal inspector who was appalled by the scam and eventually convinced Scotland Yard to investigate and arrest Hartzell in 1933. He was deported to the United States, and his trial turned into something of a circus, with Hartzell's victims staunchly defending him against all charges. Dozens of people who had been along with Hartzell for so long simply refused to believe the scheme wasn't real, that all of their dreams weren't about to come true. He was found guilty of multiple counts of fraud, and given 10 years in Leavenworth.

Amazingly Hartzell struggled to keep the scam going, even from his prison cell. But eventually, the years of lies cracked Hartzell's keen mind. According to Rayner, Hartzell died in prison believing that he was Sir Francis Drake himself.

> **CAUTION**
>
> **Don't Be a Sucker** _____
>
> Inheritance swindles like The Drake are increasingly rare, but they still pop up from time to time. At any rate, never buy into an inheritance scheme—after all, why would a total stranger cut you into their fat inheritance for just a "temporary" loan to defray expenses? (This is why God invented banks.) If you still think the offer is too good to pass up, discuss it with your personal attorney first. Maybe he or she can slap some sense into you.

Herbert H. Edwards' Heir Association

Is your last name, by chance, Edwards? It is? My goodness, you stand to become rich, and you don't even know it. Hundreds of years ago, one your ancestors, Captain Robert Edwards, used to own a slightly valuable piece of real estate. Maybe you've heard of it. It's called *midtown Manhattan*. In fact, your ancestor, Captain Edwards, owned a nice fat chunk of land where the Woolworth Building now stands and, before his death, willed it to his descendents. Or should I say, *our* ancestor. Because I'm an Edwards heir myself, and I'm involved in this association of other Edwards heirs. We're *this close* to getting the legal rights back to that land, and when that happens—which should be very soon—the payoff is going to be unbelievable. You have any idea what land like that is worth today? Billions, pal. *Billions.*

Thus went the pitch—or something like it—given by Dr. Herbert H. Edwards, a native of Cleveland, Ohio, who cooked up this plot in the 1880s. Slowly, he convinced thousands of other people who shared the last name "Edwards" (there are a lot of 'em) to cough up $26 a year and join his "Edwards Heir Association," dedicated to the legal fight of getting that uber-valuable chunk of real estate rightly returned to the Edwards clan. The association became so large and serious, it held annual conventions for its members to feast, drink, and dream of the riches that would soon be theirs. Very soon. Any week now, in fact.

 **Grifter Speak** _____

We're Robert Edwards' legal heirs
And cheerfully we take our shares
Then let us shout with joy and glee
And celebrate the jubilee.

—from a rallying party song at the annual meetings of the Edwards Heirs Association

What makes the scheme so remarkable is not the concept—people have pulled phony heir claims like The Drake and such before—but how long this thing lasted. Dr. Edwards passed it along to his son, who passed it along to *his* son. That's right. We're talking *decades*, before the U.S. Post Office finally nailed the Edwards boys on mail fraud.

I don't know about you, but this kind of scam makes me glad my last name is "Swierczynski."

Cassie Chadwick, Daughter of Andrew Carnegie

Who would give Ohio native Elizabeth Bigley any special favors? Nobody, it turned out. So in the 1890s, Bigley decided to recreate herself as "Cassie Chadwick," a mysterious high society lady who had a big secret, one she let slip to her lawyer: She was actually the illegitimate daughter of multi-millionaire Andrew Carnegie. (Today, this would be like a young woman alleging that she was the illegitimate child of Bill Gates—if one could imagine that Gates got lucky enough as a young man to produce illegitimate children.)

Now Bigley ... er, I mean, Chadwick didn't take out an ad in *The New York Times*, proclaiming herself to be Carnegie's daughter. She was more slick than that. Chadwick had her lawyer escort her to the Carnegie mansion in Manhattan, and then ran up and knocked on the door. Once inside, Chadwick tried to chat up the housekeeper for a while, then returned to her lawyer waiting outside. Along the way, she accidentally-on-purpose dropped a forged promissory note from Big Andy himself, made out to Cassie for $2 million. Chadwick swore her lawyer to secrecy; her lawyer promptly spread the word back at home in Cleveland. Suddenly Chadwick began getting what she wanted all along: special favors. Favors from bankers, who were more than happy to give the alleged Carnegie heir huge loans of millions of dollars.

The banks weren't just being nice, however; many of them slapped on huge interest charges so they could nab a piece of the famed Carnegie fortune for themselves. Too bad that in 1904—after almost 10 years and $20 million in loans later—the truth was revealed, and confirmed by Big Andy himself, who released a terse statement that read, in part: "I do not know Mrs. Chadwick." As it turned out, Chadwick/Bigley was nothing more than a Cleveland check forger who had been pardoned by the governor in 1893. But why be content with forging checks when you can claim you're related to the bank?

Bigley died, under her own name, in 1907, after serving three years in jail.

> **Con-trary to Popular Belief**
>
> One banker who had loaned $1.25 million to Chadwick was so shocked when he heard the truth about Cassie Chadwick that he promptly had a heart attack, keeled over, and died.

The Least You Need to Know

♦ Phony inventions need publicity to lure investors. Sometimes, it doesn't even matter if the publicity is bad.

♦ Victor Lustig once swindled Al Capone, and even sold the Eiffel Tower to two different scrap metal dealers.

♦ The Drake was one of the most notorious inheritance swindles in U.S. history, bilking millions of dollars from thousands of unsuspecting "shareholders" in the 1910s and 1920s.

♦ The most infamous celebrity/paternity swindle involved a woman who claimed to be Andrew Carnegie's illegitimate daughter.

Chapter 17

That's the Spirit!
Supernatural Scammers

In This Chapter

- ◆ Psychic predictions … and blackmail
- ◆ The diabolical curses of white witch doctor Edgar Zug!
- ◆ Freaky accident fakers
- ◆ The truth behind Miss Cleo

Con artists love to promise things that, for the moment, are unseen. Perhaps it's an unbelievable business opportunity. Or a fat inheritance. Or an island in the Mediterranean. Or the Brooklyn Bridge. But other con artists take this idea one step further, promising something that cannot ever be seen. I'm not talking about some stupid city bridge here, folks. I'm talking about the stuff of horror movies: ghosts, dead relatives, ominous knowledge of the future, even bodily injury. These scammers claim to have contact with The Other Side, and this special gift enables them to help you on this side of reality. (For a modest fee, of course.)

Bogus psychics and mediums—allegedly gifted people who are able to communicate with the dead—like TV's "Miss Cleo" are nothing new. They've been with us for centuries, promising all manner of important revelations and opportunities to contact the world of the undead. They might tell you, "I see dead people," but in reality, all they're seeing is dollar signs. Here are some of the most outrageous perpetrators of spiritual cons from the past 100 years.

Madam Zingara

Combine a gossip columnist with a blackmailer, and add a crystal ball and a fright wig, and you've pretty much got Madam Zingara, a scamming "spiritualist" who operated in the United States at the turn of the century. Zingara mastered a skill that all phony psychics to follow her would employ: the ability to subtly gain information from her clients, then feed it back to them in a way that sounded like a profound revelation. But Zingara's specialty was digging up a salacious detail about her victim—maybe a secret love affair, or stolen money—and then giving her victim an impromptu psychic reading. I see a man around you ... a married man ... and he's not wearing any clothes ...

Zingara's private "readings" didn't cost their victims a dime. But if they wanted those readings to remain private, the victim would have to pay up, big time. Zingara, no mentalist midget, would also work every possible angle. In the case of a young woman having an affair with a married man, she would "read" and blackmail the young lady, and do the same to her family, collecting two separate paydays. If that worked out, she'd then hit the adulterer himself, and try to exact some payment out of him.

However, this scheme once backfired on Zingara—who was born Elizabeth McMullin in 1863, but has also used the names Peet, Campbell, Sullivan, Byron, McCluskey, and Bennett—when she encountered E.T. Harlow, a clerk who'd been having an affair with a young secretary. Zingara had already swindled $258 out of the young lady when she offered to heal the man's soul with a $500 "exorcism," but that just angered Harlow, who apparently wasn't too concerned about being exposed as an adulterer. He went to the nearest police station to report Zingara and she was subsequently arrested. Another of Zingara's customers bailed her out, however, and the *pow-wower* skipped town to pull her mind games elsewhere. The "seeress" and "prophetess" finally landed

Grifter Speak

Pow-wower A popular nineteenth century term used to describe phony psychics and mediums.

in prison for good in 1900, thanks to an intrepid New York cop named M. J. Murphy who made it his personal mission to take down the phony medium. Wonder if she saw it coming?

It's a Scam

James Randi, a professional psychic-debunker, describes on his website the simple tricks "real" TV psychics use to pull the wool over their audiences' eyes. (For legal reasons, I can't reveal the names of these psychics. But if you close your eyes and clear your mind, I'll send you their names via psychic transmission. Ready? Okay ... names sent.) The most common trick is to ask questions that seem like profound statements. For instance:

Psychic: Did your husband pass quickly, or did he linger for a while?

Audience Member: Oh, (sob) yes, he died quickly.

Psychic: Yes, he's telling me, "I'm glad I didn't have to suffer long."

Note that the psychic is bringing nothing new to the conversation; the victim has revealed all. For more on psychic cons, check out www.randi.org.

Edgar Zug and Mrs. Sarah McBride

Threatening to reveal embarrassing family secrets is one thing; threatening your victim with a horrible death at the hands of evil spirits lurking in some hellish netherworld between reality and Hell is another. But that's exactly the scam Edgar Zug—allegedly American's only white witch doctor—perpetrated on hundreds of people.

Zug, along with his partner, Mrs. Sarah McBride, were perhaps the creepiest con artists in history. They dressed up in flowing black costumes and would make scary pronouncements right out of a Stephen King novel. "I see your profiles on the side of a distant mountain," Zug said to one victim, "and through the brains of these profiles, evil spirits have thrust long needles. This was done many years ago and the needles are now rusty. When these needles break, a day not long off, you both will die."

Zug and McBride first scouted out their wealthy marks—all of them on the East Coast—then gave them their spiritual reading, free of charge. Of course, the readings would reveal that some evil spell or spirit was casting dark, insidious shadows over the victims' possessions, home, even lives. The victim stood to lose everything, and the end result would be nothing less than death. The only way to ward off the absolute evil? "Buy your way out of it," Zug would tell them. "These evil spirits respect cash."

Now, even a casual reader of dark tomes like the Necronomicon could tell you that evil spirits in the black Lovecraftian ether are interested in fresh souls—"Swallow your soul, swallow your soul!" admonished one foul beastie in the 1987 horror film Evil Dead II—not U.S. currency. (What the hell would an evil spirit do with money, anyway? Go shopping on eBay?) Still, Zug and McBride would insist that only money could vanquish evil, and their frightened marks were more than willing to hand it over to save themselves. Their supernatural scheme ripped through dozens of family fortunes, until Zug and McBride encountered the Stambaughs, an elderly rich couple from Carlisle, Pennsylvania. At first, the Stambaughs were scared out of their wits, and emptied out their savings accounts and turned over property deeds to save their lives. But Zug made the mistake of getting greedy. "You're going to die," said Zug, according to Jay Robert Nash's *Hustlers and Con Men*, "unless you come up with at least another five thousand bucks." That's when the Stambaughs sought loans from friends, and one friend coaxed the truth from Mrs. Stambaugh. The friend alerted police, and Zug and McBride were quickly arrested and eventually convicted of fraud. Their case was considered the first "witchcraft" prosecution since colonial times, according to *The New York Times*. Zug admitted to taking the cash, but said he was motivated by kindness, not greed.

Plus, Zug told the court, he and his wife had been swindled by Mrs. McBride a year previous, when she allegedly told the Zugs that their child was "bewitched," and needed $500 to remove the spell. That might have been a bunch of hocus-pocus, but Zug's backstabbing did encourage other victims to pop out of the woodwork to accuse Mrs. McBride of pow-wowing.

Con-trary to Popular Belief

The opening story of horror master Clive Barker's *Books of Blood* is all about a young fake medium getting his grisly comeuppance. (Barker is the guy who gave us the Pinhead character in *Hellraiser*. Could it be anything but grisly?) At 65 Tollington Place, a boy named McNeal claims to receive transmissions from the dead, and writes their thoughts on the walls of his room. "They wrote, it seemed, whatever came into their head … Fragments of memories, and well-wishes to their living descendants, strange elliptical phrases that hinted at their present torments and mourned their last joys." Of course, McNeal is faking it, and the dead are none too happy. In fact, they're downright pissed that McNeal is putting words in their mouths. So one day, they decide to exact their revenge, and write their real stories … on McNeal's skin, and using his blood. (Told you this was going to be grisly.)

You might think this so-called "gypsy curse" scheme to be a thing of the past, but you'd be surprised to hear how often it still happens, often in tight-knit ethnic communities. Con artists still prey on certain rich, elderly—and superstitious—folks, convincing them that only money can save their souls. (Come to think of it, wasn't that the m.o. of some fraudulent preachers a while back?) Of course you know better, but you might want to check in with grandma from time to time, and make sure nobody's sticking needles in her image on the side of some dark mysterious mountain somewhere.

Exposing Mrs. Hannah Ross

When he wasn't drowning himself in a tank full of water while chained and straight jacketed, famed magician Harry Houdini had a sideline in which he exposed phony *mediums*—allegedly gifted people who were able to communicate with the dead—and other psychic fraudsters. Just months before he suddenly died of appendicitis in 1926, Houdini was petitioning Congress for the passage of an "anti-fortune telling bill" that would help prosecute fraudulent psychics. (The bill was later shot down as unconstitutional.)

Even though Mrs. Hannah Ross was scamming people 40 years before Houdini's crusade, she was exactly just the kind of medium that Houdini wanted to stop—a merciless opportunist who didn't mind toying with people's emotions, so long as it made her money. But no other phony medium would come close to matching the cruel—and as it would turn out, absurd—schemes as Mrs. Ross'. Her specialty: dead babies. Ross promised grieving parents in Boston that she could summon the spirit of their departed infant in a special spirit cabinet she had constructed. This was the 1880s, at the time when, sadly, infant mortality rates were far higher than they are today.

The parents would gather in Ross' room. The lights were extinguished, and Ross would seat herself inside a large cabinet. Then, the summoning began. Chants and prayers and incense and heavy breathing, followed by the actual manifestation of that dead infant—there, floating right in front of the cabinet! The parents would leap up and rush to their departed child, caressing and kissing it one last time before its innocent soul was called into the loving arms of God. The baby would look and feel as real as it did when it was living, with its smooth skin and sweet smell.

> ### Grifter Speak
>
> **Medium** A person with the ability to act as the conduit between the realms of the living and the dead. As you're reading in this chapter, however, rare is the medium well done. (Ba-dum-dum. Thank you, thank you. Try the veal. I'll be here all week.)

How did Ross do it? Was she actually able to summon the disquieted spirits of deceased infants? Uh, no. Ross used the same stunt that another temptress named Madonna Ciccione would use exactly a hundred years later. She used her breasts.

That's right—she actually painted the cherubic face of an infant on one of her ample breasts (it is not known whether it was the left, or right, or if she varied them), and simply poked it through a slit in a black curtain. Oh, sure the skin was smooth all right. Probably smelled sweet, too. The object that manifested itself in front of that cabinet might have otherwise inspired cries of "Oh, baby," but it wasn't a baby. Boston police exposed the scam (so to speak) and ran Mrs. Ross and her two friends out of town.

Wrecks, Broken Necks, and Fit-Throwers

Some people are uglier than others. And some people are clumsier than others. Con artist George Smith was certainly the first, and he used that fact to convince people of the second. They called him "The Human Wreck," and Smith used his gnarled body to scam transportation companies after he faked accidents.

While Smith wasn't a medium or a psychic—if he was, maybe he should have seen those buses coming—but he definitely belongs in this chapter thanks to his freak factor. According to a description in Jay Robert Nash's *Hustlers and Con Men*, the Human Wreck had missing teeth, a badly twisted spine, a missing finger on his right hand, fresh-looking wounds on his face and head, a crooked right arm and a bruised and twisted right leg. (Think Verbal Kint from *The Usual Suspects*, only beaten up and put through a Black & Decker blender.) Who could resist such a pathetic figure? In the words of one *New York Times* reporter: "He was a living demand for damages—a permanent, hobbling, pitiful protest and testimony against the recklessness and cruelty of a heartless and giant corporation."

In 1899, the 42-year-old wreck used these bodily, uh, *attributes* to put himself in harm's way, time and time again, always at the hands of transportation companies in Manhattan. No bus, train, or horse-drawn carriage was spared, and reportedly Smith would try to collect as much as $50,000 in each claim. Sometimes, though, Smith would simply present his case to a lawyer, who would quickly agree to represent this poor pathetic shell of a man, and even give him $20 advances against future settlements. (See? All lawyers aren't selfish bloodsuckers.) But then Smith and the $20 would disappear.

Not all lawyers fell for Smith's sob story. One Manhattan attorney, Morris W. Hart, thought that Smith's account of his accident was a little hazy. When Smith asked for an advance, Hart slid him a dime. Smith spit and cursed and complained about Hart's lack of … well, heart, but took the 10¢ anyway.

Another similar swindle was perpetrated by a turn-of-the-century con man named George Gray, a.k.a. "The Professional Fit-Thrower." Gray wasn't ugly like The Human Wreck, but he sure could fake a mean epileptic fit or heart attack. The 26-year-old's strategy was simple:

It's a Scam

For more devious insurance swindles, see Chapter 14.

Look for a swanky Manhattan mansion, wait for one of its wealthy owners to pop out, and then start shaking and shout, "Heart failure! Digitalis! Quick, am I dying!" (Doctors at Manhattan's Presbyterian Hospital said that Gray was so convincing, he was literally able to speed up or slow down his heart rate at will.) The panic-stricken mark would summon his servants and whisk the poor, convulsing fellow inside for some treatment. After much hullabaloo, the symptoms seemed to abate somewhat, and Gray would shamefacedly accept some money for travel and medical care from his Good Samaritan. Which, of course, is what he was after the whole time. According to Jay Robert Nash, Gray made $10,000 a year this way, which was nice money back then for a little shaking. If he had been born at the end of the following century, he probably could have given Jim Carrey a run for his money.

Gray once pulled this routine on East 69th Street in front of a businessman when a cop happened to walk by and recognized Gray from his police description. (Gray always wore an army hat, and had a prominent tooth missing.) The cop approached Gray—who admitted his identity—and started to arrest him. Nevertheless, the businessman who had been nearly swindled thought it was a shame to arrest a man in such poor condition, and pressed 50¢ into Gray's hand as he was taken away.

Finally, there was Edward Pape, who had a childhood injury that nearly snapped his neck. It was the best thing that could have ever happened to him. In adulthood, he would fling himself from trolley cars in cities across the country, allow himself to be rushed to the nearest hospital to be X-rayed, and then—lo and behold—doctors would discover a neck that was damn near broken! Pape would collect a huge fat settlement from the transportation authority, then move on to the next city to do the same thing all over again. The scheme earned this pain-in-the-neck about $75,000 a year.

Miss Cleo

Many of the examples in the chapter come from the turn of the century, which seemed to be boom times for phony psychics and mediums. Well, maybe it's a turn-of-the-century thing, but by the late 1990s, there seemed to be more psychics than ever plying their trade. One of the more infamous was a friendly woman from Jamaica named Miss Cleo.

If you've watched even an hour of daytime or late-night TV sometime before Spring 2001, you've met Miss Cleo. She's the Jamaican shaman with the huge grin, mon, who can help you with all of your relationship problems. Call her 900 number right now, mon, and for just $4.99 per minute, she'll tell you if that no-good rotten bastard is two-timing you, or if that Mr. Right you met at the corner bar is going to turn out to be Mr. Wrong.

Too bad Miss Cleo turned out to be Miss … uh, Harris.

Yep—there was no "Miss Cleo." There was, however, Youree Dell Harris, a 39-year-old actress and playwright who lived in Broward County near Los Angeles. Behind her was a company called Access Resource Services, the telemarketing firm that created the psychic service, the Jamaican angle, and even Miss Cleo's character in an effort to attract gullible marks looking for advice on life and love.

The Miss Cleo fraud had two parts. On one hand, very few callers actually got to speak to Miss Cleo herself, or even another alleged psychic. At first, the company claims, they had a team of "in-house psychics" manning the phone banks. But the volume of calls to Miss Cleo became so great, her parent company Access Resource Services decided to hire nearly 1,000 "readers"—people who would work from home and read to callers from a prepared script. There was "no experience necessary," according to the ads. (Can't predict the future? Can't even guess what you're going to have for lunch today? No worries! You're perfect for the Miss Cleo Team!) Callers who expected to speak with an authentic Jamaican shaman would be very disappointed. Plus, the readers were instructed to keep callers—who were paying $4.99 per minute—on the horn for at least 19 minutes, otherwise, they might not get any more work from Miss Cleo.

But that wasn't even the worse part. The other sting was an alleged phony billing scheme where people were billed for calls they didn't make, while others—calling for a "free consultation"—were kept on hold for over an hour, and then charged $300 for dead air. When "customers" wouldn't pay up, they'd receive a collection letter from Miss Cleo herself. "Taking responsibility for your actions is an important step in your spiritual journey," it read. That might explain how the company glommed over $1 billion from 6 million customers over the past couple of years.

In 2001, the FTC swooped down on Miss Cleo and her company, charging her with fraud, and a host of civil fraud lawsuits followed. (Actually, Miss Cleo—or the actress who portrayed her—was protected from any suits or criminal charges, because she was solely an employee of Access Resource Services.) Missouri Attorney General Jay Nixon made it his personal mission to put the company out of business, charging Access with eight charges, including false advertising, civil fraud, and violating that state's "no-call law." In October 2002, Nixon finally got some satisfaction: The owners of "Miss Cleo" pleaded no contest to charges of felony fraud in a St. Louis courtroom, and were slapped with a $50,000 fine. Miss Cleo, for her part, has been off the phone (and the air) since spring 2002. According to my trusty crystal ball, her future is indeed murky—other states have followed Missouri's lead.

Don't Be a Sucker

In many cases, phone bills with weighty Miss Cleo—or other psychics—charges are thanks to kids, who see the number and decide to have some fun and goof around with the voice on the other end of the phone. They don't need a psychic, however, to predict their future once their parents see the bill: life indoors with no phone and no PlayStation 2. Don't want your kids pulling the same stunts? Most phone services have "900" number blocks; call your local telephone carrier to find out how to activate it.

The Least You Need to Know

♦ Psychics use sneaky questions to sound like they're revealing secrets from The Other Side.

♦ Make sure your elderly relatives aren't falling for the so-called "gypsy curse swindle," in which evil spells are lifted ... for a price.

♦ Brace yourself: Some folks go to horrific extremes to fake accident injuries for insurance money.

♦ Come on, mon! Hang up on phony phone psychics like Miss Cleo.

Chapter 18

The Crooks in the Gray Flannel Suits

In This Chapter

- ◆ William Miller, the real originator of the Ponzi Scheme
- ◆ Meet the greatest check forgers who ever wielded a pen
- ◆ Ferdinand W. Demara Jr. the so-called "Great Impostor"
- ◆ "The Deacon" and "Yellow Kid" team up

You've already read about the infamous Charles Ponzi—the smooth-talking investment scammer who took the "rob Peter to pay Paul" idea to dizzying extremes—back in Chapter 13. Now get ready to meet some of his colleagues—smooth-talking guys who have pulled scams that make Enron and WorldCom look like a corner bodega stick-up. Businesses have always been ripe targets for scam artists, and these guys made scams their business.

In this chapter, you'll read about canny business scammers, genius bad check passers, brilliant impostors, and even a pair of con men whose favorite target was other con men. These are no fly-by-night con artists pulling short cons on the sidewalk; these men lived the life. (In some cases, lives.)

William "520 Percent" Miller

The first time he was fleeced, William Miller was a 24-year-old bookkeeper living with his pregnant wife in a small apartment in Brooklyn. It was 1899. Miller worked for a tea company near Wall Street, and he heard wild stories about stock brokers making it rich by playing the market. With a baby on the way, Miller desperately needed the cash. So he borrowed $100 from a local legbreaker and ran to the nearest investment house. Unfortunately, the investment house he chose was crooked. The broker talked Miller into buying a stock that was "certain to rise," but actually was due for a fall. (The broker bought at the lower price, and pocketed the difference—it was a typical *bucket house* scam from the early days of Wall Street.)

Grifter Speak

Bucket House or **Bucket Shop** A turn-of-the-century term for crooked stock brokers (or more often, con men posing as brokers) who sell worthless or phony stock to unsuspecting marks.

Six days later, the broker told Miller the bad news: His investment was gone. The next day, the legbreaker came looking for his money. Miller was desperate. So, he did what any man under pressure would do: He turned to Benjamin Franklin for inspiration.

WM. F. MILLER

Investments

"The road to wealth is as plain as the road to market."

—Benjamin Franklin

This was the sign Miller hung in the front window of his apartment. His first "clients" were students of a Bible-study class Miller taught. "It's not fair that the Morgans and the Goulds and the Vanderbilts are making so many millions when us little people are making so little. So I've decided to do something about it." Miller claimed that he'd picked up a trading secret by hanging around Wall Street, and was prepared to offer his clients a 10 percent return on their investments. Only he didn't mean 10 percent annually. Miller meant 10 percent in one week. When one Bible student did the math—520 percent a year!—a nickname was coined, and a scam was launched.

Miller's strategy was a classic Ponzi scheme, years before there was even a Charles Ponzi. (I guess it sounds better than "Miller Scheme.") He would pay off his original investors with proceeds from later investors. As word of the incredible paydays spread, Miller had even more investors. Original investors were even funneling their money back to Miller to make even more money. Miller started doing direct mail pitches and advertising in the newspaper. He bought two new suits and rented a ground-floor office around the corner from his apartment. (All of the noise from investors was waking up his newborn son, William Jr.) Over the course of 11 months, Miller managed to save $480,000 for himself, a far cry from the $15 a week he was pulling down as a bookkeeper for a tea company.

Like any Ponzi scheme, it was only a matter of time before Miller's little investment enterprise imploded. But before that could happen on its own, two other con artists swooped in like vultures and circled the slightly-naive Miller. Bankers—who were suddenly losing business to Miller and his scheme—had put pressure on the New York City D.A. to investigate Miller. Word got out, and not long after, a political fixer named T. Edward Schlesinger showed up at Miller's rented office. "You've got a problem, son," said Schlesinger, who looked to be in his late 50s. "I know what you're pulling, because I've been pulling the same scam myself, on a smaller scale." Unless you listen to me, Schlesinger continued, you're going to end up in jail.

Schlesinger said he could keep the D.A. and the cops off Miller's back in exchange for part of Miller's take. The older con man took Miller to meet with Robert Ammon, a Manhattan lawyer whose office reeked of whiskey. Ammon's solution: incorporate. "Then you take all you want and never pay it back," advised the lawyer. Of course, this was nothing but a ruse. When it looked likely that the law was coming to arrest the three of them after all, Ammon advised that both Miller and Schlesinger give their money to him for safe keeping. "Things are bad enough," Ammon said. "But they'll be worse if they catch you with the money." Schlesinger agreed, and went off to fetch the $240,000 he'd accumulated. That was the last time Miller ever saw T. Edward Schlesinger, who promptly took the money, traveled to Germany, and spent the rest of his life there fishing.

Miller, however, dutifully handed his share, roughly $250,000, over to Ammon, then took more of his lawyer's advice and fled to Canada. Police were able to lure him back, however, by telling him that his infant son was sick—he'd better come back quick. Miller, now more the dupe than con artist, fell for it. He was arrested and sentenced to 10 years. (Ammon was also arrested for his role in the scheme and sent away to Sing-Sing.) Upon Miller's release in 1909, life returned to normal. Amazingly, his former employer at the tea company rehired him as bookkeeper. And one day, he returned home from work to discover that his wife was pregnant.

Alexander Thiel

The career of America's boldest check forger began with a framed copy of the Declaration of Independence. It was 1930. Alexander "Whitey" Thiel was working in a Chicago speakeasy when he looked up and saw a tattered copy of the Declaration hanging on the wall. Bored, Thiel decided to play a little game. He stared at one of the signatures—John Hancock's, appropriately enough—then tried to duplicate it from memory on a piece of paper. When Thiel went back to check, he was stunned at how closely he'd nailed it. Thiel tried more signatures, working his way down the list of Founding Fathers, experimenting with how long he needed to memorize the signature. Three minutes was quickly shortened to two. Then one. Then 30 seconds. Next, he tried to see how long he could go between memorization and forgery. First, it was an hour. Then two. Then 12. Twenty-four. The limit of his amazing powers of graphic duplication seemed to be 72 hours—after that, things got a little fuzzy. But 72 hours would be plenty.

At age 40, a check forger was born.

Before that epiphany, Thiel was a small-time burglar, gambler, and narcotics user who had served time in reform school before going to work for the Chicago underworld. He knew he'd never succeed at the straight life. Thiel's father had tried and saw his life savings wiped out by a 1904 bank crash. "I was only fourteen at the time," Thiel would say later, "but I decided then and there that banks and bankers were no damned good and I'd get even with them some day."

Boy, did he. Instead of picking up the tommy gun, Thiel picked up the pen. His first target: Manhattan real estate mogul Messmore Kendall. First, he bribed an elevator boy to gain access to Kendall's office late at night. Once inside, Thiel studied Kendall's signature on a cancelled check, and ripped out two blank checks from the checkbook. On the attached stubs, Thiel used a rubber stamp to print the word IMPERFECT. No one—certainly not Kendall—would miss the checks now. Finally, Thiel used the check-printing machine in Kendall's own office to create two checks, one for $76,000 and another for $86,000.

Later, under the assumed name of Joseph J. Collins, Thiel would open up a new bank account with the first forged check, and then add to that deposit later with the second. No one suspected a thing. Kendall himself didn't even notice the missing checks until he saw his bank statement weeks later. But by that time, it was too late: "Collins" had already withdrawn most of the money from his account.

This would become Thiel's usual pattern: Sneak into a business to gain access to blank checkbooks, forge a check or two, then deposit them under a phony name and business. Over his 13-year career, Thiel used phony checks to steal a total of anywhere from $600,000 to $1 million, and for the longest time police had only the vaguest description of their suspect, who they dubbed "Mr. X." (Most bank tellers could only remember that the man in question looked an awful lot like actor John Barrymore.) Thiel was so good, and skilled at so many different things—forgery, burglary, impersonation—police actually believed that he was the leader of a gang of check forgers.

Con-trary to Popular Belief

Witnesses told police that Alexander Thiel had an uncanny resemblance to actor John Barrymore. Once, the real John Barrymore showed up in his New York bank to cash a check. The teller squinted, looked at the wanted poster of Thiel tacked next to his desk, then immediately called police. It took the flustered Barrymore quite some time to explain that he was indeed who he claimed to be, and not some evil genius check forger.

Thiel never tried for as big a jackpot as the Kendall heist again—stealing such huge amounts repeatedly would be risky—but he found it just as effective to pull smaller scores. Wanted posters with a police artist's sketch of "Mr. X" were distributed to banks across the country. In November 1937, a New York City police officer finally received their first solid lead on the mysterious Mr. X. A phone number led the cops to a securities dealer who knew of a guy who fit the description, and a swift arrest was made. The only problem: The guy they arrested wasn't Thiel. It was a man named Bertram Campbell, who had the unfortunate luck of looking slightly like John Barrymore, and having paid off some creditors in the recent past with $100 bills. (During Thiel's most recent score, he had walked away with a great deal of $100 bills.) Once bank tellers identified Campbell as Mr. X, it was all over—despite Campbell's insistence that they'd arrested the wrong guy.

Meanwhile, Thiel read about the capture of "Mr. X." with a queasy stomach. He was glad it wasn't him behind bars, but he had never intended for an innocent man to take a fall for him. Thiel fired off a series of anonymous letters to the New York City D.A., detailing why Campbell couldn't be Mr. X, but nobody in the office paid much attention. Thiel worked more forgery jobs in hopes that authorities would see that they had the wrong guy locked up, but nothing doing. (Campbell would end up serving his full term of four years in jail.)

The law finally caught up with Thiel in the strangest way. Seems that handwriting wasn't Mr. X's only obsession; he had a fondness for drugs, too. (Much of Thiel's forgery proceeds were used to feed his addiction.) In 1943, Thiel was holed up at a rehab clinic in Kentucky. Meanwhile, the FBI had joined the hunt for Mr. X, and sent his signatures to their handwriting analysis section, which recognized certain minor characteristics. At first, they tried to match those characteristics with criminal signatures they already had on file, but no luck. Finally, someone had the idea to match the signature against the narcotics files, because—like Thiel—many check forgers were drug users. That's when law enforcement finally came up with a real name and face for Mr. X, and Thiel was arrested soon after.

There are two curious footnotes to Thiel's story. Thiel and Campbell eventually met face-to-face. "I'm sorry for all the trouble I caused you," said Thiel. Campbell, who might have been forgiven for hauling off and slugging the real Mr. X in the kisser, simply shrugged. "I supposed you couldn't help it."

After nine years of jail, Thiel emerged from prison an old man. He made a run at the straight life, but at age 75, couldn't resist one last forgery. He made out a bogus check for $100. By the time the police found him, Thiel was ready to cash it all in. This last quote may be apocryphal, but according to some, Thiel told the arresting officers: "Give me a pen and a blank check and I'll square my bill with the undertaker now."

Con-trary to Popular Belief

Another infamous check forger was a short wily Canadian named Ralph Wilby. In 1941, Wilby was an auditor at the William T. Knott Management Company in Manhattan, which cut and printed $40 million worth of checks each year for 14 different department stores. Wilby, an experienced scammer, took the job under an assumed name, then used the IBM check machine to cut a fat check to another alias. Wilby would take that check to a bank in another city to open an account. When the bank asked for a reference, Wilby would supply his real name at the Knott Company. The letter would arrive days later, Wilby would give his alias a glowing reference, and the account would be opened. To cover the losses on the books, Wilby would steal little amounts from the department store clients in the form of fake fees and charges.

Over the next two years, Wilby stole an estimated $400,000 from Knott using this method. He was so good at covering his tracks that his scheme might have gone on for years, if not for the poor choice of one of his aliases: "Mr. H.B. Hecht." It was a German surname at the time—World War II—when Germans who opened fat bank accounts in American cities then disappeared were considered suspect. The trail led the FBI back to Wilby, who then pulled the ultimate financial scam: He convinced the Knott company to give him $10,000 in exchange for returning most of the stolen loot (which he had buried in tin cans outside of his house). Knott agreed, and upon Wilby's release from prison, he had ten large to start over.

Ferdinand Waldo Demara Jr.

You're in the middle of the Korean War. You've been shot to hell. There is a bullet in your chest, millimeters away from piercing your heart. A Royal Canadian Naval medical officer leans over you, tells you not worry. Your fellow soldiers crowd around, watching nervously. You pass out, all without realizing that the friendly medical officer really isn't in the Royal Canadian Navy. And he really isn't a doctor. He's a high-school dropout.

In fact, the only medical training he has came from a book he read on the boat ride over from Canada.

This was just one of the many jaw-dropping impersonations of Ferdinand Waldo Demara, Jr., an impostor from Canada who assumed various professions not so much for profit, but "rascality—pure rascality," he claimed. Demara's life story became a book (by Robert Crichton) and eventually the 1960 Tony Curtis flick, *The Great Impostor.* Born in Lawrence, Massachusetts in 1921, Demara grew up believing that there had to be a way to succeed in various careers without going through all of that pesky schooling and training. Luckily, Demara had a photographic memory, which enabled him to absorb vast amounts of material just by looking at it for a minute or so. This, along with his ability to forge documents, is how he fooled people into thinking he was a Trappist monk, law student, cancer researcher, hospital orderly, soldier, sailor, jail warden, deputy sheriff, schoolteacher, and yes, a doctor with the Royal Canadian Navy. (Don't worry—that wounded soldier, a South Korean fighter, survived the operation.) Throughout the 1940s and 1950s, Demara served the occasional light jail sentence, but nothing too severe, simply because Demara largely seemed to be in it for the recognition, not the money. (Although he did steal, forge, and embezzle.)

For all of his free-wheeling, fun-loving impersonations, however, Demara died a lonely, bitter guy. He felt he never received the recognition he deserved for his wild accomplishments; a doctor friend of Demara's said he was a "broken man who thought his talents were wasted." He died of a heart attack on June 8, 1982. (One hopes that Demara had a real doctor attending his dying needs.)

Grifter Speak

Never before had [Demara] felt, at the same instance, such an impostor and such a complete, lonely, isolated fraud. There was no place to run and no place to dodge what he had to do and no assurance that he could find the courage or whatever ingredient it would take to begin surgery on the three Koreans who lay on bunks, drugged by heavy doses of morphine.

—from *The Great Impostor,* by Robert Crichton (1959)

> **Con-trary to Popular Belief**
>
> Sterling Clifford Weyman (birth name: Steve Weinberg) was another amazing impostor, assuming the roles of doctor, lawyer, diplomat, Naval officer, disc jockey, headmaster of a school for the hearing impaired, and the "official greeter" for New York City over a 30-year period. His specialty was posing as delegates for foreign leaders. In 1915, he once posed as the attaché for Queen Marie of Romania, and requested the privilege of personally inspecting the USS Wyoming. The Navy was happy to oblige the Royal Queen of Romania, and Weyman was whisked aboard for a tour. Afterward, he threw a huge party for Navy brass at New York's Hotel Astor. "Just send the bill to the Romanian Consulate in Washington," he told the hotel manager. A few days later, Weyman's photo—as the attaché from Romania—appeared in *The New York Times*. "Wait a second!" cried one Brooklyn cop when he saw the paper. "That's that nut from Brooklyn—up to another imposture."

"The Deacon" and the "Yellow Kid"

Flimflamming is usually a lone wolf profession: one con man against the world. But Fred "The Deacon" Buckminster and Joseph "Yellow Kid" Weil found strength in numbers.

In 1908, Buckminster was actually a Chicago vice cop who had a warrant to arrest Weil for a phony waterproofing swindle he was pulling. (Remember Harry Holland's "Magical Preserving Fluid" from Chapter 16? Same city, same scam. Some things never change.) As Buckminster was escorting Weil to the precinct house, the so-called "Yellow Kid" pulled out $10,000 and handed it to the officer. Buckminster asked Weil where the money came from, and Weil was honest. "Scams," he said. Buckminster didn't have to be told twice. He joined forces with Weil, and together teamed up for decades of impersonations and swindles—mostly targeted at other con men or people looking to make a crooked buck.

Sometimes, it would be gambling scams. Just like in the Paul Newman/Robert Redford blockbuster *The Sting*, Weil and Buckminster would create a phony gambling parlor—complete with fake pony races, and full of phony customers—just to fleece the living daylights out of one victim. Other gambling scams took advantage of the telecommunications of the day: the wire. Instantaneous transmission of information (such as, say, horse race results) was not possible back in the early part of the twentieth century; there was no radio, no TV, no AOL "Instant Messaging." Gambling parlors relied on the results coming from via telegraph, or "wire." Weil and Buckminster cooked up many ways to beat the wire. Sometimes, they would intercept the information at the Western Union office before it made its way to the betting parlor, then place money on the winning horse before the bookie halted bets. In one ingenious scam that could have only worked back then, Buckminster bribed a railroad engineer to "toot" the winning results of a race as his train passed the gambling parlor. Now that's what I call getting "railroaded."

Other times, the duo used completely original scams, such as the Pedigreed Pooch Swindle. First, a duded-up Weil would take a carefully-coiffed dog with a ribbon that read FIRST PRIZE into a bar. (This only sounds like the set-up to a joke; trust me, it's a con game.) Weil would then explain to the bartender that he was late for a business meeting with a bank that didn't allow dogs, and offer the bartender $10 to watch him. Bartender would say, sure. A short while later Buckminster would burst in, then let his eyeballs pop out of his head when saw the dog. "My God! I've been looking for that breed for years!" Buckminster would offer the bartender $100 on the spot to buy it. The bartender would say no, the dog wasn't his. Buckminster would keep upping the ante—$200, $300, $500—until the bartender seemed interested. As a show of good faith, Buckminster would hand the bartender $50 as a security deposit until he returned with $450 more.

The original owner—Weil—would then return, looking depressed. Seems that the business meeting didn't work out quite the way he'd thought, and he was suddenly short on cash. Predictably, the bartender had the perfect solution. "Sell me your dog, then! I'll give you $100 for it!" Weil would hem and haw until the price reached $250. Still, a nice profit, the bartender would think. The deal was done. Weil would take the cash, then later meet up with Buckminster to split the proceeds. Sure, they'd be out the $50 investment, but there was still $200 in clear profit, all for a gussied-up mutt they found on the street. (In case you haven't guessed, the ribbon was a fake, too.)

Con-trary to Popular Belief

When I see a crook, I see nothing but dollar signs.

—Fred "The Deacon" Buckminster

I never cheated an honest man. Only rascals.

—Joseph "Yellow Kid" Weil.

Both partners pulled scams to their dying day. At age 76, Buckminster agreed to write his memoirs for a detective pulp magazine. The payment? $100. But "The Deacon" altered the check to make it look like $1,000, and then cashed it. (The publishers never bothered to press charges; they must have realized they got what they asked for when employing a con artist.) Weil's last swindle was claiming to live to a 100. Sure, he died in 1976, and was born in 1875. But that birth date was a later invention; early records show that Weil was born in 1877. Weil scammed the record books by two years. Here's looking at you, "Kid."

The Least You Need to Know

◆ The so-called "Ponzi scheme" was first used by William "520 Percent" Miller in 1899—30 years before Ponzi.

◆ An innocent man was sent to prison for Alexander Thiel's check forgeries.

◆ Ferdinand W. Demara Jr., was a brilliant impostor who once performed heart surgery on a wounded soldier—without any medical training.

◆ Fred "The Deacon" Buckminster and Joseph "Yellow Kid" Weil teamed up to scam other con artists.

Chapter 19

The Late and the Great

In This Chapter

- Will the real Howard Hughes please stand up?
- Frank Abagnale: Catch him if you can
- Ivan "the Terrible" Boesky
- Meet the 16-year-old who conned Oprah
- Crazy Eddie's insane accounting practices

If you're thumbing through the first three chapters of this section, you might get the impression that all of the great con artists lived at least 100 years ago. While it's true that the Golden Age of the Con lasted roughly from the turn of the century through the 1930s, that doesn't mean that the celebrity scam artist is a thing in the past. Want proof? Check out the recent Steven Spielberg/Tom Hanks flick, *Catch Me If You Can*, which is all about the exploits of real-life 1960s con artist Frank Abagnale. Better yet, read this chapter, in which I'll tell you about Abagnale and four other latter-day flim-flammers who are all destined to go down in infamy. (If not in a Spielberg flick.)

Clifford Irving

Being expected to cough up a book manuscript can do strange things to your head. (Believe me.) But that still doesn't explain the bizarre lengths Clifford Irving went to produce a fake autobiography of reclusive billionaire Howard Hughes.

Don't get me wrong; this Hughes book deal was a fat one. In 1971, publisher McGraw-Hill offered $500,000 to Irving for the exclusive "authorized" biography of Hughes, one of the most enigmatic—and wildly stinking rich—men on the planet. People had a hard time getting within 100 yards of Hughes, let alone reporters, let alone writers hoping to write a book about him. (He hadn't spoken to the media since 1958. An "authorized" biography means that the subject is fully cooperating with the author; if you don't have your subject's input and okay, you have to label your bio "unauthorized." If you're writing your own life story, it's generally "authorized," because you'll presumably have your own cooperation. (Horror writer Robert Bloch, author of *Psycho*, impishly labeled his autobiography *Once Around the Bloch* as "unauthorized.")

Now there was one problem with Irving writing Hughes' "authorized" bio: Irving had never met the man. But to make it seem like he had full cooperation, Irving hired a research assistant named Richard Suskind and got to work. Irving forged letters from Hughes to himself, detailing their meetings and agreements. (Irving copied these and mailed them to his editors at McGraw-Hill.) Irving and Suskind did a ton of research, poring over books, articles, and even testimony Hughes once gave to Congress. They took what they learned and dictated it into tape recorders, as if interviews had taken place, then painstakingly transcribed those tapes into a 950-page typescript. (Irving copied this and mailed it to his editors at McGraw-Hill, too.) The phony biographer took trips, and sent his editors postcards about how well things were going with Mr. Hughes. Irving also nabbed a copy of another Hughes biography—not yet published—that was full of insider information based on interviews with Hughes's number two man, Noah Dietrich. Irving filched details, and presented them as his own material from interviews with Hughes. It was a hell of a lot of work for a fake.

Con-trary to Popular Belief

Before tackling the Hughes bio, Irving had one other non-fiction book to his credit: a biography of a Hungarian art forger. The title? *Fake!*

Then came the financial part of the scam. You see, that $500,000 advance was to be divided between Irving and Hughes, with the billionaire getting most of the money. (Isn't that always the case?) McGraw-Hill would be awfully suspicious if their check to Mr. Hughes was never cashed. So, Irving convinced his third wife Edith to open a Swiss bank account under the name "H. R. Hughes," and then convinced McGraw-Hill that Hughes was hoping for a little more advance money. Despite the fact that Hughes could shovel huge piles of cash into a tree chipper for weeks and not worry about going broke, McGraw-Hill believed Hughes might bolt if they didn't cough up more dough. The advance was raised to $750,000, and immediately sent out a check for $50,000 to "H. R. Hughes." Two more checks—one for $275,000, and another for $325,000—followed as the manuscript neared completion, and it all went into that Swiss bank account controlled by Irving. That wasn't the only source of cash out of this Hughes deal. *Life* magazine offered up thousands for the right to excerpt *The Autobiography of Howard Hughes*, the Book-of-the-Month club came up with $350,000 to feature it as their monthly selection, and Dell Publishing ponied up $400,000 for the paperback rights. Now $1.5 million might be chump change to a guy like Hughes, but it was more money than most writers could ever hope to see.

How did this brilliant scheme finally unravel? In exactly the way you might expect. Howard Hughes heard about the book when McGraw-Hill formally announced it in December 1971, and promptly hit the roof. He ended his media boycott and called an editor he knew at *Time* magazine to blow the whistle.

The really strange part? It took a while before Hughes could convince people that Irving was a fraud. The forged letters were inspected by the top handwriting analysis firm in the United States, and proclaimed to be the real thing. Irving passed a lie detector test. Hughes had a telephone press conference, but Irving insisted it was someone doing a bad impersonation. Suddenly, Howard Hughes probably regretted being such a recluse. When it came time to prove his identity, no one would quite believe him.

The Swiss bank account was the nail in Irving's coffin—investigators traced the money through "H. R. Hughes" back to Edith Irving, and the scam was over. McGraw-Hill dropped the manuscript into the trash—never to be released—and in March 1972 Irving was charged with conspiracy, fraud, and perjury. *Time* magazine named Irving their "Con Man of the Year." Irving spent seven months in federal prison, then went on to write another book about his experience as a scam artist. It was titled *What Really Happened*, and presumably every word came from Irving himself. But you never know.

Frank W. Abagnale

Catch him if you can—by the time you read this, the story of Frank W. Abagnale will be familiar to millions of heartsick teenaged girls. That kind of thing happens when Leonardo DiCaprio portrays you in the film version of your life.

Abagnale is the Great Impostor (see Ferdinand Waldo Demara in Chapter 18) of our generation, only with a much happier ending. While Demara ended his life on a sad, slightly desperate note, Abagnale turned his life of scamming around into what he calls "laying down the positive con." In short, he's made a latter-day career of lecturing businesses about how to avoid getting suckered by con artists like himself. His 1980 memoir, *Catch Me If You Can,* was turned into the 2002 Steven Spielberg film of the same name, starring DiCaprio as Abagnale and Tom Hanks as Carl Hanratty, the FBI agent who pursues him. Abagnale's 2001 book, *The Art of the Steal,* is a detailed guide to corporate scams that no business owner or manager should be without.

Long before the positive cons and Hollywood attention, however, Abagnale was a freewheeling flimflammer operating two distinct scams in the late 1960s. On one hand, he operated as a master impostor, posing as an airline pilot, a pediatrician, an assistant district attorney, a stockbroker, and a professor. To fuel these flights—and quite often it was literally a flight—of fancy, Abagnale also passed tons of bad checks, totaling at least $2.5 million. What makes Abagnale's accomplishments even more impressive is that during his five years on the con, he was pretty much a teenager. He started pulling scams at 16, and ended up hunted by the FBI by age 21.

The impersonations actually began as a result of small-time bad check writing—or "paperhanging," as it was called on the streets of New York City. Abagnale was a 16-year-old runaway, passing a couple of rubber checks in small amounts here and there, getting them cashed at hotels throughout Manhattan with a phony ID he created. Then one day he spied a flight crew leaving a swank New York Hotel—pilots and stewardesses, all in their immaculate gold-piped uniforms, smiling as if they owned the world. A light bulb popped. Being part of a flight crew meant instant respect. Respect meant you could cash bigger phony checks at hotels all around the world.

Abagnale decided he would become a pilot. Completely winging it, the teenager cold-called Pan Am posing as a pilot who had his uniform stolen, and found out where he could find a temporary replacement. To "pay" for the uniform, he filled out a Pan Am supply form with phony info and employee ID numbers, completely off the top of his head. (The fact that the form had five boxes for the employee ID number helped him conclude that—duh—Pan Am employee numbers had five digits.) Uniform in hand, Abagnale did more research, calling Pan Am and pretending to be a high school newspaper reporter looking to do a story of the lives of airline pilots, and asked to speak to a real one. That subsequent conversation taught Abagnale all he needed to know about impersonating a pilot, and even scamming a free flight to any destination in the country. "Deadheading," explained the patient pilot. "If my boss told me tonight that he wanted me in L.A. tomorrow to fly a trip out of there, I might fly out there on Delta, Eastern, TWA, or any other carrier connecting with Los Angeles that could get me there on time." All you needed, explained the pilot, was the pink form. Simply bring your pilot's license to any airline counter, and you could fill one out.

Abagnale had the uniform and the inside info; all he needed was the Pan Am ID and pilot's license. Faking an ID was easy enough—he simply called a firm that specialized in creating IDs for companies, and pretending to be the president of "Carib Air," asked to see examples of pilot's IDs. The ruse worked so well, the firm owner even helped Abagnale make up a sample ID, complete with his photo and personal info, to show his "colleagues" back at Carib Air. For the license, he simply found a mail-order service that specialized in making plaques that duplicated pilot's licenses for people to hang on their walls. Abagnale supplied the bogus info, the service made up the plaque, and a printer reduced the plaque to a wallet-sized card. Abagnale congratulated himself. He was now a pilot, all without spending a single hour in flight school.

> **Grifter Speak**
>
> In a certain sense, I'm still a con artist. I'm just putting down a positive con these days, as opposed to the negative con I used in the past … One of the nice things about my new life is that I'm making more money trying to prevent fraud than I ever did by committing fraud. Going straight does pay.
>
> —Frank W. Abagnale in *The Art of the Steal* (2001)

Anybody can fake a conversation for a short period of time. But it takes a particular mad genius to be able to pull off these kinds of information-gathering conversations, time after time, in a variety of professional fields—including law, medicine, and academia. His technique was deceptively simple, and actually, reporter-like: Question until you find the information you need to take the next step. And the next step. And the next step. Until the next thing you know, *The New York Times* is calling you "The Great Impostor" and you're known throughout the 50 states as "The Highwayman."

Abagnale was finally nabbed when a stewardess recognized his handsome mug from a wanted poster, and French police arrested him. After stints in French and Swedish jails, Abagnale was extradited to the United States. He briefly escaped custody twice, but ended up arrested for good in New York City, right in front of the Waldorf-Astoria Hotel, by two plainclothes detectives who recognized him. Sometimes, fame can be the worst thing for a con artist.

Barry Minkow

In 1984, Barry Minkow was a slightly geeky 16-year-old who desperately wanted to do something that would impress girls. Some kids in his position join rock bands;

others try to make athletic teams. Instead, Minkow decided to become the Carpet Cleaning King of California.

Hey, to each his own.

The business started out legit: Minkow borrowed $1,400 from a buddy to buy cleaning gear, then booked jobs out of his mom's garage. Minkow had the experience; cleaning carpets had been his after school job, and his mom had done phone soliciting for the same business. He decided to call the business ZZZZ Best, mostly to get that coveted "last listing in the phone book" spot. But as it turned out, Minkow didn't need a gimmick like that. Word spread of this spunky kid from Reseda, California operating his own business, and soon he was hiring more employees, and after that, investors came knocking. ZZZZ Best made the local news, then national news, culminating in an *Oprah* appearance. "Celebrity was a tool to attract money," Minkow recalled years later to the London newspaper *The Guardian*. "It wasn't like the mayor sent in a team of accountants to audit my books before he declared Barry Minkow Day, when the impression the investors got was that he did." (Minkow wasn't kidding; the mayor of L.A. actually did this.) "When I did *Oprah*, the impression was given that they'd checked me out, but of course, they hadn't."

Things got out of hand, and soon Minkow was lying about the profits ZZZZ Best was pulling in. How did he fake profits? The same way he had faked profits from the very beginning: stealing. You see, Minkow was burglarizing money orders from liquor stores, fraudulently applying for bank loans, pulling credit card scams on his customers, and eventually, using the classic Ponzi tactic of courting investors, then paying those investors back with money from later investors. And as buzz about ZZZZ

Con-trary to Popular Belief

Like other infamous con men, Minkow now lectures businessmen and his church members on the evils of greed. Minkow, however, likes to give his lectures while dressed in his orange prison jumpsuit. "Look," he tells them, "I know you think you can be one good trading day away. But if you lie, you're going to be wearing this jumpsuit for eight Super Bowls."

Best grew, it wasn't hard to find those later investors. A month after the company went public in 1986, the value of the company jumped from $64 million to $100 million. Meanwhile, ZZZZ Best—the actual cleaning part of the business—began to exist in theory only. There were no teams of carpet cleaners scouring the rugs of California residents; nor any restoration teams rehabbing buildings, as Minkow had announced at one point. During one frenzied month, Minkow rehabbed an entire building in 20 days (the actual work was done by an outside company), just to fool a team of accounting auditors.

But ZZZZ Best finally went bust in 1987, after a reporter named Daniel Askt started poking around when he heard stories of customers being falsely charged on their credit cards. Minkow, then 20, was charged with stock fraud and sentenced to seven and a half years in jail—"Real prison, too, not 18 months in a golf-course camp," Minkow hastens to add. These days, Minkow is a senior pastor at the Community Bible Church in San Diego, California. He's been paying back the investors he conned, anywhere from $750 to $2,000 a month.

Ivan Boesky

If you play a word association game and start with "1980s corporate greed," it probably won't be long before somebody mentions "Ivan Boesky." The Detroit-born stock speculator was the poster boy for bad-boy Wall Street deals of that decade, and for good reason. Boesky's $2 billion was earned illegally, and even after it was all over, "Ivan the Terrible" was able to hold on to a considerable fortune.

How? Boesky's game was "arbitrage," where speculators bet on whether or not a certain company is going to merge with another, or be acquired during a hostile takeover. From the mid-1970s to the mid-1980s, Boesky seemed to be a master of the game, building his own $700,000 arbitrage firm up into a billion-dollar enterprise. But in reality, Boesky was cheating at the game. He was guilty of insider trading, in which he paid millions of dollars to sources in exchange for illegal information, such as whether or not a certain company was going to merge with another. (Kind of takes "speculation" out of the whole deal, doesn't it?) Boesky's scheme was uncovered when SEC investigators caught one of his sources, Dennis Levine, trading secrets with other speculators. Levine was squeezed, and sold Boesky down the Hudson River. Boesky, in hopes of a lighter prison sentence, offered to sing louder, and even agreed to make phony deals over the

Grifter Speak

Greed is all right, by the way. I want you to know that. I think greed is healthy. You can be greedy and still feel good about yourself.

—Ivan Boesky, in his 1985 commencement speech to the University of California-Berkeley's School of Business Administration.

Grifter Speak

It was this incredible feeling of invulnerability. That was the insanity of it all. You get bolder and bolder, and it gets easier, and you make more money and more money, and it feeds upon itself. And looking back, I realize I was sick, that it became an addiction, that I lived for the high of making those trades, of doing the next deal, making the bigger deal.

—inside tipster Dennis Levine on *60 Minutes*

phone to trap other insider traders. The ensuing scandal was the Enron and WorldCom of its day, and it pretty much destroyed Levine's investment banking firm, Drexel Burnham Lambert.

In the end, Boesky slipped by with a three-year prison term and a $100 million fine. To anybody who's ever agonized over a $25 parking ticket, that sounds like a lot. But not when you consider that—minus the penalty—his net worth was still a billion bucks and change.

"Crazy" Eddie Antar

It was 1987. I was an impressionable 15-year-old geek who had saved up all summer to purchase my first Commodore 64. (Told you it was 1987.) A home computer, of course, is only fun with software, and I was intrigued by a new store that had opened up not too far from my neighborhood. Crazy Eddie's, it was called. It was an electronics and appliances shop that boasted the lowest prices possible. Their prices were so insanely low, the pitch went, that their owners must be in dire need of shock therapy. The TV ads certainly didn't convince you otherwise. In 30-second spots, pitchman "Crazy Eddie (actually, actor Jerry Carroll) screamed and ranted and frothed at the mouth about how low his prices were; America hadn't seen such a lunatic pitchman since the Hawaiian Punch guy went around beating the crap out of innocent fruit juice drinkers.

I was 15. I was sold. I rode my bike to the Crazy Eddie's store, and indeed, the prices for computer games were low. Hell, on my newspaper bundling salary, I'd be able to afford a new game every two weeks! Crazy Eddie was a-okay in my book.

That's because I was 15, and I wasn't a Crazy Eddie's investor. If I were, and it were 1987, I'd personally want to strap Eddie and his cousin Sam to the electric chair.

> **Grifter Speak**
>
> I'm INSANE!!!! How can I offer these prices? Because I'm totally nuts! I'm INSA-A-A-A-A-ANE!
>
> —Jerry Carroll, in a "Crazy Eddie's" TV spot

That's because the Antars took advantage of the late 1980s Wall Street boom in which investors were more than happy to throw cash at anything that seemed to be making a profit. When the Antars decided to take Crazy Eddie's public—in other words, offer stock to investors to expand the business—it was easy to show tremendous growth. The Antars simply stopped skimming as much as they used to from the business. (As it turned out, the cousins had skimmed money from their own business for years, helped in part by avoiding those pesky sales taxes.) When the brothers let the money sit, sales appeared to jump from $29 million to $46 million in just one year. Wall Street went … well, nuts. Crazy Eddie went public.

The only problem with such explosive growth is that investors expect more of the same the next year. To duplicate the illusion, the Antars cooked up imaginary merchandise, and even moved products around to different stores in the chain to make it seem like there was more inventory. The Antars also employed a clever money scheme called the "Panama Pump," in which skimmed money was sent to Israeli banks, then routed to Panama—which uses U.S. currency and has very strict banking secrecy laws—and in turn, pumped back into Crazy Eddie's, in the form of purchases by check. Auditors somehow missed these kinds of schemes, even though the check "purchases" were often for $100,000 or more. No matter how "insane" the prices, who on earth walks into a Crazy Eddie's and buys a hundred grand worth of boom boxes and Commodore 64s?

Such tricks worked in 1986, but by 1987 a little bit of sanity had set in. The SEC started to investigate the cousins for cooking the books, and by the time the government had levied a $73 million judgement against the cousins, Eddie Antar had fled the country. Sam was left behind; in exchange for his cooperation, he received six months of house arrest, and had to perform 1,200 hours of community service. (Today, he routinely lectures groups on investment fraud.) Eddie surfaced in Israel in 1992, and was extradited back to the United States to face conspiracy and racketeering charges. He was sentenced to seven years in jail—not the nearest insane asylum.

The Least You Need to Know

- Clifford Irving tried to pass off his fake Howard Hughes biography as "authorized," even though he'd never met the reclusive billionaire.

- Frank Abagnale is probably the most infamous con man in recent memory, but now he uses his skills to prevent fraud, not perpetrate it.

- Barry Minkow, at 16, became the Charles Ponzi of his generation.

- Ivan Boesky was guilty of insider trading—using illegal tips to make stock purchases.

- "Crazy" Eddie Antar and his brother used a 1980s Wall Street boom and shady accounting practices to defraud their investors.

Part 5

Reversal of Fortune: Stinging Con Men

You didn't think this book would have a downbeat ending, did you?

Sure, con artists get away with millions of dollars. They pull the wool over our eyes more often than a sweater salesman. They have deep hearty laughs at our expense as they sip single-malt scotches at their annual Con Artists Convention at swank hotels across the country. They delight in their sheer genius, in their utter superiority over us dumb suckers.

But sometimes, the suckers get revenge. Here's what happens when a fool-proof scam doesn't exactly go the way it should, thanks to the vigilant—and sometimes sneaky—efforts of various law enforcement agencies and watchdog groups, from your local boys in blue to the D.A.'s office all the way up to the FBI and the National Consumers League. And here's who to call if you are scammed and want a little payback for yourself.

Chapter 20

The Law Strikes Back

In This Chapter

- ◆ How law enforcement beats con men at their own game
- ◆ Why the government is trying to scam you
- ◆ When cops swindle fugitives and crooks

To catch a crook, sometimes you have to operate like a crook. This is especially true when trying to capture a skilled con artist, whose most powerful weapon is the ability to tap dance around the truth. Many con games, by their very design, are set up to avoid contact with the law, discourage the mark from reporting it to the law, and be confusing enough to perhaps allow the con to wiggle out of prosecution by the law. Well, to paraphrase Sean Connery in *The Untouchables*, you can't be bringing a knife to a gun fight. And that means you have to fight con artists with the tools of their own trade: lies, deceptions, and double-crosses. It can be controversial, but sometimes law enforcement agencies will set up their own scams and con games, all for the purpose of educating would-be marks or flushing out the bad guys. Here are some of the ways this happens.

The Reverse Sting

In Seattle, the local food stamp fraud ring was a well-oiled machine. Street addicts eagerly ripped open their monthly benefits envelope, then made a beeline for their nearest "runner." The runner would purchase the food stamps at half the face value—which was fine with addict, because you couldn't buy heroin with food stamps, anyway. It was like the government giving you money to shoot up. The runner than sold the stamps to middlemen for a bit more than he bought them, and the middlemen did the same with local merchants downtown. The merchants would then redeem the stamps with the federal government, and make a nice fat profit for practically nothing.

A local businessman noticed runners buying food stamps from addicts and was disgusted, according to the *Seattle Post-Intelligencer*. "These criminals were taking advantage of alcoholics and drug addicts," he said. "I wanted to make sure that food stamps went to people who needed them, not to support drug and alcohol addictions." So he reported the scam to the D.A.'s office, which then coordinated a massive sting operation to smash the ring to pieces. Cops pulled on ratty clothes and posed as Seattle street addicts, and over the course of nearly two years sold over a quarter of a million dollars worth of food stamps. These were no ordinary food stamps, though. They were traceable, and when certain downtown merchants tried to redeem them, it was all too clear who was involved in the fraud ring. Dozens of people were arrested and charged with unlawful use of food stamps—a felony—which can be punishable to up to five years in the slammer.

Going undercover to smoke out criminals is a time-honored law enforcement tradition. Most undercover operations are variations of the impostor cons we discussed in Chapter 10—cops pretend to be someone they're not (street addicts, fences, drug dealers, businessmen) to gain the confidence of criminals and gather evidence that will eventually be used to prosecute them. Yes, note the word *confidence*. When you boil them down, undercover operations are con games, only used for the forces of good rather than the forces of greed.

Law enforcement will also play the role of the sucker to expose and arrest con artists. Take one national-level work-at-home scheme that was busted up by the FTC and Justice Department in June 2002. At first, the deal sounded great to Bob Keith: receive discounted music CDs, then sell them at a nice profit. *We will show you step by step how to earn $150,000 per year just by working a few hours per week*, the classified

> **Grifter Speak**
>
> **Sting** 1. (noun) the point in a con game where the mark's money is taken. 2. (person) Former lead singer of The Police who is best known for his adult contemporary hits and his marathon Tantric sex sessions with his wife.

ad read. *Imagine that!* There was only one problem. "I got recordings from artists that have been dead for 30 years," Keith told the Associated Press. The Philadelphia man lost over $13,000 in the scam.

So investigators took Bob's place and answered the same ad, then listened to the same sales pitch. The investigators were encouraged to talk to other former customers who made a killing using their work-at-home program. As it turned out, those other customers were shills, reading from carefully-prepared scripts. The company was slapped with fraud charges and a lawsuit. And that was only one of 77 work-at-home scam operations in 16 states that was targeted in the sting. The m.o. in every single sting was the same: Pose as a customer, listen to the pitch, gather evidence, then file charges.

In another case, this one in San Francisco in 1997, a woman was contacted by a con artist who was encouraging her to claim serious injuries after a minor car accident. The woman, who smelled a scam, called her local prosecutor's office, and they quickly arranged a sting. An undercover investigator took the woman's place when meeting with the con artist, who explained how it all worked. The con artist—who in this case happened to be a lawyer—set up agreements between health care workers and the alleged victims. When the insurance companies were confronted with phony medical records and were forced to pay up, the cash was split three ways: a third to the "victim," a third to the health care worker, and a third to the con artist, who was also referred to as the "capper."

"I can see you're hurting," said the capper in this case, according to an article in *The San Francisco Examiner*. "I can tell your neck is injured by the way you move."

"But I feel fine," responded the investigator, still posing as the woman.

"Keep complaining," said the capper. "They cannot tell you what you feel. Just keep complaining you're a victim of a violent crime of DUI."

The capper in this case was part of an insurance fraud ring that used stolen accident reports from the San Francisco PD to identify accident victims. Thanks to the undercover work—and to one honest woman reporting the scam in the first place—seven members of the ring were charged with 73 felony counts of insurance fraud and workers' compensation fraud.

Con-trary to Popular Belief

For another classic tale of con men getting stung, see "Credit Declined" in Chapter 4, in which a ring of would-be credit card thieves used stolen digits to order tons of expensive computer hardware, but received a pile of junk instead.

Sometimes, investigators will pose as both victims *and* crooks to catch still another crook. (You with me? Good.) The best recent example is the Durascam sting operation, which was launched by California's four major FBI offices and state investigators. The medical fraud was fairly insidious: Some medical supply companies and clinical labs would collude with clinic workers in an effort to exaggerate the need for wheelchairs, or oxygen tanks, or other health equipment that the patient didn't need. As a result, patients (and their medical insurance companies) were socked with huge bills, and crooked supply companies and labs enjoyed the profits.

How did the FBI decide to fight it? By setting up their own clinic.

They called it Western Comprehensive Care, and based it in Encino, California in 1998. The clinic's employees were actually FBI agents, and retired agents were recruited to play the role of "patients." Soon, crooked companies started crawling out of the woodwork, approaching agents with promises of kickbacks for playing along. "Agents actually received about $180,000 in kickbacks," said FBI Agent Daniel M. Martino in the *Los Angeles Times*. The result of the two-year sting operation was dozens of arrests, making it the largest undercover medical fraud inquiry in U.S. history.

Grifter Speak

Keep complaining. They cannot tell you what you feel.

—insurance scam artist to a car accident "victim."

Not only was the sting successful, but it was a big hit with the retired FBI agents, who were all too happy to be back in action, even if it was simply posing as an ordinary schlub with artery trouble. "They were unbelievably eager to do this," said Martino. "We needed a cadre of people we could trust. And who better than ex-agents?" Let this serve as a warning to con artists: Not only is the entire FBI after your swindling butt, but the legion of FBI retirees, as well.

The Government *Is* Out to Get You

When the government isn't busy trying to fool con artists, it also spends a lot of time trying to con innocent American citizens. Yes, you read that correctly. The government—*your* U.S. government—is looking to make you its next patsy.

But it's for your own good. As you read in earlier chapters, there are thousands of phony stock scams out there. The Securities and Exchange Commission (SEC) says it grapples with 40,000 phony stock complaints at any given time. It tries to warn consumers about these scams, but let's face it—who has time to read do-gooder pamphlets or visit Internet fraud tip sites?

So instead the SEC decided to take the message to the people who need it the most—consumers who fall for stock scams. In the fall of 2001, a bunch of clever wags at the SEC with a very dark sense of humor cooked up McWhortle Enterprises, a Washington company that claimed to have come up with a handheld "biohazard" detector. Worried about anthrax in your office or smallpox in the water cooler? Worry no more. All McWhortle needed, according the pitch on the company website, was $63 million in operating capital to make the detector a reality. McWhortle said that the SEC was giving them early approval for the company's initial public offering (IPO), and those who jumped on board were very likely to earn obscene amounts of money. The company was even lucky enough to have a story appear on P.R. Newswire, a popular newswire of business press releases. It seemed as if the more paranoid the country, the better it was for McWhortle Enterprises.

> **Don't Be a Sucker**
>
> Want to screw with the minds of your closest frien ... er, I mean, help your friends learn the perils of falling for an Internet stock scam? Direct them to www.mcwhortle.com, and tell them what a great deal it is. Then sit back and watch the fun ensue.

"Biohazard" was apparently a magic word, because in three days McWhortle's site recorded over 15,000 hits. Those 15,000 would-be investors were disappointed, however, when they clicked the "INVEST NOW!" button and were told that McWhortle was a scam. Instead of big bucks, visitors were given tips on detecting stock scams. The SEC received a bunch of comments from those would-be investors via e-mail. "I hated your website," typed one. "I am a professional short-seller, and I saw a wonderful opportunity to make a killing—only to discover that it wasn't just a fraud, but a fraud of a fraud. How am I supposed to make a living?" It's a shame people don't appreciate a good old-fashioned "tough love" lesson from the SEC.

The SEC's little scam was a big success and led to the creation of other fake sites, operated along with help from the Treasury Department and other law enforcement agencies. Needless to say, the SEC is not revealing exactly which other investment sites are frauds. Keep this in mind the next time you're tempted by an amazing stock opportunity—it could very well be the SEC, trying to teach you a lesson. (That lesson, in case you missed it the first time, is that almost all too-good-to-be-true investment schemes are just that, so avoid 'em.) For more on investment scams, see Chapter 13.

Arresting Developments: When Cops Pull Scams

By now, it should be clear that law enforcement officials across the country are very fond of pulling con games. Like all confidence men, cops have a particular favorite con game that they love to pull. It's an oldie but apparently a goodie, because crooks keep falling for it. Let's call it the old, "Come On Down, You've Won A Prize" scam.

It all begins with a list. Maybe it's a list of people who have 10 or more unpaid parking tickets. Or maybe it's a list of 50 fugitives, all wanted in connection with various violent crimes. Cops are faced with these lists all of the time, but sometimes lack the resources—or time—to round everyone up. Or in the case of violent fugitives, the risks are too great, and the manpower too limited. Still, violators of the law must be brought to justice. What do you do in that case?

Why, you award them fabulous gifts and big cash prizes!

Okay, not really. But the fugitives don't know that. They receive a phone call, or a piece of mail from GBJS Enterprises that says they've won something—concert tickets, an all-expense paid vacation, a brand new car. To claim their prize, they simply have to report to a certain office downtown and bring their driver's license and winning prize claim number. When the fugitives arrive, however, they're not greeted by the leggy blondes or streaming balloons and confetti. Instead it's a burly cop with thick, hairy arms, reading them their Miranda rights. If the fugitives look closely at their prize claim number, they might discover that it's actually their Identification Order number, the number the FBI uses to track fugitives. And the name of that prize company? Well, GBJS Enterprises may actually stand for "Going Back to Jail, Sucker."

The Feds originally cooked up this highly-effective scam, but over the past decade it has found its way down to the local level. In 1996, the Dallas Marshal's Office created a sting operation to catch people with outstanding traffic warrants. First they compiled a list of people who had at least five misdemeanor warrants. The total came to 5,481. Each person received a letter from "PYT Enterprises," which said that they'd won free concert tickets, but also had a chance at winning a new car. (True to form, the prize claim number was each offender's warrant number.) Simply call to make an appointment, the letter read, and you can come in to claim your prize. "We had to go great lengths to make this look like a legitimate contest," said Dallas Marshal Ron Cornelius to the *Fort Worth Star Telegram*. The Dallas Marshals borrowed an office in an industrial park, as well as a white 1996 Ford Mustang GT to show on-site.

All of the house dressing apparently paid off for the Marshal's Office. Over 200 people called to inquire about the prizes, and 48 of them actually showed up at the "PYT Enterprises" office to receive their tickets. When the offenders arrived, they were given a music preference survey to fill out—meanwhile, the cops were busy verifying identities and the validity of warrants. Forty of them turned out to be on their list. (Eight others had tagged along with friends, hoping to cash in.) Two people were even caught with drugs on them, and subsequently arrested. "Greed is the word that surfaced most often," said Cornelius. "People who were arrested said, 'I shouldn't have been so greedy.'" The sting was a smashing success. According to the Fort Worth Star Telegram, it only cost $1,500 in overtime, and resulted in clearing 245 outstanding felony traffic warrants, which had a value of over $63,000.

Grifter Speak

I shouldn't have been so greedy.
—traffic offenders, after falling for a concert ticket scam set up with the Dallas Marshal's Office

Cops have used prize-giveaways, job interviews, free barbecues, lotteries, auctions, and more to lure in the fugitives. These kinds of stings are time-savers—one stop shopping for rounding up all manner of offenders and fugitives—but they can also save lives. How? By taking the fugitive, who may be armed or prone to violence when cornered, out of his own environment.

Con-trary to Popular Belief

Some fugitives are captured in jeans and t-shirts; others, in their pajamas as they're dragged screaming from their beds. Still other fugitives, however, get dressed up in a sharp suit, clean shirt, and freshly-pressed tie. That's because they've been lured to their arrests by the promise of a job interview, a common police scam. Instead of tax forms and a 401K, the would-be applicant is given handcuffs and deluxe accommodations at the Gray Bar Hotel.

Back in the 1980s, U.S. Marshals came up with a particularly clever sting method: package delivery. One phony service was called "FIST Bonded Delivery Service," with FIST standing for "Fugitive Investigative Strike Teams." FIST would show up at the fugitive's last known address to deliver a package full of "valuable merchandise." If the fugitive happened to be there, the "delivery man" (actually, a U.S. Marshal) would ask if the fugitive wouldn't mind coming out to the van to pick up his package—it was quite heavy. Once the fugitive was safely out of the house, and more importantly, away from any weapons or accomplices, the delivery man would slap on the cuffs and read the fugitive his Miranda rights. "By asking the fugitive out of the house, it erases the obvious perils of having to break in and search for someone who probably is armed and willing to shoot policemen," explained one U.S Marshal to the Associated Press.

If the fugitive wasn't home, the delivery man would leave a note with a phone number to arrange delivery. Once the fugitive called, "FIST" would arrange a delivery time, and would remind the fugitive to have good identification on hand to be able to receive the package. Good ID, of course, made it all that easier for a "delivery man" to make a positive ID of his fugitive. The motto should have been "Package Delivery Stings: When You Absolutely, Positively Have to Catch Your Fugitive."

Con-trary to Popular Belief

The American Civil Liberties Union (ACLU) once said that prize stings were "deceptive," and actually defraud criminals because no actual prizes are given. Either the stings should be halted, or the prizes should actually be awarded, claimed some ACLU members. "I think that it would be in order that they live up to their claim," said one. "If a merchant or business person has to do it, I think that certainly is in order."

The Least You Need to Know

♦ Law enforcement agencies find it useful to target con men by running stings and posing as criminals or victims to catch their quarry.

♦ Some scams you encounter might be run by the government—to help prevent real fraud.

♦ Cops sometimes use scams to catch hard-to-find fugitives.

Chapter 21

Where to Go If You've Been Scammed

In This Chapter

- ◆ Should you think local, or go federal?
- ◆ A rundown of the agencies that police fraud
- ◆ The best anti-fraud consumer and watchdog groups

For every type of scam under the sun, there seems to be an individual agency out there to deal with it. (Just type in the word "fraud" in your favorite Internet search engine, and see how many organizations and groups pop up.) Trying to sort out one fraud agency from another can be very confusing. If you're scammed, who do you call? The local police? The Better Business Bureau? The FBI? The National Guard? The French Foreign Legion? Mommy?

In this chapter, I'll try to clear up some of the confusion and help you navigate your way through the law enforcement jungle. I'll also walk you through the three levels of fraud-busting agencies: the local guys, the Feds, and finally, the nonprofit consumer watchdog groups.

Who You Gonna Call, Sucker?

It's bad enough that you've been swindled. Now you have to figure out who to call to report the scam, and see if anything can be done to recover your money. "One reason scams can be so frustrating is that the victim is often confused about where to go," says retired FBI agent Mike Connelley. "The victim can wind up making numerous phone calls, and it's easy for him to think that various agencies are giving him the run around, that no one is interested in his problem."

That's how it can feel, sure. But don't take it personally. Investigating fraud is not so clean-cut.

Think about it from the law enforcement point of view. Local police departments, district attorneys and FBI regional offices receive hundreds of thousands of fraud-related calls every year. And each time, the cop/attorney/agent picking up the phone has to satisfy his own series of questions: Is this caller legit? Or is this a scam artist trying to cover his own tracks? Then there's the jurisdictional mess. Do we have a specific statute or law that covers this alleged scam? Even if the answer is yes, the law enforcement agency still has another decision to make. Is this scam significant enough—significant in terms of money lost, or public pressure, or number of people swindled—to justify the time and resources it will take to investigate it?

"If the complaint is based on weak jurisdiction, not much good physical evidence, witnesses who can't recall the incident in much detail, or there's a small dollar loss," explains Connelley, "that just makes it easier for the law enforcement agency to say 'no.'" This is not because the law doesn't care that you've been scammed. But the reality is that they have limited budgets and manpower, and they're forced to apply those resources where they think they can make a difference.

What does this mean for you? Well, this makes it all the more important to guard yourself from scams in the first place. (And you've taken that step by plunking down your hard-earned cash for a copy of this book.) If you've been swindled, write down as much information as you can about what happened:

1. **Who** was involved—names and descriptions, if possible.

2. **What** happened, from initial contact to final sting.

3. **Where** it happened—phone, or street corner, or in your workplace.

It's important not to let your pride get in the way. Sure, nobody likes to be fooled. At least if you're mugged, you've got righteous anger on your side—you want payback, and you want it now. Successful con games, however, are designed to make the victim feel weak or stupid, and as a result, hesitant to go to the authorities. Don't give in to this. As soon you can, take notes, then make your first phone call.

Who do you call? For most small-time scams, it's best to start local, and that means your local police department.

Your Local Police Department's Bunco Squad

Most big city police departments have some kind of fraud division, typically called the "bunco squad" or perhaps "fraud detail" or the "fraud unit." Typically they deal with things like adoption scams, carnival cons, phony charities, check kiting, counterfeiting and forgery, illegal gambling, and a variety of street cons (pigeon drops, shortchanging, etc.). "The key here is dollar loss," explains Connelley. "Small dollar loss is a local problem, while big dollar schemes get the attention of the Feds."

Call the main number, and ask for officers who deal with fraud cases. If you live in a suburban area or a small town, there's a good chance your local police department won't have the budget or manpower for a separate bunco squad. In that case, look up the number for …

Your District Attorney

Either your local D.A. works jointly with your local PD, or they'll have their own "special operations" or "consumer fraud" unit to deal with scams. If the scam involves other counties, the D.A. might link up with their counterparts in those counties. The D.A.'s office might handle the same scams as a police bunco squad, but they also investigate slightly larger scams, such as real estate fraud, Ponzi schemes, and retail cons.

If the fraud is big enough—meaning it involves a number of victims in a number of different counties—the D.A. might seek the involvement of your state's attorney general. Don't bother calling the attorney general first; his or her office will almost always direct you back to the local level. The attorney general will only jump in when the sheer size of the scamming operation is too big for a lone D.A.'s office to handle, or when public outcry is so great that it demands the attorney general's special attention. (That, or the scam is a hot

> **Don't Be a Sucker**
>
> Remember that an absurd number of con artists get away with their crimes because they make their marks feel stupid or weak—and as a result, reluctant to report their crimes. You're not stupid, or weak. You've simply let your guard down, and someone took advantage of that fact. Report the jerk.

topic, and it's an election year. Color me cynical, but that's the way it sometimes works, folks.)

> **Don't Be a Sucker** _____
>
> Should you call the cops or the FBI? The rule of thumb is the dollar loss. If you've lost a relatively small amount of money, call the police. But if you've been swindled out of thousands of dollars, and the perpetrators are in another state, and you suspect you're only one of many, call the nearest FBI office. (You can find a list of regional FBI headquarters at www.fbi.gov.)

For anything larger than a street scam, however—especially business or real estate fraud—you might consider contacting a lawyer first. A good lawyer can help you map out your options and help you contact the right law enforcement agency. "Nobody likes to pay attorney bills," says Connelley, "but in all honesty, that's where you should go for the best advice. The more the victim has lost, the more you should be seeking your own good legal advice from a competent attorney."

Whether you go with a lawyer or not, sometimes a scam is too big for the local guys to handle. In these cases, it's time to call out …

The Big Guns: Federal Agencies

There are a number of federal agencies that track and try to squelch specific kinds of scams. As I've mentioned, these aren't the guys to call if someone's scammed you out of $10 on a street corner, or taken you for an expensive ride down Three Card Monte Boulevard. "If the scheme has an interstate flavor to it—if there are multiple states involved, and large dollar amounts, or it involves the U.S. mail or banks or stock, call the Feds," advises Connelley.

The Federal Bureau of Investigation (FBI)

You think your particular fraud case has that "interstate flavor"? Call the FBI first. Yes, they're incredibly busy fighting terrorists these days, but they still are the nation's premier crime-fighting agency. The FBI handles a host of scams, including check kiting, counterfeiting and forgery, gambling cons, insurance fraud, investment scams, Ponzi schemes, and telemarketing scams. You can find a listing of the FBI's regional offices at www.fbi.gov. If, however, your scam involves the Internet—and with over 16,000 Internet fraud complaints in 2001 alone, it just might—you should check out …

The Internet Fraud Complaint Center (IFCC)

Founded in May 2000, the IFCC is a joint venture of the FBI and the National White Collar Crime Center. Its goal: to provide a national "clearinghouse" of Internet fraud. If you see something suspicious on the Internet, or believe you've been scammed, log on to www.ifccfbi.gov to report it. The site walks you through the process, step by step, and takes no more than 10 minutes. The IFCC takes it from there, deciding on which level enforcement agency—local, state, or federal—is best equipped to investigate the suspected fraudster.

> **CAUTION**
>
> **Don't Be a Sucker**
>
> Finding the right agency to report a fraud *can* be confusing. But not in the case of Internet scams or identity theft. Two relatively new organizations have sprung up to deal with these burgeoning cons. For all Internet con games, go to www.ifccfbi.gov, and for identity theft, call 1-877-FTC-HELP or log on to www.ftc.gov/ftc/complaint.htm.

The Federal Trade Commission (FTC)

This is the agency that enforces consumer protection laws. If someone has swiped your identity (see Chapter 4 for more), you want to get in touch with the FTC. They won't be able to go after the perpetrators—that falls to other enforcement agencies—but they can help you rebuild your financial life. *Contact:* 1-877-FTC-HELP (382-4357). 600 Pennsylvania Avenue, NW, Washington, D.C. 20580. www.ftc.gov/ftc/complaint.htm or www.ftc.gov/ftc/consumer.htm.

> **Con-trary to Popular Belief**
>
> Two years ago, the FTC let loose the hounds—they created a "fraud lab" that used search robots to comb the Internet for fraudulent ads and services. Not only do the robots detect the suspicious material, but they instantly copy it, making it easier for prosecutors to offer up the evidence later.

The U.S. Secret Service

Sure, they're supposed to come between a bullet and the President of the United States, but they're also looking out for you, too. Because they're part of the Treasury Department, the Secret Service is charged with investigating crimes against financial institutions, including counterfeiting, forgery, money laundering, and bank and computer fraud. They also take a keen interest in the so-called "419 Scam," which you read about in Chapter 5 ("Out of Africa"). *Contact:* 202-406-5708, www.treas.gov/usss.

The Internal Revenue Service (IRS)

Your favorite bloodsucker ... er, I mean, revenue service has been fighting fraud since July 1, 1919. That's when the IRS—then called the Bureau of Internal Revenue—hired six tough Postal Inspectors to investigate fraud. These guys were good. They used tax fraud to put many famous gangsters in prison, including Al Capone. (If you've ever seen *The Untouchables*, you know that it was tax fraud that finally tripped up Big Al.) The IRS Criminal Investigation Division—now employing 2,800 special agents—is still as tough as ever. In 2001, IRS investigators looked into 3,283 cases. About two-thirds of those resulted in convictions. Has some slimeball been embezzling from your company? Sic the tax boys on 'em. Ditto if you've been swindled by a phony charity. Contact: 1-800-829-1040, www.irs.ustreas.gov.

Consumer and Watchdog Groups

Sometimes, citizens have to take crime-fighting into their own hands, Charles Bronson-style. (Okay, maybe not Charles Bronson-style—his character in the *Death Wish* series was a bit of a nutcase.) Instead of getting a gun, angry fraud victims have gotten organized, forming various watchdog groups that aim to educate the public about scams, prevent them, and support those people who have fallen victim to them. So if local law enforcement or the D.A.'s office isn't too interested in hearing your story, one of these organizations might be.

The National Consumers League

For over 100 years, the watchdogs at the National Consumers League have been watching our backs. If you work in the U.S. or have ever purchased something in the U.S., the NCL is on your side. (They're the guys who helped create a "minimum wage" for hard-working Americans in 1938.) More recently, the nonprofit organization has instituted an excellent anti-fraud hotline and website dedicated to preventing and reporting scams:

- ◆ **The National Fraud Information Center (1-800-876-7060)** is a toll-free hotline established in 1992 and dedicated to helping victims of phone and Internet fraud. An offer sound fishy to you? Give the hotline a ring, and ask the NFIC's advice. If you think you've been scammed, call the same number to report it. All fraud reports are sent quickly—within minutes—to federal enforcement agencies, including the FTC and your local attorney general.

◆ **Internet Fraud Watch** (www.fraud.org) is an off-shoot of the NFIC, but specializing in web scams. Here, you can report fraud using an online form, read tips about the latest 'Net scams, and check the latest fraud statistics and trends. This is an incredibly useful site, and one that very much came in handy as I wrote this book.

For more info: National Consumers League, 1701 K Street, N.W., Suite 1200, Washington, D.C., 20006. 202-835-3323. Fax: 202-835-0747. www.nclnet.org

The Better Business Bureau (BBB)

One-stop shopping for consumers who think they've been swindled by a retail store or company, the Better Business Bureau has been looking out for consumers since 1912. Contact the Council of Better Business Bureaus, which will direct you to your local BBB—there are 145 of them, scattered throughout the United States. Call 703-276-0100, or find them on the web at www.bbb.org.

Association of Certified Fraud Examiners

This is the professional organization of guys who go after fraud and white-collar crime for a living. There are over 26,000 "CFEs"—Certified Fraud Examiners—who are trained to prevent and spot all manner of business bunco, from embezzlement to asset misappropriations to faulty financial statements. If you're a small business owner, you should definitely check out the ACFE website, which is full of great fraud-busting tips. (For instance, companies who install an internal "fraud hotline"—a number employees can call to blow the whistle—have cut their financial losses in *half*.) *Contact:* 1-800-245-3321. www.cfenet.com.

Don't Be a Sucker

Still stuck? Need to complain to somebody, but don't quite think any of the previously mentioned agencies will do the trick? Log on to the Consumer Action website at www.pueblo.gsa.gov/chr/corpormain.htm. The site is full of contacts for banks, BBBs, associations, etc., where you can lodge a complaint about a particular service or product. (Still can't find what you're looking for? Try Dial-A-Prayer.)

American Association of Retired Persons (AARP)

As you've read back in Chapter 2, con artists love to target the elderly. That really makes the AARP angry—after all, they're a national organization of Americans 50 years or older—and they've fought back with a number of excellent education programs and tips. *Contact:* 1-800-424-3410. www.aarp.org.

The Least You Need to Know

◆ Con artists count on you feeling too embarrassed to report a scam.

◆ If your dollar loss is small, call local police; if it's large, call the Feds.

◆ In large business fraud cases, enlisting a lawyer can be a smart move.

◆ Various watchdog groups support victims of fraud.

Con Man Glossary

Con artists seem to speak a different language from the rest of us; expert linguists have identified some "scam-ese" terms and offered the following translations:

419   The section of the Nigerian criminal code that deals with fraud; also refers to the letter/e-mail scam that targets U.S. businessmen.

actual fraud   A scheme intentionally designed to cheat somebody.

addict   A mark who falls for scams time and time again.

autograph   A scam in which a con artist asks for someone's John Hancock, then uses that signature on a check.

badger game   A scam in which sex is used as a lure, and then an angry husband/parent shows up, demanding money.

beef   When a mark complains to the police.

big con   Any con game in which a mark is sent away to collect money (also called "put on the send"), as opposed to the short con, which a con artist tries to take the money a mark has on him.

block hustle   When a con artist makes it clear that he's selling stolen merchandise, making it extremely unlikely that you'll contact the authorities after he swindles you.

blute   Fake clippings from a newspaper, used in big con games.

broad   A playing card.

broad tosser   Slang for a three-card monte operator.

bucket shop or bucket store   A turn-of-the-century term for crooked stock brokers (or more often, con men posing as brokers) who sell worthless or phony stock to unsuspecting marks.

bunco   Synonym for a con, fraud, or scam; *bunco artists* pull scams, while *bunco squads* (cops) try to prevent scams and catch bunco artists.

C-gee   A con artist.

cackle-bladder   A rubber pocket used to fake a bloody wound or gunshot; typically used by con men to scare away a mark after he's been suckered.

cannon   Pickpocket.

chill   When a mark loses interest in a con game.

cold deck   A marked deck that is slipped in during a game. Also known as a "cooler."

come-on   When a con artists pitches his story to a mark.

con   Short for confidence game. In *The Big Steal*, linguist David W. Maurer limits the definition to any swindle where the mark knows he stands to profit by being dishonest.

constructive fraud   Swindling somebody with misleading words or actions.

convincer   Small winnings/money that encourages a mark to keep himself involved in a con.

cramming   When a salesperson tries to pack in extra services into an existing order.

curdle   When a con game goes awry.

cyberbazaars   Online trading places where stolen credit card numbers are offered to the highest bidder.

dollar store   A shop that features goods at very discounted prices, but is actually meant to attract marks for short or long cons.

el toro y la vaca   Spanish for "the bull and the cow," this refers to the method of driving in front of a vehicle, then slamming on the brakes, for sole purpose of causing an accident. The bull is the insured car; the cow is the car full of potential "victims." Also known as the "swoop and squat."

flash   Expensive-looking carnival prizes that will attract suckers.

flat game   The carnival word for a game of skill or chance that might or might not involve skill or chance. These games can flatten your wallet.

flattie   The guy who operates a flat (fixed) game.

fraud   Intentional deception to cause a person to give up property or some lawful right.

gaffed   When a flat game is tilted heavily in favor of the carnival operator.

good deal syndrome   When people, looking for bargains, open themselves up to being swindled.

grifter   Someone who makes a living swindling or scamming people, usually with a series of short cons.

heavy rackets   Crimes that involve violence or force; the opposite of the con or swindle.

hep   To be wise to a con artist's tricks. This word is thought to have originated with Joe Hep, who ran a Chicago saloon where many grifters hung out.

hype   Slang term for a shortchange artist.

identity theft   When a con artist uses your personal data—a Social Security number, credit card accounts, birth dates—to create a shadow identity, which then buys merchandise, takes out loans, and makes other financial transactions.

juice   Marked cards.

lapping   A business scheme in which an employee uses stolen money to cover an earlier theft; the process is repeated until he quits or is caught.

less-cash deposit scheme   When a scammer uses a discarded deposit slip to present a bogus check to a bank, then asks for a certain amount of money back (less-cash) right away.

live one   A player with money.

lot lice   Carnival-goers who stroll around but never play games of chance.

mark   The victim of a con game.

mechanic   A skilled con artist who knows how to manipulate a deck of cards.

Michigan roll   The fake roll of money flashed to marks in Pigeon Drop schemes. Often it's real money on top, but shredded newspaper or bogus bills stacked beneath. Also known as *boodle*, *flash roll*, or *nut*.

occupational fraud   The technical term for using your job to swindle money out of your employer.

one-liner   A short con.

panel game   A scam in which sex is used as a lure, and then a thief sneaks into the room through a hidden panel and steals money and jewelry from the preoccupied victim.

paper player   A con artist who uses marked cards.

pigeon drop   A "found money" scam in which an unsuspecting passerby is encouraged to offer up "good faith" money, only to have it swindled away from him.

pow-wower   A popular nineteenth century term used to describe phony psychics and mediums.

put the finger on   When con men identify a likely mark.

shill   A con artist's co-conspirator.

shoulder surfing   The method a con artist uses to watch a victim's hand movements to learn their secret PIN and credit card numbers.

short con   Any con game in which a con artist tries to take the money a mark has on him, as opposed to the big or long con, in which the mark is sent away for more money.

slamming   When a salesperson switches your long distance telephone service without your permission.

slum   Cheap carnival prizes you'll receive on the off-chance that you *do* win.

snake oil   Slang for bogus health cures or products.

stacking   How a card mechanic organizes a deck of cards.

sting   When a mark's money is taken.

stress   The "time is running out! act now!" part of a scam.

sucker list   A phone/mailing list that includes the name, address, phone numbers, and other personal details about anyone who may have fallen for a telemarketing scam in the past.

swap   When a con artist trades what is promised with something of much lesser value.

take a fall   To be convicted of a crime.

touch   The money taken from a mark.

Further Readings

In my opening letter, I mention that there is no such thing as *The Great Book of Cons*—a compendium of every con game ever invented. That may be true, but some of these books come close. If you're intrigued by the world of the confidence man—and really want to arm yourself in case he comes skulking your way—I heartily recommend these titles. (I've even thrown in a couple of choice con men novels, if your taste in fiction runs toward the criminal end of the spectrum.)

Abagnale, Frank W., with Stan Redding. *Catch Me If You Can*. New York: Broadway Books, 2000. Perhaps the best, most suspenseful first-person account of a modern day con artist.

———. *The Art of the Steal*. New York: Broadway Books, 2001. Here, Abagnale opens up a virtual treasure chest of business and financial cons. There are so many secrets revealed, it's not clear if this is meant for businesses to protect themselves, or to give a low-level grifter an advanced education.

Asbury, Herbert. *The Gangs of New York*. New York: Alfred A. Knopf, 1972. Read all about the scams being perpetrated in nineteenth century Manhattan. (Coincidentally, Martin Scorcese's version of this book stars Leonardo DiCaprio, who also stars as con artist Frank W. Abagnale in *Catch Me If You Can*.)

Bellin, Andy. *Poker Nation: A High-Stakes, Low-Life Adventure into the Heart of a Gambling Country*. New York: HarperCollins, 2002. This memoir is flush (sorry) with cool stories from the world of backroom, high-stakes poker. If you're a five-card stud fan, run straight (sorry again) to your bookstore to pick up a copy.

Cannell, Stephen J. *King Con*. New York: Avon Books, 1998. The same man who gave us *The Rockford Files* and *The A-Team* delivers this snappy novel about a grifter seeking revenge against the mobsters who put him in the hospital.

Easley, Bruce. *Biz-Op: How to Get Rich With "Business Opportunity" Frauds and Scams*. Port Townsend, Washington: Loompanics Unlimited, 1994. Here's a rare volume—a guidebook for people who want to pull frauds and scams. Then again, I'd expect nothing less from the ever-irreverent Loompanics people.

Faron, Fay. *Rip-Off: A Writer's Guide to Crimes of Deception*. New York: Writer's Digest Books, 1998. This book is part of Writer's Digest "Howdunit Series," aimed at mystery writers who are looking to add a bit of hardcore realism to their stories and novels. Still, this is a highly useful compendium of con games, and the fiction stuff is kept to a minimum. Highly recommended.

Henderson, M. Allen. *Flimflam Man: How Con Games Work*. Boulder, Colorado: Paladin Press, 1985.

———. *Money for Nothing: Rip-offs, Cons and Swindles*. Boulder, Colorado: Paladin Press, 1986.

Hynd, Alan. *The Confidence Game: Kings of the Con*. New York: Tempo Books, 1970. An obscure but fun collection of 10 con man stories, originally written for *TRUE—The Man's Magazine* and *True Detective Magazine*.

———. *Murder, Mayhem and Mystery*. New York: A.S. Barnes & Co., 1958. A collection of … well, murder, mayhem and mystery, with a bunch of great con man tales thrown in for good measure.

MacNee, Patricia J. *The Crime Encyclopedia: The World's Most Notorious Outlaws, Mobsters and Crooks*. Woodbridge, CT: UXL, 2002. Only one section of this thick, fat, true crime book is dedicated to con artists, but it's still very much worth your time.

Marlowe, Dan J. *Four For the Money*. Greenwich, Connecticut: Gold Medal, 1964. A riveting crime novel about a con man who runs operations in a backwater Nevada gambling town while waiting for a team of heisters to show up. This Gold Medal paperback classic is hard to find, but don't let that stop you from hunting down a copy.

Maurer, David W. *The Big Con: The Story of the Confidence Man*. New York: Anchor Books, 1999. This is a reprint of perhaps the best sociological study of confidence men and their swindles, originally published in 1940. It was the source for the con man film classic, *The Sting*.

Nash, Jay Robert. *Hustlers & Con Men*. New York: M. Evans and Company, 1976. Profiles of American con artists since the Mayflower, written by the country's best-known true crime writer. Highly recommended.

Ridley, John. *Love Is a Racket*. New York: Knopf, 1999. A black comedy about a failed screenwriter who becomes a drunken grifter, trying like hell to pay back a $15,000 debt before someone breaks more of his fingers.

Sifakis, Carl. *Frauds, Deceptions and Swindles*. New York: Checkmark Books, 2001. A nifty encyclopedia-style collection of frauds and con games throughout history.

Slim, Iceberg (Robert Beck). *Long White Con*. New York: All America Distributors Corp., 1998. In this novel, Slim—author of the infamous crime saga *Pimp*—traces the career of a scammer as he graduates from short to long cons.

Smith, Lindsay E., and Detective Bruce A. Walstad. *Sting Shift: The Street-Smart Cop's Handbook of Cons and Swindles*. Littleton, Colorado: Street-Smart Communications, 1989.

Stapinski, Helene. *Five-Finger Discount: A Crooked Family History*. New York: Random House, 2001. Ever wonder what it would be like to grow up in family full of grifters, swindlers, and robbers? Stapinski does the work for you in this bittersweet (and warped) memoir.

Swierczynski, Duane. *This Here's A Stick-Up: The Big, Bad Book of American Bank Robbery*. Indianapolis, Indiana: Alpha Books, 2002. Not exactly about con games, but read it anyway. It makes a great Mother's Day present!

Thompson, Jim. *The Grifters*. New York: Vintage Black Lizard, 1963. Perhaps the best—certainly best known—book about small-time con artists trying like hell to land the big score.

Walker, Kent (with Mark Schone). *Son of a Grifter: The Twisted Tale of Sante and Kenny Kimes, the Most Notorious Con Artists in America*. New York: William Morrow, 2001. A page-turning account of that rarest breed of con artists: remorseless killers. In this case they were mother and son, no less.

Wells, Joseph T. *Frankensteins of Fraud*. Austin, Texas: Obsidian Pulishing, 2000. Wells, the creator of the Association of Certified Fraud Examiners, offers up this detailed history of twentieth century white collar criminals.

Whitlock, Chuck. *Scam School*. New York: Macmillan, 1997. Usually, the words "As Seen on Oprah!" sends me hiding beneath the nearest table. But this is a rare exception: A smart, no-nonsense, expert looks at the most common confidence games, written by a guy who makes it his business to bust scams. Highly recommended.

———. *Easy Money*. New York: Kensington Books, 1994.

Swierczynski's "Spot-the-Scam" Quiz

Do you have what it takes to see a swindle coming from a mile away? Take this short quiz to find out.

Instructions: Think about what you've learned in this book and try to pinpoint what kind of scam might be in play. Then, check your answers. Give yourself 10 points for each correct answer.

1. You're working at the cash register at a Quik-Pump-Mart. A guy comes up, slaps a tin of breath mints on the counter (cost: 65¢), then hands you a $20 bill, and asks for his change back in a specific order. What scam might he be trying to pull?

   A. Counterfeit bill-passing

   B. Shortchanging

   C. A "hey dude, smell-my-breath" swindle

Answer: B. Shortchangers often try to pay for inexpensive products with large bills, then try to confuse the clerk with weird change requests.

2. You're bored one day. You start paging through your local phone directory, looking for your own name. (Everyone likes to see their name in print.) To your surprise, you discover you're not listed. Normally, to "de-list" your number, you have to pay a fee. What might be going on here?

   A. You have a disgruntled ex working at the phone company.

   B. Someone went back in time and shot your grandfather.

   C. An identity theft is at work.

Answer: Could be C. Sometimes, if an identity theft has wormed his way into your life, he'll de-list you, so it'll take creditors longer to reach you, which means he'll have more time to perpetrate his scam.

3. An e-mail pops into your IN box. "Earn $50,000 in Just Six Weeks," the e-mail proclaims. Sounds pretty good. But there's something missing from the ad. Something that probably makes this offer illegal. What is it?

   A. The number/percentage of people who actually earned $50,000 in just six weeks.

   B. The name and contact number of the person in charge.

   C. The fine print that reads: "Work may involve smuggling heroin for North Jersey mobsters."

Answer: A. If the business can't prove that others have actually made this much money in the time promised, it's a scam.

4. An e-mail pops into your IN box. It's from the IRS. They're now doing e-audits, and need you to submit your Social Security number and bank account information right away, using the handy form attached. You should …

   A. Comply immediately, because the IRS has super-satellites that can stop a human heart with a tiny laser beam.

   B. Erase it, and suffer the dire consequences.

   C. Scratch your head, because as far as the IRS knows, you "died" in that car crash 15 years ago.

Answer: B, because there won't be any "dire consequences." The IRS is mean, but not mean enough to do "e-audits." This is a scam artist trying to steal your personal info. Never give out personal info to anyone via e-mail—legit companies will never ask you for info this way.

5. It's 9:05 P.M. The phone rings. It's a telemarketer. You're annoyed, because the call interrupted your viewing of *Survivor: Kandahar*, but you can hang up without guilt. Why?

   A. Telemarketers like it when you hang up on them. It's all part of the slightly sadomasochistic game they play.

   B. You recognize the caller's voice; it's your brother-in-law Ray.

   C. Legit telemarketers are only allowed to call between 8 A.M. and 9 P.M.

Answer: C. It stinks, but telemarketers are allowed to call you 13 out of the 24 hours in a day. But you can—and should—ask to be removed from their lists. By law, they must do so, and not call you again. If they do, call the Federal Trade Commission's toll-free complaint line: 1-877-FTC-HELP (1-877-382-4357) to report the company.

6. You read an ad for an amazing weight-loss regimen that involves heat beads, fuzzy dice, and a bottle of supplements. But unless some other element is involved, it's probably a scam. What is that element?

   A. Regular exercise and dietary changes.

   B. A doctor with a Harvard Medical School degree and/or an *Oprah* appearance under his belt.

   C. Genuine angora on that set of fuzzy dice.

Answer: A. There is no "miracle" weight loss program that doesn't involve exercise or dietary changes (but usually both). Save your money.

7. You buy a Rolex on the street from some guy in a trench coat. But there's something odd about this Rolex, which leads you to believe it might be a fake. What's odd?

   A. The second hand ticks along, instead of sweeping around in a smooth, continuous motion.

   B. Rolex is spelled "Roleck's."

   C. Unlike most conventional timepieces, this watch features a thirteenth hour.

Answer: All of the above, although the first (A) is the easiest way to spot a fake Rolex.

8. You're working as a computer dealer. A guy comes in, dressed to the nines, and wants to buy the best laptop in the joint—complete with a DVD burner, wireless interface, coffee cup holder, the works. He hands you a check for $2,699, and you notice that the check register number is 162. An alarm goes off in your head. Why?

   A. The laptop he's trying to purchase actually costs $3,699.

   B. A low register number means the account is new.

   C. You were born in January 1962. Obviously, this man is a foreign operative, sending you a signal after all these years.

Answer: B. New accounts aren't necessarily bad, but it could be a shell account, opened with a minimum deposit ($200) that can't possibly cover the value of the check. Don't accept such checks unless you can verify the amount is in the account.

9. You're in a fender bender with another car. Fortunately, you're fine, but you can't say the same for your beloved Chevy Corsica. You start to exchange insurance info, and the other party hands you an address. You should worry if the address …

   A. … Is a P.O. box or hotel room.

   B. … Is a California address.

   C. … Reads, "Bradbury City, Mars."

Answer: A. A nonpermanent address could mean you've been targeted by insurance fakers, who use a temporary address to file dozens of phony claims. But B might be cause for alarm, too—a third of all fraudulent accident claims come from California.

10. Your spouse is plotting to murder you for the insurance money. (Hey, we've all been there.) What can you do to help investigators nab him/her after your death?

    A. Make sure your policy is rather new—less than two years old.

    B. Jack up the policy amount to something absurd ($5 million) considering your station in life (counter jockey at the Quick-Pump-Mart).

    C. Try to be murdered in a foreign country.

Answer: All of the above. New, fat policies are almost always suspect, as are foreign death certificates, which are easier to fake. Plus, you might try manifesting yourself to your spouse after death, wailing and moaning about revenge, as she's driving her car up a winding mountain road, or something.

Scoring

0 to 20 points: Wow! You did really great on this quiz! Tell you what. Take your wallet and drop it into a big manila envelope. Address the envelope to Duane Swierczynski, c/o Alpha Books, and send it to me express mail. I'll be sure to give you a special prize.

30 to 50 points: Not bad. Go to your nearest t-shirt shop. Ask them to custom-print you a shirt that says: SCAM ME—I WON'T KNOW THE DIFFERENCE! Wear it as often as possible.

60 to 80 points: Nice work. Apparently, you're one of those people who can be fooled only some of the time. Stay away from the phones and people in overcoats, and you should be fine.

90 to 100 points: Impressive! Con artists should steer clear of you. If con artists were vampires, you'd be Wesley Snipes.

Index

C

D

J-K

Check Out These
Best-Selling
COMPLETE IDIOT'S GUIDES®

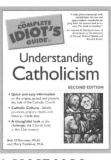

Understanding
Catholicism
SECOND EDITION

1-59257-085-2
$18.95

Learning
Spanish
THIRD EDITION

0-02-864451-4
$18.95

The
Bible
SECOND EDITION

0-02-864382-8
$18.95

Being a
Groom
SECOND EDITION

0-02-864456-5
$9.95

Grammar
and Style
SECOND EDITION

1-59257-115-8
$16.95

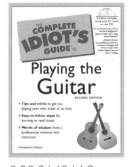

Playing the
Guitar
SECOND EDITION

0-02-864244-9
$21.95 w/CD

Personal Finance
in Your 20s & 30s
SECOND EDITION

0-02-864374-7
$19.95

Knitting and
Crocheting
SECOND EDITION
Illustrated

1-59257-089-5
$16.95

The Perfect
Resume
THIRD EDITION

0-02-864440-9
$14.95

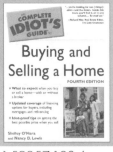

Buying and
Selling a Home
FOURTH EDITION

1-59257-120-4
$18.95

Low-Carb
Meals

1-59257-180-8
$18.95

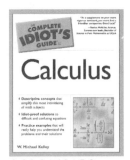

Calculus

0-02-864365-8
$18.95

More than *450 titles* in *30 different categories*
Available at booksellers everywhere

ALPHA